Inquire
A Student Handbook for 21st Century Learning

Teacher's Guide
to the Student Handbook

Robert King, Christopher Erickson, and Janae Sebranek

Created by
Thoughtful Learning

Distributed exclusively by

ZB **Zaner-Bloser**

Acknowledgments

Inquire is a reality because of the collaborative efforts of our hardworking team of educators, students, researchers, writers, editors, and designers. Their critical and creative thinking, as well as their problem-solving and communication skills, made this resource possible.

The *Inquire* Team

Steven J. Augustyn   Mark Lalumondier   Jean Varley
Tim Kemper   Cindy Smith   Jeanne Yost
Lois Krenzke   Lester Smith   Claire Ziffer

A special thanks goes to Cindy Smith, project-based instructor at Karcher School in Burlington, Wisconsin. In addition to providing guidance and feedback on *Inquire*, Ms. Smith graciously allowed the team to field-test the material in her class. Her insights and those of her seventh- and eighth-grade students greatly improved *Inquire*. To them, we say "Thank you!"

Inquire on the Web

This book is just the beginning! Visit thoughtfullearning.com to find dozens of downloadable templates and forms, additional models and projects, links to great resources, and much, much more.

Trademarks and trade names are shown in this book strictly for illustrative purposes and are the property of their respective owners. The authors' references herein should not be regarded as affecting their validity. Wikipedia is a registered trademark of the Wikimedia Foundation. Microsoft and PowerPoint are either trademarks or registered trademarks of Microsoft Corporation in the United States and/or other countries.

Copyright © by Thoughtful Learning

Distributed in the U.S.A. exclusively by Zaner-Bloser, Inc., 1-800-421-3018, www.zaner-bloser.com.

Each copy master in this book may be reproduced, with the copyright notice, without permission from the publisher. No other part of this work may be reproduced or transmitted in any form or by any means, electronic or mechanical, including photocopying and recording, or by any information storage or retrieval system without the prior written permission of Thoughtful Learning unless such copying is expressly permitted by federal copyright law. Address inquiries to Permissions, Thoughtful Learning, PO Box 460, Burlington, Wisconsin 53105.

ISBN 978-14531-0888-8

1 2 3 4 5 6 7 8 25170 18 17 16 15 14 13

ISBN (online) 978-14531-0889-5

Printed in the U.S.A.

SUSTAINABLE FORESTRY INITIATIVE — Certified Chain of Custody — Promoting Sustainable Forestry — www.sfiprogram.org — SFI-01042

Thoughtful Learning
www.thoughtfullearning.com

Dear Educator:

You face unprecedented challenges in preparing your students for life in a changing world. Thank you for taking on these challenges. Please know that *Inquire* is an innovative resource that will guide and enrich your instruction along the way.

Inquire can help your students . . .

- **build 21st century skills** such as critical and creative thinking, problem solving, understanding media, and collaborating;
- **sharpen their study skills** such as reading to learn, improving vocabulary, note taking, and taking tests;
- **develop inquiry skills** such as questioning, planning, researching, creating, improving, and presenting; and
- **create amazing projects,** from writing and Web projects to design and performing projects.

Whether you teach in a traditional classroom or in an inquiry- or project-based environment, you'll find that *Inquire* helps your students develop the literacy and learning skills they need. And whether you teach math, science, social studies, language arts, or research skills, you'll discover that *Inquire* can help your students flourish. As you know, students who can think deeply, solve problems, and work with others will excel not only in your classroom, but also in life.

Thank you for helping to shape the future!

Best regards,

Chris Erickson
President/Author

Table of Contents

Overview

What is the *Inquire* program?

The *Inquire* program helps students think and learn, with a focus on 21st century skills, basic study skills, literacy, the inquiry process, and classroom projects. The program consists of a *Student Handbook,* a *Teacher's Guide,* and *Inquire Online.*

Why is *Inquire* important?

With the current emphasis on critical thinking, problem solving, media literacy, and thoughtful learning, *Inquire* is an indispensable guide for students and an invaluable resource for teachers.

How can *Inquire* be used?

Inquire can serve well in the regular classroom as well as in the inquiry-based, problem-based, and project-based classrooms. It is also a natural fit for research courses or classes that teach 21st century skills or basic study skills. (See pages 26–34 in this guide for more.)

Who should have a copy of the *Inquire Student Handbook*?

Inquire works best when every student has a copy to use across the curriculum and later at home. It is designed for students in grades 9–12, but as there are no grade designations in the book, it can serve students in other grades as appropriate. *Inquire* is also a useful in-class resource for classrooms that cannot provide copies to all students.

What goes with the *Inquire Student Handbook*?

This *Teacher's Guide* introduces you to *Inquire,* shares the pedagogy that prompted its development, offers planning and instruction guidelines, and provides chapter-by-chapter lesson plans. *Inquire Online* provides the *Student Handbook* and *Teacher's Guide* in online delivery, with many added links, resources, templates, and downloads. The *Inquire* Web site (thoughtfullearning.com) offers additional teaching ideas, articles, resources, and more.

How should I get started?

- First, page through the *Inquire Student Handbook* to appreciate the depth and breadth of the information included.
- Then read the opening chapter to get a look at content presentation. (You will find it friendly, complete, and easy to follow.)
- Next, review or skim the opening section of the *Teacher's Guide* (pages 1–60) and at least one of the lesson-plan chapters (pages 61–303) to understand how best to use *Inquire.*

Pedagogy Behind *Inquire*

Inquire reflects the best research on instruction, including 21st century skills, critical thinking and problem solving, inquiry-based instruction, and project-based education. This section in the *Teacher's Guide* highlights the key pedagogical schools of thought that make *Inquire* so important and timely.

Why are the 21st century skills so important?

"The current and future health of America's 21st century economy depends directly on how broadly and deeply Americans reach a new level of literacy—21st century literacy—that includes strong academic skills, thinking, reasoning, teamwork skills, and proficiency in using technology."

This key pronouncement comes from the 21st Century Workforce Commission National Alliance of Business, but it reflects the thinking of many important organizations, both private and public, interested in preparing students and citizens for life and work in the 21st century.

One key organization, the **Partnership for 21st Century Skills,** is a public-private meeting of the minds that has developed a model of learning for the 21st century. This model has become a template for preparing students for learning, literacy, and life skills at all levels of education and in the development of core standards to guide instruction for this generation of students. *Inquire* addresses the skills identified in this important model. (See pages 52–54 in this guide for correlations to the 21st century skills.)

21st Century Skills in *Inquire*

Learning Skills

- Critical thinking
- Creative thinking
- Problem solving
- Communicating
- Collaborating
- Building arguments

Literacy Skills

- Information literacy
- Media literacy
- Technology literacy

Life Skills

- Flexibility
- Initiative
- Social skills
- Productivity
- Leadership

How can Bloom's taxonomy direct instruction?

Key features in any model of 21st century skills are critical thinking, creative thinking, and problem solving. On the one hand, today's students need to approach learning more thoughtfully and deliberately; on the other hand, they need to apply creative thinking skills to solve problems and complete projects.

The challenge for educators is deciding where to begin and how to practice thinking skills in content-area instruction. Bloom's revised taxonomy classifies the basic thinking behaviors and can serve as a blueprint for educators as they plan thoughtful curriculum and instruction.

Bloom's taxonomy has guided thoughtful instruction for many years; the revised taxonomy, shown below, is even more valuable and applicable to 21st century instruction. *Inquire* teaches specific strategies for critical and creative thinking based on Bloom's revised taxonomy of thinking.

Blooms Revised Taxonomy in *Inquire*

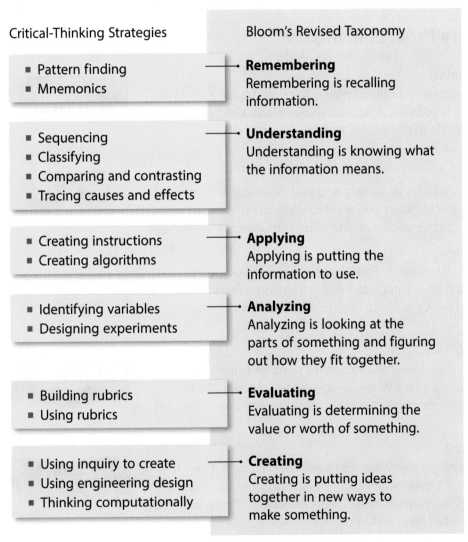

Critical-Thinking Strategies

- Pattern finding
- Mnemonics

- Sequencing
- Classifying
- Comparing and contrasting
- Tracing causes and effects

- Creating instructions
- Creating algorithms

- Identifying variables
- Designing experiments

- Building rubrics
- Using rubrics

- Using inquiry to create
- Using engineering design
- Thinking computationally

Bloom's Revised Taxonomy

Remembering
Remembering is recalling information.

Understanding
Understanding is knowing what the information means.

Applying
Applying is putting the information to use.

Analyzing
Analyzing is looking at the parts of something and figuring out how they fit together.

Evaluating
Evaluating is determining the value or worth of something.

Creating
Creating is putting ideas together in new ways to make something.

Why is inquiry-based instruction pedagogically sound?

Inquiry-based instruction is a teaching technique that promotes many of the 21st century skills, including critical thinking, problem solving, and collaborating. This method of instruction was initially common in the science curriculum and is now used in all content areas. In fact, inquiry-based schools are designed to promote student-generated, hands-on learning.

Inquiry-based instruction increases students' interest in learning while helping them retain what they have learned and internalize lifelong learning skills. It also reflects the problem-based approach used in the workplace.

The key to using the inquiry approach successfully is to put in place a process that will carry students through their inquiries. Part II of *Inquire* covers the inquiry process as shown below. In addition, the project guidelines in Part III of the book follow the steps in the inquiry process.

The Inquiry Process in *Inquire*

Questioning
You're just starting out, so now is the time to ask questions. Anything is possible. Ask creative questions, simple questions, deep questions. Imagine, wonder, dream, brainstorm, hope.

Question

Planning
Next, choose one possibility and plan how you will make it happen. Decide what you want to do, what your goals are, how much time you have, and what resources are available.

Plan

Researching
Then do the research. Follow your plan, use your resources well, and gather complete information and helpful details. This will involve working with media, technology, and people.

Research

Creating
As you create, use your discoveries to make something new and amazing. Build. Write. Design. Sculpt. Record. Don't worry about perfection at this point. Just get something out there.

Create

Improving
After creating something, you need to evaluate it. Does the end product meet your goals? Does it do what you want it to do? What works well? What could work better? How can you improve what you created?

Improve

Presenting
Once your work is ready, present it to your audience. Afterward, ask yourself if the work is everything you wanted it to be. What did you learn as you worked on this project?

Present

Why does project-based instruction connect with students?

Project-based instruction is an interdisciplinary approach to teaching that promotes 21st century literacy and learning. This approach increases student interest, allows for practicing 21st century skills, and promotes both self-directed learning and teamwork. Project-based instruction is closely connected with inquiry-based instruction in that students develop projects using the inquiry process and 21st century skills.

Traditional classroom teachers often assign projects after introducing new content. Teaching teams often plan interdisciplinary projects that connect key concepts in all of the represented content areas. Project-based schools are built entirely, or almost entirely, on student-directed learning.

Part III of *Inquire* offers students a wide variety of project ideas, from writing projects to Web projects, from audio-visual projects to performing projects.

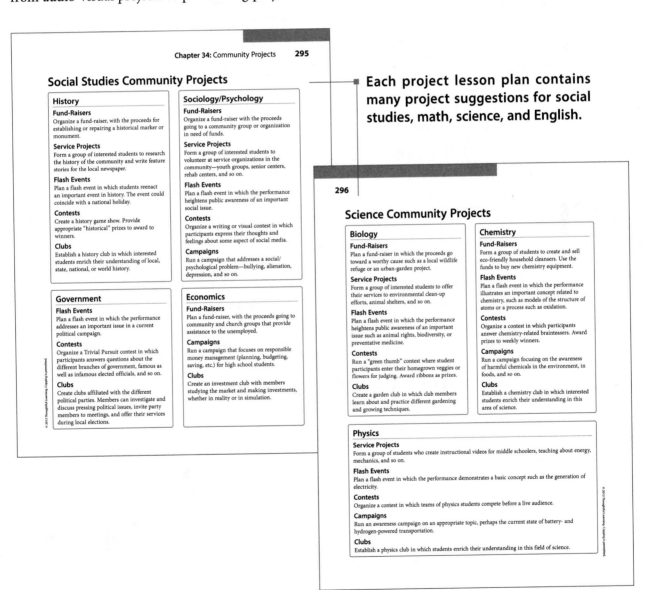

Each project lesson plan contains many project suggestions for social studies, math, science, and English.

How do 21st century skills, inquiry, and projects interconnect?

Students need 21st century skills like critical and creative thinking, communicating, and problem solving as they work through the inquiry process. Students use the inquiry process to develop projects, and projects help students learn core content.

This chart shows the special relationship between 21st century skills, the inquiry process, and content-based projects.

Part I: 21st Century Skills

- Critical thinking
- Creative thinking
- Problem solving
- Communicating
- Collaborating
- Building arguments
- Information literacy
- Media literacy
- Technology literacy
- Financial literacy

Part II: Inquiry Process

- Questioning
- Planning
- Researching
- Creating
- Improving
- Presenting

Part III: Projects

- Writing
- Graphing
- Web developing
- Audio-visual
- Design
- Performing
- Community

Across the Curriculum

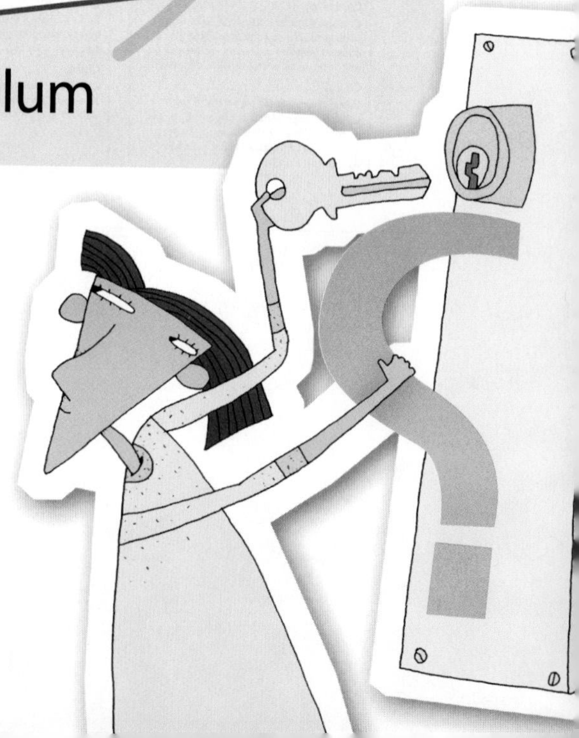

Quick Tours of *Inquire* and Ancillaries

The *Inquire Student Handbook* teaches 21st century skills, inquiry, and projects. The material is presented in an easy-to-follow format. Once students get to know *Inquire*, they will be able to find information quickly and efficiently—a key feature of any useful resource.

The *Inquire Teacher's Guide* helps you use the *Student Handbook* in the classroom. Just follow the headings and questions to find what you need. Beyond that, the *Inquire* Web site is easy to navigate and provides a wealth of resources and links. This section highlights the main features in each of these resources.

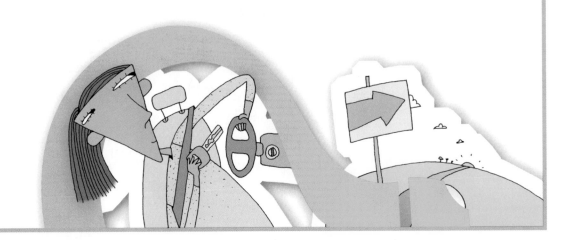

What is included in *Inquire*?

Inquire is organized in three parts. Part I covers 21st century skills and traditional study skills. Part II covers the inquiry process, and Part III provides examples of a wide variety of projects.

Part I: Building 21st Century Skills

This section covers 21st century learning and literacy skills. If students follow the strategies in each chapter, they will become better thinkers and learners now and for years to come. These skills will also prepare them to use the inquiry process discussed in Part II and to create the projects outlined in Part III.

Chapters in This Section

Part II: **Using the Inquiry Process**

This section leads students through the steps in the inquiry process, from questioning to creating to presenting. As students learn about this process, they will apply many of the skills that they learned in Part I. They will also use the inquiry process to complete the projects in Part III.

Chapters in This Section

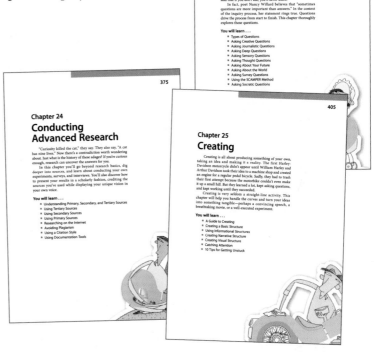

Part III: **Developing Projects**

This section offers dozens of project ideas—writing projects, graphing projects, design projects, community projects, and much more. Each specific project includes guidelines, visuals, and examples. Listed below are the types of projects covered in Part III, but these are just starting points. Let inquiry guide your students as they make these projects their own.

Chapters in This Section

A Closer Look at the *Student Handbook*

These two pages identify important elements and features that help students do their best thinking and learning with *Inquire*.

■ **Engaging chapter openers and illustrations connect with students.**

■ **Clear headings and explanations make *Inquire* easy to use.**

67

Chapter 5

Communicating

So far in this book, you've focused on thinking—the ways in which you explore, develop, and compose ideas. Communicating takes thinking to the next level. If thinking is composing, communicating is the concert. The ideas are no longer confined to your own head. You "play" them for someone else, who listens, thinks, and responds with new ideas—and maybe even cheers.

Communicating is a back-and-forth process that involves speaking and listening. When you speak, you are the performer, and when you listen, you are the audience. Then the roles reverse. To communicate well, you need to speak and listen effectively in a variety of situations. This chapter will show you how.

You will learn . . .

- Understanding the Communication Situation
- Listening Actively
- Reading Faces and Body Language
- Speaking
- Speaking One-on-One
- Speaking in a Group
- Speaking to an Audience
- Overcoming Stage Fright
- Listening and Speaking Terms

Chapter 1: Overview of 21st Century Skills   9

Literacy Skills

You live in the information age, which means that you consume and produce information at a faster rate than any generation before.

Information, Media, and Technology Literacy

Information literacy begins with understanding the many forms that information takes. Information comes in pictures, diagrams, PSAs, Web pages, billboards, bank statements, train schedules—anything that people create to communicate. The communication situation is the key that can unlock these media and help you understand the message.

| Sender | Message | Receiver |
| Context | Medium | |

- **Sender:** Who created this message? Is the sender one person, a group, unknown? What authority does the sender have?
- **Message:** What is the subject? The main point? The purpose? What ideas support the main point? Is the message reliable?
- **Medium:** What medium is used? How public is it? What strengths does the medium have? What weaknesses?
- **Receiver:** Who is reading, hearing, or viewing this message? Is the receiver one person, a group, unknown? How will the receiver feel about the message? What should the receiver do with the message?
- **Context:** In what place and time was the message created? In what place and time will it be received? What came before? What should come after?

Financial Literacy

You may already have a job, or you may be searching for one. Jobs involve a set of challenges and responsibilities. You need to acquire these skills:

- ☑ Fiscal responsibility
- ☑ Career planning
- ☑ Money management
- ☑ Credit and debt management
- ☑ Risk management
- ☑ Saving and investing

Your Turn

1. Think about a message you recently received. Use the questions above to analyze each part of the communication situation.
2. What medium do you prefer for casual messages: talking face to face, texting, phoning, using social media? Why do you prefer this medium?
3. What career are you aiming for? Look online to find the starting yearly wage for that job. Divide that number by 12. Where do you want to live? Look online to find average monthly prices for apartments. How much money will be left after you've paid your rent? Consider how far that money will stretch to cover your other expenses.

53

Problem Solving as Inquiry

Over the last few pages, you've walked through the problem-solving process. Problem solving is actually a version of the inquiry process. The two processes are charted side by side here to illustrate the comparison.

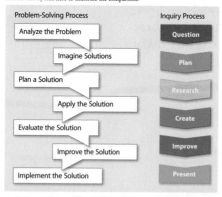

On the next pages, you will see how the inquiry process takes a number of different forms in science, math, social studies, and language arts.

Your Turn **Problem Solving in History:** Choose a historical catastrophe such as the Black Plague, World War I, or the Great Chicago Fire. What causes led to the catastrophe? What effects resulted? If you had a time machine, could you avert the catastrophe? How?

Problem Solving in Science: Think of a modern problem that science could solve, for example, pandemics, increasing energy needs, or protection from Earth impactors. Use the process above to sketch out a possible scientific solution.

Everyday Problem Solving: Think about your daily activities—getting ready for school, taking on a new assignment, trying out for a team or a play. How many of these processes require inquiry and problem solving?

■ **Thoughtful graphics serve as effective instructional tools.**

116

Developing Good Habits

Your brain is very practical. Its first job is to keep you alive. Its second job is to keep you connected to other people, which is part of staying alive. Its third job is to learn things. Not surprisingly, your brain mostly wants to learn things that connect you to other people and keep you alive. To be ready to learn, you must be healthy, happy, and socially connected. Developing the following 10 critical habits will ensure that you are ready to learn.

(Brain diagram labeled: Learning, Connected, Alive)

10 Critical Habits for Learning

1. **Sleep.** Get eight hours of sleep whenever possible.
2. **Eat.** Have a balanced breakfast each morning.
3. **Move.** Exercise your body to increase blood circulation to your brain.
4. **Connect.** Share what you learn with friends and family.
5. **Relax.** Find a way to feel safe and comfortable so that you can learn.
6. **Work.** Set goals, and work to achieve them.
7. **Wonder.** Nurture curiosity, which is a key to learning.
8. **Discover.** Seek answers and put new ideas together.
9. **Create.** Bring new ideas and inventions into the world.
10. **Share.** Apply your ideas to make a difference in the world.

Your Turn Rate how often you practice the 10 critical habits for learning, from 1 (rarely) to 5 (always). Then choose two habits that need more attention, and tell how you will improve each.

```
                (Rarely) ──────────────▶ (Always)
 1. Sleep     1......2......3......4......5
 2. Eat       1......2......3......4......5
 3. Move      1......2......3......4......5
 4. Connect   1......2......3......4......5
 5. Relax     1......2......3......4......5
 6. Work      1......2......3......4......5
 7. Wonder    1......2......3......4......5
 8. Discover  1......2......3......4......5
 9. Create    1......2......3......4......5
10. Share     1......2......3......4......5
```

- Visual depictions throughout *Inquire* help students grasp abstract concepts.

358

Scheduling Time

Schedule your project's tasks on a calendar. If the due date is fixed, begin with that date and work backward, dividing the available time between the various tasks. If, on the other hand, the project's due date is open, list the first task with an estimate of how long it will take, the second task with its estimate, and so on. There may be some overlap on the schedule, especially if team members work simultaneously on different tasks.

Using a Calendar

Use an actual calendar or simply list your tasks along with their dates. If possible, post tasks on a shared online calendar application. An online calendar allows you to display tasks in various views: by month, week, day (even hours), or as a dated agenda.

Month View

Sun	Mon	Tue	Wed	Thu	Fri	Sat
27	28 Begin research	1	2	3 Finish list	4 Send requests	5
6	7 Assign teams	8 Begin interviews	9	10	11	12
13	14	15	16	17	18	19
20	21 Finish interviews	22 Assess results	23	24 Create story	25	26
27	28 Start edit	29	30	31	1 Video due	2

Agenda View

Date	Task
Feb. 28	Research the subject.
Mar. 3	List veterans and caregivers in our area.
Mar. 4	Request interviews.
Mar. 7	Assign interview teams.
Mar. 8	Begin the interviews.
Mar. 21	Finish interviews.
Mar. 22	Evaluate the results.
Mar. 24	Create a cohesive "story" for our video.
Mar. 28	Edit the video.
Apr. 1	Present the video in class and post it online.

Making Adjustments

As your project unfolds, keep track of your progress with each task.

- **Speed up if you find that you are falling behind.** This may require either assigning more resources (perhaps asking for help) or reevaluating the task itself. Deadlines are important.
- **Slow down if you find that time permits.** This may allow you to go into more depth or to reassign resources. (For example, if you finish the background research in less time than anticipated, you could dig deeper or help a team member gather more data.)
- **Revise your schedule if necessary.** Due dates (deadlines) are sometimes extended if a strong case can be made. If problems arise, speak with your instructor early on.

Your Turn Use a calendar application to schedule your project's tasks, or plot them on a paper calendar. (See thoughtfullearning.com/h358 for a template and links.)

- Point-of-use practice helps students understand new skills.

Part III:
Developing Projects

P
Bu

P
Us

- Helpful color coding identifies the three main parts of *Inquire*.

What is included in the *Inquire Teacher's Guide?*

The *Inquire Teacher's Guide* is divided into two main parts. Part I introduces you to the *Inquire Student Handbook* and helps you implement instruction thoughtfully and meaningfully. Part II provides chapter-by-chapter lesson plans.

Part I: Presenting Inquire

- Overview
- Pedagogy Behind *Inquire*
- Quick Tours of *Inquire* and Ancillaries
- Using *Inquire* for Planning and Instruction

- Assessing Student Work
- Correlations for *Inquire*
- Research Guide to *Inquire*

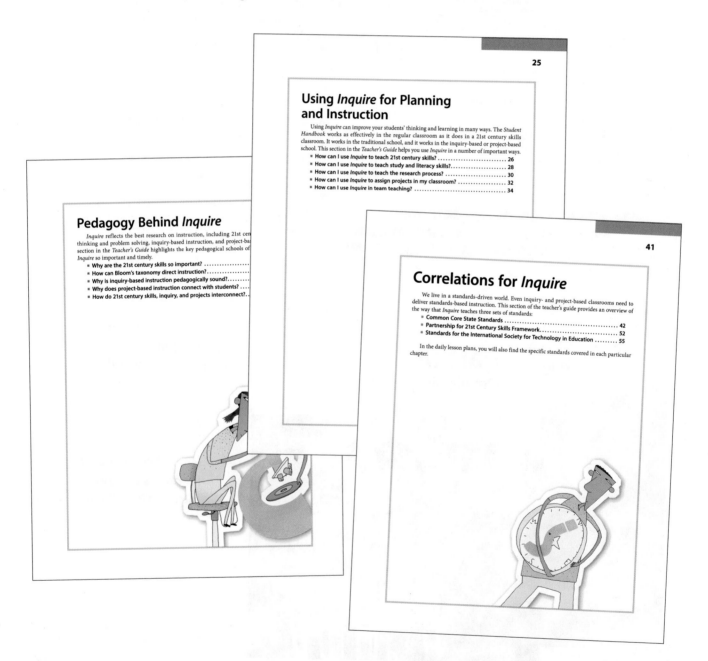

Using *Inquire* for Planning and Instruction

Using *Inquire* can improve your students' thinking and learning in many ways. The *Student Handbook* works as effectively in the regular classroom as it does in a 21st century skills classroom. It works in the traditional school, and it works in the inquiry-based or project-based school. This section in the *Teacher's Guide* helps you use *Inquire* in a number of important ways.

Pedagogy Behind *Inquire*

Inquire reflects the best research on instruction, including 21st cen[tury] thinking and problem solving, inquiry-based instruction, and project-ba[sed] section in the *Teacher's Guide* highlights the key pedagogical schools of *Inquire* so important and timely.

Correlations for *Inquire*

We live in a standards-driven world. Even inquiry- and project-based classrooms need to deliver standards-based instruction. This section of the teacher's guide provides an overview of the way that *Inquire* teaches three sets of standards:

In the daily lesson plans, you will also find the specific standards covered in each particular chapter.

Part II: Chapter-by-Chapter Lesson Plans

- Outcomes and Correlations
- Daily Lesson Plans
- Extension and Review
- Content-Area Minilessons
- Team-Teaching Suggestions
- Cross-Curricular Project Ideas

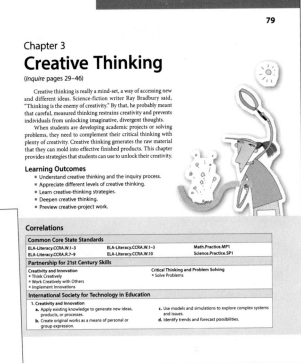

79

Chapter 3

Creative Thinking

(*Inquire* pages 29–46)

Creative thinking is really a mind-set, a way of accessing new and different ideas. Science-fiction writer Ray Bradbury said, "Thinking is the enemy of creativity." By that, he probably meant that careful, measured thinking restrains creativity and prevents individuals from unlocking imaginative, divergent thoughts.

When students are developing academic projects or solving problems, they need to complement their critical thinking with plenty of creativity. Creative thinking generates the raw material that they can mold into effective finished products. This chapter provides strategies that students can use to unlock their creativity.

Learning Outcomes
- Understand creative thinking and the inquiry process.
- Appreciate different levels of creative thinking.
- Learn creative-thinking strategies.
- Deepen creative thinking.
- Preview creative-project work.

Correlations

Common Core State Standards		
ELA-Literacy.CCRA.W.1–3	ELA-Literacy.CCRA.W.1–3	Math.Practice.MP1
ELA-Literacy.CCRA.R.7–9	ELA-Literacy.CCRA.W.10	Science.Practice.SP1

Partnership for 21st Century Skills	
Creativity and Innovation	**Critical Thinking and Problem Solving**
• Think Creatively	• Solve Problems
• Work Creatively with Others	
• Implement Innovations	

International Society for Technology in Education
1. Creativity and Innovation
a. Apply existing knowledge to generate new ideas, products, or processes.   c. Use models and simulations to explore complex systems and issues.
b. Create original works as a means of personal or group expression.   d. Identify trends and forecast possibilities.

80

Lesson Plan: Creative Thinking

Special Note: This chapter contains many "Your Turn" activities—perhaps too many to assign during a one-week chapter review, but enough to offer your students an excellent choice.

Day 1
1. Ask students if this statement—*Peanut butter tastes like first grade*—reflects a critical or a creative mind at work. Point out that creative thinking often involves making new connections.
2. Ask for a volunteer to read page 29 and the introduction on page 30 aloud. Share a story of creative thinking in action, such as the history of Velcro (details for which can easily be found online).
3. Then discuss the rest of the page and have students complete the "Your Turn" activity.
4. Discuss "Creative-Thinking Strategies" and the "Your Turn" activity on page 31. Consider assigning all or part of "Abundance and Novelty," page 45.

Day 2
5. Discuss pages 32–33 with your students. Have them complete one or both of the "Your Turn" activities, depending on the time available.
6. Discuss pages 34–35 with your students. Point out that each of these imaginative activities can improve their understanding of a topic. Either ask students to complete one or more of the "Your Turn" activities on their own, or work on the "Forced Connections" activity (page 35) together as a class. Ask for student input and write their ideas on the board.

Day 3
7. Discuss pages 36–37 with your students. Have them complete one or more of the "Your Turn" activities, depending on the time available.
8. Discuss pages 38–39 with your students. Either ask them to complete one or more of the "Your Turn" activities on their own, or engage the class in a discussion about a topic you are currently studying. Ask a number of Socratic questions about the topic (page 38) and write students' ideas on the board. Continue the discussion as long as time permits.

Day 4
9. Discuss pages 40–41 with your students. Have students complete one or both of the "Your Turn" activities.

Day 5
10. Discuss pages 42–43 with your students. Have students complete the "Your Turn" activities on both pages.
11. Also discuss page 44. Assign the "Your Turn" activities as homework in order to complete students' preview of creative-project planning.

Extension: Creative Thinking

Name _____ Date _____

Your Turn Think creatively about the common, ordinary paper clip by completing the following activities. You will focus on remembering, understanding, and applying (*Inquire* pages 32–37).

1. Generate your initial thoughts about a paper clip by completing a cluster about it (page 32).

_____
_____
_____
_____
_____

2. Next, think metaphorically about a paper clip by creating a simile, a metaphor, another analogy, and a symbol for it (page 34).

_____
_____
_____
_____
_____

3. Then compose a square-peg question about a paper clip using the sentence formula on page 36. Answer the question in as many ways as you can.

_____
_____
_____
_____
_____

Follow-up: Write freely for 5 to 8 minutes, highlighting the discoveries you have made about paper clips with the three creative strategies above.

_____
_____
_____
_____

A Closer Look at the Lesson Plans in the *Teacher's Guide*

These two pages take a closer look at special features that make the *Teacher's Guide* work well for you.

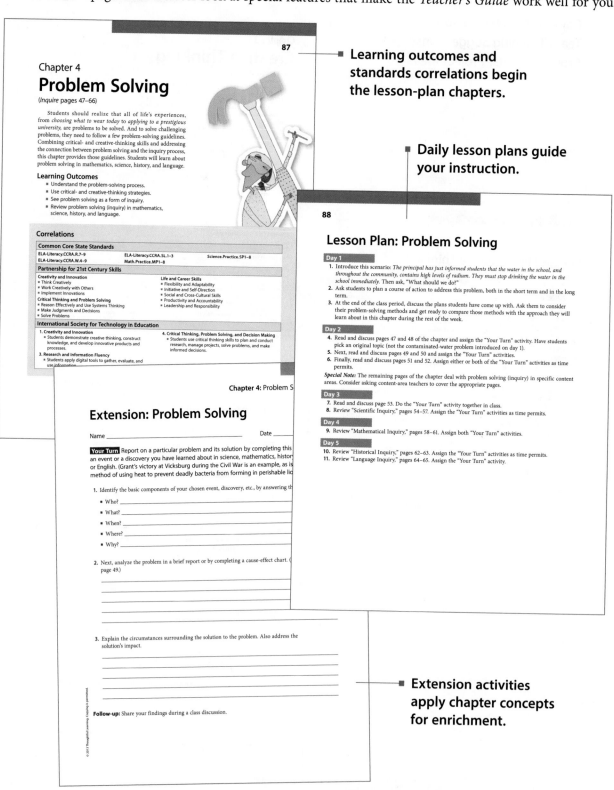

- Learning outcomes and standards correlations begin the lesson-plan chapters.

- Daily lesson plans guide your instruction.

- Extension activities apply chapter concepts for enrichment.

Chapter 4: Problem Solving **91**

Science Minilessons: Problem Solving

Analyzing a Problem

Controversy exists over parents choosing not to have their children inoculated for contagious childhood diseases.

RESEARCH this controversy online and in print materials.

DISCUSS it with a small group of classmates.

Then **ANALYZE** the issue using a cause-effect chart. (See *Inquire* page 49.)

PROPOSE a reasonable solution to this problem.

Designing an Experiment

Late in the warm season, many inland freshwater lakes suffer from algae blooms.

RESEARCH the issue to learn what, if anything, is being done about it.

Working in a small group, **DESIGN** your own experiment to explore/solve this problem. (See *Inquire* page 55.)

SHARE your experiment design with the other groups for discussion.

Extension: **CARRY OUT** your experiment if possible.

Questioning (Inquiry)

Suppose you are interested in the phenomenon of absolute or perfect pitch. More specifically, you want to know how it is measured.

LIST questions that would get such a project underway.

Then **CONDUCT** some initial research.

IDENTIFY two problems that you would likely face if you were to carry out an experiment that measures absolute pitch.

Scientific Inquiry

In at least some states, vending-machine operators are now required to post the number of calories in soft drinks available for purchase. Suppose you have two questions about this information: (1) How is the calorie count determined? (2) How accurate are the numbers?

USE the scientific method to determine your own calorie count. (See *Inquire* page 54.)

PLAN at least the first three steps.

Extension: **CARRY OUT** your experiment if possible.

Imagining and Planning Solutions

Driving at night is a serious problem for many drivers, especially when it is snowing or raining.

CLUSTER possible solutions to this problem. (See *Inquire* page 50.)

COMPARE clusters with a classmate.

DECIDE together on the best solution.

Then **CHECK** online to see what science and engineering experts are doing about this problem.

Designing an Experiment

Suppose you are interested in astronomy, especially in meteor showers.

RESEARCH meteor showers online.

INVESTIGATE specifically how you can track them.

DESIGN an experiment and carry it out. (See *Inquire* page 55.)

REFLECT on how well the problem-solving method worked for you.

- Minelessons allow you to use the chapter content across the curriculum.

- Team-teaching suggestions for projects help teachers collaborate.

280

Team-Teaching Suggestions

Design projects often involve drawing, drafting, measuring, using proportions, rapid prototyping, building, bench testing, and similar experimental activities. These projects may also require unfamiliar tools and materials, as well as special work and storage space. As a result, some design projects are best done in collaboration with teaching partners. Here are some suggestions.

An Art Partner

An art instructor can be invaluable for projects that involve lots of graphic design, especially when it comes to theater costumes and sets. Graphic design also plays a major role in print layout, from the artwork of a book cover to the font choice of the text inside. Game designs also require a strong graphic sense to help create a pleasurable experience. Even blueprints, models, tools, and machines benefit from an artist's vision.

A Theater Partner

Many of the design projects described in this chapter find perfect application in a theater setting. For any play, actors must be costumed with clothes and jewelry. Printed posters, flyers, and programs (perhaps even T-shirts for advertising) must be developed. Stage sets must be drawn and constructed. A play can even provide a reason for a more formal blueprint or diorama. Theater instructors are used to managing these various elements that go into making a production.

An Industrial Arts or an Engineering Partner

For the "heavier" projects in this chapter—especially tool and machine designs—an industrial instructor or an engineering specialist can be of great assistance. Such a partner is best prepared to instruct students in safety procedures and in proper uses of tools and equipment. The instructor or specialist can also best explain the creation and use of blueprints and prototypes.

Chapter 32: Design Projects **281**

Social Studies Design Projects

European History

Poster
During much of medieval history, kings and queens ruled Europe, and the British royal family still enjoys much popularity.

Decide whether you support monarchy or oppose it. Create a poster to express your views.

T-Shirt
The Industrial Revolution transformed the Western World, creating both wealth and misery. If you lived in an agricultural community that was industrializing, would you support the change oppose it?

Design a T-shirt expressing your position for or against the Industrial Revolution.

U.S. History

Game
The Jamestown Colony and the Plymouth Settlement were established and developed in very different ways.

Choose one of the colonies and create a board game or card game to simulate the establishment of that settlement.

Blueprint or Scale Model
From grade school on, most students know of Christopher Columbus' *Niña, Pinta,* and *Santa Maria.* These ships were actually quite small and open to the elements.

Research the design of one of these ships and create a blueprint or scale model to show how it was built. Present your design to the class.

World History

Poster
Create a brochure that captures the essence of a ruler's reign.

Costume
Hold a costume party that portrays a historical period. Discuss the relation of fashion to the character of the time period.

Game
Design a game that communicates important facts about your favorite civilization.

Scale Model
Study the sketches of Leonardo Da Vinci's inventions, from flying machines to tanks to giant crossbows. Create a blueprint or prototype of one of his inventions.

- Cross-curricular project ideas suggest assignments in math, science, social studies, and language arts.

What features are included in *Inquire Online*?

This digital version of the *Student Handbook* is delivered on the Web and has the following features:

- **Each page of the print edition appears in a format that can be projected on a screen or Smart board.**

- **Fully searchable text lets you find what you need instantly. Bookmarks let you find it again.**

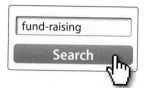

fund-raising

Search

Bookmark This!

Inquire To Organize a Fund-Raiser

1. **Question** the situation for the event.
   - **Subject:** What will the fund-raiser be about? Will it have a theme? How will you raise money? Is it a one-time event, or is it one that happens often?
   - **Purpose:** Why are you putting on the event? How much money do you wish to raise? Why should people participate?
   - **Audience:** Who will attend the event? What do they expect? What response do you want from them?

2. **Plan** the event by completing a planning sheet. (See page 573.)
   - **Fund-raiser ideas:** Raffle, car wash, battle of the bands, dance marathon, beach clean-up, walk-a-thon, chili cookoff, youth-mentorship program
   - **Organize:** Recruit a team of people to plan and carry out the event.
   - **Materials:** List materials you will need and plan how to obtain them.
   - **Budget:** Fill out a budget sheet. (See page 574.)

3. **Research** the event.
   - **Arrange** to use the location you need for your event. Assign team members to reserve the space. Then decide how the space will be set up for the event.
   - **Publicize** the event using posters, fliers, social media, and other creative forms of publicity (see page 428).

4. **Create** the event, considering the following roles for team members.
   - **Budget committee** to keep track of expenditures, ticket sales, and donations
   - **Publicity team** in charge of creating publicity materials and building awareness for the event
   - **Host** to guide the group through the event
   - **Entertainers** for the event (DJs, actors, and so on)
   - **Cooks/servers/dishwashers** for food events
   - **Refreshment** people to provide and sell refreshments
   - **Runners** in charge of retrieving new materials and doing other odd jobs during the event

5. **Improve** your event.
   - **Evaluate** the event.
     Did the event fulfill its goals and objectives?
     Did it focus on an appropriate idea or activity? How much money did it raise? Did enough people attend or give money? How could it be improved next time?
   - **Improve** the event by adding value, removing inefficiency, rearranging the sequence, and reworking parts to make them more effective.

6. **Present** the results of the fund-raising event, including earnings generated, in a newsletter, school calendar, social media post, blog, or school newspaper article.

Additional Resources

Web page: Event Planning Tips (California Libraries)

Web site: How to Plan a Sustainable Event (Sustainable Communities Online)

Web site: Popular Youth Fundraising Ideas (United Way)

Web site: Creative Fundraising Ideas (Buzzle)

Web site: Ashoka's Youth Venture

Planning Sheet template

Event Budget Sheet template

Event Work Roster template

- **Live links provide easy navigation.**

Planning Sheet: Fund-Raiser

...nning sheet lays out the most important details for planning an event, ..., goal, objectives, tasks, time, team members, and tools. The following ... is a fund-raising idea that came from the "Save Our Animal Shelter" ... (pages 286–287).

Save Our Animal Shelter Planning Sheet

Host a fund-raising dance to support the local animal shelter.

...tives: **Who?** Eleventh-grade students, faculty, and animal shelter employees will organize the event. We'll ask local businesses to sponsor the dance.

What? To run a successful dance we'll need a DJ, decorations, chairs, tables, refreshments, and event T-shirts.

Where? The school gymnasium.

When? Saturday, September 22, from 8:00 p.m. - 10:30 p.m.

How? We'll divide the tasks among interested 11th-grade students.

	Time:
	Sept. 4
Host dance kick-off meeting in the activity center.	Sept. 4
Plan the budget. Research music options.	Sept. 4
Reserve the gymnasium and disc jockey.	Sept. 9
Create publicity materials (posters, fliers, T-shirts).	Sept. 4 - Sept. 22
Visit local businesses; make a pitch for sponsorships.	Sept. 9 - Sept. 22
Reserve tables and chairs. Purchase decorations.	Sept. 17
Set up and decorate the gymnasium.	Sept. 21
Host the dance!	Sept. 22
Clean up and return equipment and materials.	Sept. 23
Present earnings to the animal shelter	Sept. 25
	Sept. 25

Students—Jamie Pollin (host), Tyrone Long, Selena Gelhart, Tameka Dubay, Josh Muller, and Neva Patel. Faculty—Mr. Meadow, Mr. Kaufmann, and Mrs. Kresken. animal shelter employees—Nicole Sullivan and Rodrigo Flores

...quipment: DJ equipment and microphone
...and drink: Fresh fruit, veggies, water, and punch
...Materials: T-shirts, decorations, tables, chairs, cups, and plates

- **Additional models, projects, and resources assist further exploration.**

What features are included in the *Inquire Online Teacher's Guide?*

The *Inquire Online Teacher's Guide* includes the same great content as the print addition, with the following additional features:

- **Links allow direct access to the** *Student Handbook.*

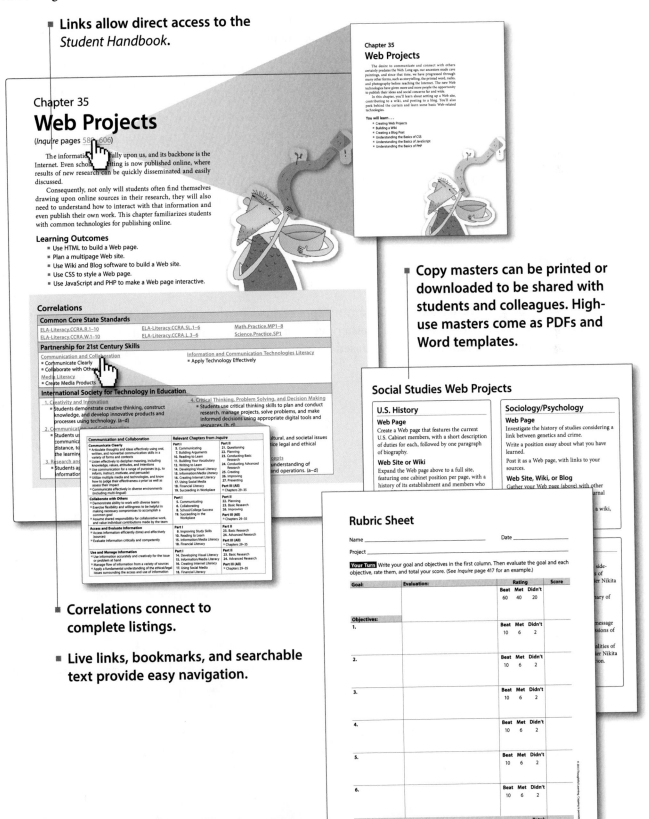

Chapter 35
Web Projects
(Inquire pages 586–606)

The information is fully upon us, and its backbone is the Internet. Even scholarly writing is now published online, where results of new research can be quickly disseminated and easily discussed.

Consequently, not only will students often find themselves drawing upon online sources in their research, they will also need to understand how to interact with that information and even publish their own work. This chapter familiarizes students with common technologies for publishing online.

Learning Outcomes
- Use HTML to build a Web page.
- Plan a multipage Web site.
- Use Wiki and Blog software to build a Web site.
- Use CSS to style a Web page.
- Use JavaScript and PHP to make a Web page interactive.

Correlations

Common Core State Standards

ELA-Literacy.CCRA.R.1–10	ELA-Literacy.CCRA.SL.1–6	Math.Practice.MP1–8
ELA-Literacy.CCRA.W.1–10	ELA-Literacy.CCRA.L.3–6	Science.Practice.SP1

Partnership for 21st Century Skills

Communication and Collaboration
- Communicate Clearly
- Collaborate with Others

Media Literacy
- Create Media Products

Information and Communication Technologies Literacy
- Apply Technology Effectively

International Society for Technology in Education

1. Creativity and Innovation
- Students demonstrate creative thinking, construct knowledge, and develop innovative products and processes using technology. (a–d)

2. Communication and Collaboration
- Students use...

3. Research and...
- Students ap...

4. Critical Thinking, Problem Solving, and Decision Making
- Students use critical thinking skills to plan and conduct research, manage projects, solve problems, and make informed decisions using appropriate digital tools and resources. (b, d)

- **Correlations connect to complete listings.**

- **Live links, bookmarks, and searchable text provide easy navigation.**

Chapter 35
Web Projects

The desire to communicate and connect with others certainly predates the Web. Long ago, our ancestors made cave paintings, and since that time, we have progressed through many other forms, such as storytelling, the printed word, radio, and photography before reaching the Internet. The new Web technologies have given more and more people the opportunity to publish their ideas and social concerns far and wide.

In this chapter, you'll learn about setting up a Web site, contributing to a wiki, and posting to a blog. You'll also peek behind the curtain and learn some basic Web-related technologies.

You will learn . . .
- Creating Web Projects
- Building a Wiki
- Creating a Blog Post
- Understanding the Basics of CSS
- Understanding the Basics of JavaScript
- Understanding the Basics of PHP

- **Copy masters can be printed or downloaded to be shared with students and colleagues. High-use masters come as PDFs and Word templates.**

Social Studies Web Projects

U.S. History

Web Page
Create a Web page that features the current U.S. Cabinet members, with a short description of duties for each, followed by one paragraph of biography.

Web Site or Wiki
Expand the Web page above to a full site, featuring one cabinet position per page, with a history of its establishment and members who...

Sociology/Psychology

Web Page
Investigate the history of studies considering a link between genetics and crime.

Write a position essay about what you have learned.

Post it as a Web page, with links to your sources.

Web Site, Wiki, or Blog
Gather your Web page (above) with other...

Rubric Sheet

Name _____   Date _____

Project _____

Your Turn Write your goal and objectives in the first column. Then evaluate the goal and each objective, rate them, and total your score. (See *Inquire* page 417 for an example.)

Goal:	Evaluation:	Rating			Score
		Beat	Met	Didn't	
		60	40	20	
Objectives:					
1.		Beat	Met	Didn't	
		10	6	2	
2.		Beat	Met	Didn't	
		10	6	2	
3.		Beat	Met	Didn't	
		10	6	2	
4.		Beat	Met	Didn't	
		10	6	2	
5.		Beat	Met	Didn't	
		10	6	2	
6.		Beat	Met	Didn't	
		10	6	2	
				Total:	

What features are included on the Thoughtful Learning Web site?

The Thoughtful Learning Web site is a dynamic, evolving resource for teachers, students, parents, and administrators. The site includes the following features:

- **Articles** about 21st century skills, inquiry, and project-based learning give you deep background understanding of the pedagogical foundations of the program.

- **"In the News"** guides you to many valuable sites for information about 21st century skills, inquiry, and project-based learning. You'll find amazing projects, instructional videos, helpful hints, powerful research, and much more.

- **The Thoughtful Learning blog** includes posts about inquiry, critical thinking, creative thinking, problem solving, and instruction in 21st century skills.

- **Personal learning network opportunities** abound. Follow the @InquireBook Twitter feed and connect with us on Facebook for the latest articles on 21st century learning, projects in the curricular areas, and inquiry events. You'll also get a chance to talk with the authors of the book and join them in discussions with other educators.

- **Product information** helps you learn more about *Inquire* at different grade levels and lets you peruse other learning resources from Thoughtful Learning.

- **The calendar of events** features upcoming appearances by the authors of *Inquire* at conventions such as NCTE and ASCD, as well as other events around the world that feature 21st century learning, inquiry, and project-based learning.

Using *Inquire* for Planning and Instruction

Using *Inquire* can improve your students' thinking and learning in many ways. The *Student Handbook* works as effectively in the regular classroom as it does in a 21st century skills classroom. It works in the traditional school, and it works in the inquiry-based or project-based school. This section in the *Teacher's Guide* helps you use *Inquire* in a number of important ways.

How can I use *Inquire* to teach 21st century skills?

You can teach 21st century skills in two stages.

- In the first stage, introduce the 21st century skills, either one right after another (see the chart below), or as needed throughout the school year.
- In the next stage, provide regular opportunities to apply the skills as you cover your content-area curriculum.

*So think introduction **and** application when you address any of these skills.*

Suggested Sequence: Introducing the Skills

Here is a suggested timetable for nine weeks of 21st century skills instruction (one 45-minute class per day, five days per week). The chart identifies the pages in the *Teacher's Guide* that provide day-by-day lesson plans for each chapter as well as the location of each skill in the *Inquire Student Handbook*.

Week	Skills Unit	TG Pages	*Inquire* Pages
1	**Overview of 21st Century Skills**	63–70	3–10
2	**Critical Thinking**	71–78	11–28
3	**Creative Thinking**	79–86	29–46
4	**Problem Solving**	87–94	47–66
5	**Communicating**	95–102	67–82
6	**Collaborating**	103–110	83–94
7	**Building Arguments**	111–118	95–114
8	**Succeeding in School and College**	119–124	115–126
9	**Succeeding in the Workplace**	189–194	315–332

21st Century Skills in Action

Integrating 21st century skills into the curriculum is really quite simple when you use *Inquire* as your guide. Watch for teachable moments when students can use skills to enhance their learning. Here are example teachable moments in three content areas.

Critical Thinking in American Literature

Imagine that you are having a discussion about the "Great American Novel" and one student asks why *The Great Gatsby* makes the cut but *Twilight* does not. Instead of simply saying that one is a classic and the other a pop phenomenon, you can challenge your students to determine the criteria for evaluating literary greatness and use what they find to develop rubrics.

Application: As a class, brainstorm the traits of a great American novel. Have a student write on the board all ideas offered in good faith. Then, working individually, in pairs, or in teams, have students select the key traits of a great American novel and use them to construct a rubric, using the approach shown on pages 22–23 of *Inquire*. Have students present their rubrics to the class, and have the class select the best one to use for evaluating novels. Use the rubric for all novels read by the class.

Creative Thinking in Current Events

Suppose that you are studying a contentious current issue, such as the Israeli/Palestinian conflict. You are leading a discussion of the situation, and students' positions are becoming pretty heated. Instead of changing the subject or just asking students to "agree to disagree," you can get them to think in new and creative ways about the situation by using perspective shifting.

Application: Using the lower half of *Inquire* page 35 as a guide, ask students to list their key characteristics: age, gender, nationality, religion, personality, and current mood. Ask students to reflect on how these characteristics help shape their opinions about the contentious issue. Then ask students to shift their perspectives by writing a second list and changing some or all of the characteristics. Ask students what they would think of the situation if they had these differing characteristics.

Problem Solving in Physics

Just before each school year, the Earth sweeps through the trail left by a comet, creating the Perseid Meteor Shower. As your students arrive in your physics classroom, you can share with them images of the meteor shower and explain that the comet debris impacts the Earth's atmosphere like bugs hitting the windshield of a car. Then ask students if they can figure out how much these yearly impacts slow the Earth's revolution around the sun. At first, they will have no idea how to figure out such a puzzle, but when you introduce the concept of inquiry to them, they will be emboldened to find ways to figure the problem out.

Application: Lead your class through *Inquire* pages 54–57, and tell your students that you want them to think like physicists, using science and math to solve problems. Ask them what the constants and variables are in the case of the comet debris and the revolution of the Earth. Ask them how they can use basic physical principals such as the conservation of motion to determine the effect of impactors on the Earth's speed.

How can I use *Inquire* to teach study and literacy skills?

As with 21st century skills, you can teach study and literacy skills in two stages.

- In the first stage, introduce the study skills, either one right after another (see the chart below), or as needed throughout the school year.
- Then provide regular opportunities to apply the skills as you cover your content-area curriculum.

*So think introduction **and** application when you address any of these skills.*

Suggested Sequence: Introducing the Skills

Here is a suggested timetable for nine weeks of study and literacy skills instruction (one 45-minute class per day, five days per week). The chart identifies the pages in the *Teacher's Guide* that provide day-by-day lesson plans for each chapter as well as the location of each skill in the *Inquire Student Handbook*.

Week	Skills Unit	TG Pages	*Inquire* Pages
1	**Improving Study Skills**	125–130	127–140
2	**Reading to Learn**	131–136	141–158
3	**Building Your Vocabulary**	137–142	159–178
4	**Writing to Learn**	143–148	179–202
5	**Taking Exit and Entrance Exams**	149–154	203–216
6	**Developing Visual Literacy**	155–162	217–236
7	**Improving Information and Media Literacy**	163–168	237–256
8	**Creating Internet Literacy**	169–176	257–268
9	**Developing Financial Literacy**	183–188	291–314

Study and Literacy Skills in Action

The best way to practice study and literacy skills is in the context of learning across the curriculum. Here are examples of applying study skills in content areas.

Reading to Learn in World History

Suppose your next unit of study focuses on the Enlightenment, with readings from the textbook and treatises from John Locke, Thomas Paine, and David Hume. To help students prepare for, carry out, and reflect on their reading, teach the reading-to-learn strategies included in chapter 10 of *Inquire*.

Application: Whenever students receive a new reading assignment, have them use the SQ3R approach outlined on page 143 of *Inquire*. Students should survey the document, looking at titles, headings, graphics, and organization. Next, they should question the document, thinking about who wrote it, when, where, and why. Only then should they carefully read the work. Afterward, they should recite the main point of the document and the key arguments in each part of it. Finally, they should review the reading and discuss it with others.

Improving Your Vocabulary in Biology

Help students grasp and remember the many vocabulary terms in biology by assigning them to keep a vocabulary notebook; use a dictionary; and explore the prefixes, roots, and suffixes of new terms.

Application: Read "Keeping a Vocabulary Notebook" (*Inquire* page 160) and assign students to do so. Also discuss *Inquire* pages 161–163 and 166–177. Then, when you introduce new terminology, tell students to record it in their vocabulary notebooks.

- Ask them to use context clues to come up with an initial definition of the term.
- Have them check prefixes, roots, and suffixes for a more complete idea.
- Then have them look up the word in their textbook glossary or a dictionary.
- Ask students to relate the term to others that they have learned.

Developing Visual Literacy in Algebra

Mathematical data is often presented in the form of tables, charts, graphs, and other visual elements. As a result, students need to know how to read and interpret many forms of graphics, drawing from them the essential information.

Application: Lead students through "Understanding Information Graphics" (*Inquire* pages 228–234). Then take students to the library or media center and send them on a scavenger hunt to find one example of each type of graphic.

- Ask each student to choose one graphic of interest and to extract mathematical data from it.
- Have students use the data to create a mathematical expression, such as a ratio, a percentage, a sum, a multiplier, or other function.

How can I use *Inquire* to teach the research process?

Part II of *Inquire* focuses on inquiry and research. It helps students form powerful questions to guide their research, plan how they will find information, perform basic and advanced research, and use what they find to create a research-based project. Whether you teach in a traditional classroom or an inquiry- or project-based setting, you'll find that the skills in Part II equip students to ask questions, find answers, and report them effectively.

Suggested Sequence: Teaching Inquiry and Research

Use the suggested sequence below to lead students through the process of inquiry and research. Start by introducing the process and teaching strategies for questioning. Then take a week to explore the different types of projects provided in Part III of the *Student Handbook*. Designate which projects students can choose from. During the rest of the quarter, lead students through the rest of the chapters in Part II as they work on their research projects.

Special Note: The guidelines for the projects in Part III follow the steps in the inquiry process presented in Part II of the *Student Handbook*.

Week	Research Units	TG Pages	*Inquire* Pages
1	**Understanding the Inquiry Process**	203–208	335–342
2	**Questioning**	209–214	343–354
3	**[Part III Project Review—List Possible Projects]**	253–314	429–604
4	**Planning**	215–220	355–362
5	**Conducting Basic Research**	221–226	363–374
6	**Conducting Advanced Research**	227–232	375–404
7	**Creating**	233–238	405–414
8	**Improving**	239–244	415–422
9	**Presenting**	245-250	423–428

Research Skills in Action

Research skills derive from the inquiry process, which begins with questioning. When students learn to frame their own questions, they naturally seek answers, which is the research process. Here are suggestions for using research skills in the content areas.

Questioning in Chemistry

Imagine that you are presenting the Periodic Table of the Elements. You could lecture about how it is set up, indicating why hydrogen appears at the top right and helium at the top left and why elements are grouped in families in various sectors. Or you could ask students to use inquiry and research to find the answers for themselves.

Application: Lead students through "Asking Deep Questions" on *Inquire* page 347. Then ask them to take 5 minutes to write down deep questions about the Periodic Table of the Elements.

- Have students volunteer their questions while a designated student writes them on the board (leaving out repeats).
- Ask each student to choose two deep questions from the list to research.
- Provide time on computers or in the library or media center, allowing students to research answers.
- Afterward, have them present their answers to the class.

Researching in Language Arts

Suppose that you are discussing with your students the research process, in particular evaluating sources of information. This issue has become important because of the wealth of information sources, some of them unreliable, on the Internet. When you are ready to discuss this issue, use chapter 24 in *Inquire* as a guide.

Application: Carefully review "Understanding Primary, Secondary, and Tertiary Sources" on pages 376–377 in *Inquire* with your students. Then ask students, individually or in pairs, to identify two reliable sources of each type for a given research topic. Afterward, ask them to share their findings with the class.

Planning and Improving in the Arts

Often in art class, you as the instructor must define the parameters of success for a specific project. You can help students develop their inquiry and research skills by involving them in the process of devising the rubric they will use.

Application: At the beginning of a new art project, introduce the type of work that students will be doing, whether drawing, painting, sculpting, molding, designing, or whatever. Present specific excellent examples of the outcome that you seek. Then ask students to help you plan the project.

- Lead students through "Setting Your Goal" and "Defining Objectives" on pages 356–357.
- Have the class collaboratively create a goal and objectives for the project.
- Lead students through "Evaluating" on pages 416–417.
- Have the class fill out rubric sheets for the coming project.
- Use the rubric sheets to guide students as they develop and assess their work.

How can I use *Inquire* to assign projects in my classroom?

No matter how you approach instruction, you should review all of the project possibilities offered in Part III of *Inquire*. Please keep the following points in mind when reviewing this part.

- Guidelines and at least one model are provided for each type of project.
- Some of the ideas work well for short-term projects; others are long-term projects.
- The guidelines and models serve as starting points; students should adapt, expand, and combine project ideas to make them their own.

Short-Term Projects

This chart lists possible short-term project ideas in Part III that could be implemented across the curriculum. Short-term projects can usually be completed in one to three class periods.

Science	Social Studies	Mathematics
An **observation report** about a recent science conference A **diagram** of a prokaryotic cell An **infographic** about the loss of coral reefs A **proposal** for a large-scale experiment	A **report** recapping a political convention An **email** to a student in another country A **round table** reenacting the Treaty of Versailles A **table** containing information about population ranges	A **podcast** about the invention of the concept of zero A **pie graph** of the budget for a fund-raiser **Instructions** for solving a trinomial equation A **budget sheet** for a school dance
Government	**Language Arts**	**Health**
A **survey** about candidates in an election A **letter** to the editor of a newspaper A **campaign speech** for a social movement A **time line** of the amendments to the Constitution	A **narrative** telling what happened to a character after the story closed A **Web page** reviewing a novel A **play** dramatizing a key scene from a novel A **round table** between the major characters in a Shakespearean play	A **news report** about a recent drug recall A **line graph** tracking calorie consumption over a week A **PSA** about drinking enough water A **persuasive poster** to destigmatize mental disorders

Long-Term Projects

This chart lists possible long-term projects in Part III that could be implemented in any content area. Long-term projects usually take at least a week to complete. As the chart below shows, a long-term project may incorporate multiple short-term projects.

Scale Model (*Inquire* pages 540–545)		
Blueprint	Flowchart	Instructions
Diagram	Letter	Table

Web Site (*Inquire* pages 592–595)		
Blog/Wiki	Web Page	Proposal
Graph	Contest	Slide Show
Paragraph	Infographic	Podcast

Campaign (*Inquire* pages 582–585)		
Brochure	Instructions	Proposal
Contest	Letter	Poster
Diagram	Live Interview	PSA
Email	News Report	Speech
Flash Event	Paragraph	Table
Graph	Play	Time Line
Infographic	Podcast	T-Shirt

Play (*Inquire* pages 566–568)		
Poster	Blueprint	Scale Model
Brochure	Narrative	Time Line
T-Shirt	Event	Podcast

Rube Goldberg Machine (*Inquire* pages 546–548)		
Blueprint	Scale Model	Instructions
Speech	Summary	Letter
Time Line	Observation Report	Flowchart
Proposal	Club	

Documentary (*Inquire* pages 518–519)		
Instructions	Scale Model	Digital Story
Play	Email	Time Line
Event	Poster	Blueprint

How can I use *Inquire* in team teaching?

When you work in a teaching-team situation, the team members can provide support, ideas, and feedback, reinforcing the learning across the curriculum. The most effective way to teach 21st century skills and study skills is in a team environment, and *Inquire* will make this job a lot easier.

What does team teaching with *Inquire* look like?

Of course, every team is different, but here's one example of how a team might use *Inquire* across the curriculum for a lesson in problem solving—one of the 21st century skills.

Team Meeting: Initiate Instruction

The team meets to set their goals for introducing their students to problem solving. One teacher is chosen to anchor the group. All teachers collaborate to think of ways to introduce or incorporate problem solving into one or more lessons.

Anchor Teacher

The anchor teacher—perhaps a literacy coach or a language arts teacher—teaches *Inquire* pages 47–53, the first part of the chapter on problem solving.

Math Teacher

As a warm-up, the math teacher covers *Inquire* pages 58–61, "Mathematical Inquiry." Then he or she has students apply these concepts in a lesson.

Science Teacher

As a warm-up, the science teacher reviews *Inquire* pages 54–57, "Scientific Inquiry." Then she or he has students apply this material in a lesson.

Social Studies Teacher

The social studies teacher uses the instruction on pages 62–63 in the *Inquire Student Handbook* for an activity on global problems. The class picks one problem and uses the steps in the *Student Handbook* to come up with possible solutions.

Team Meeting: Review and Extend

The group meets again to review how well the problem-solving material has worked so far and to discuss the next phase of instruction.

Assessing Student Work

Inquire helps you track your students' progress as they learn skills and create projects. In this section of the *Teacher's Guide,* you'll see how learning outcomes and formative assessment opportunities are built into the skills chapters of *Inquire.* You'll also discover the summative assessment supports in the *Teacher's Guide.* Finally, note how the planning and rubric sheets in the *Student Handbook* can help your students and you track progress on individual and collaborative projects.

How can I assess students' skills?

Inquire includes a number of features to help you assess students' learning of 21st century skills, study skills, and inquiry skills. Follow these steps:

Step 1: Match learning outcomes to standards.

Read the "You will learn..." list of learning outcomes at the beginning of the *Inquire* chapter you are teaching. Cross-check this list against the standards you need to teach. Pages 42–51 in the *Teacher's Guide* correlate *Inquire* chapters to common standards.

■ **Common Core State Standards**

Communicate Clearly
- Articulate thoughts and ideas effectively using oral, written, and nonverbal communication skills in a variety of forms and contexts
- Listen effectively to decipher meaning, including knowledge, values, attitudes, and intentions
- Use communication for a range of purposes (e.g., to inform, instruct, motivate, and persuade)
- Utilize multiple media and technologies, and know how to judge their effectiveness *a priori* as well as assess their impact
- Communicate effectively in diverse environments (including multi-lingual)

Collaborate with Others
- Demonstrate ability to work with diverse teams
- Exercise flexibility and willingness to be helpful in making necessary compromises to accomplish a common goal
- Assume shared responsibility for collaborative work, and value individual contributions made by the team

Step 2: Assess formatively.

Assign the "Your Turn" activities that appear throughout the *Inquire* chapter you are teaching. These activities allow students to practice skills and allow you to formatively assess student progress. To assess their understanding, read what students write, and listen to their discussions. Then provide feedback.

You will learn . . .
- Critical Thinking and the Inquiry Process
- Critical-Thinking Strategies
- Remembering
- Understanding
- ~~plying~~
- ~~lyzing~~
- ~~uating~~
- ~~ating~~

■ *Inquire* **Learning Outcomes**

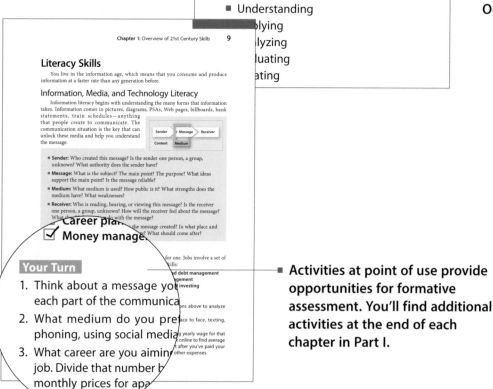

■ **Activities at point of use provide opportunities for formative assessment. You'll find additional activities at the end of each chapter in Part I.**

Step 3: Assess summatively.

When you have finished teaching a skills chapter, you can assess your students' learning using the review activity provided along with the daily lesson plans in the *Teacher's Guide.* Treat this review as a chapter test to measure learning, or use it as a soft assessment, letting students reflect on what they have learned.

90

Review: Problem Solving

Name _____ Date _____

Your Turn Answer the following questions.

1. How is creative thinking part of the problem-solving process?

2. Which graphic organizer works well to analyze a problem? Describe it.

3. What role does a trait evaluation play in the problem-solving process?

4. Problem solving is actually a version of which other process?

5. Scientists follow the scientific method to carry out experiments (and solve problems). Name the steps in this method.

Reflect: Consider how both critical and creative thinking are a part of the scientific method.

240

Evaluating Media Messages

The fact that media messages are constructed means that they can also be deconstructed, or separated into parts. The checklist below relates to the five parts of the communication situation—sender, message, medium, receiver, and context (see page 68). Asking questions about a message in the context of these parts will help you to analyze and evaluate it. The pages that follow will delve deeper into each checklist question.

Media-Message Evaluation Checklist

Sender ➤ Message ➤ Receiver
Context Medium

Sender
☑ 1. Who created the message? Is the source reliable? Was it by a news organization, a public citizen, or an advertiser? (See page 241.)

Message
☑ 2. What does the message say (subject, main point, support)? (See page 242.)
☑ 3. Is the information fair and logical? (See page 243.)
☑ 4. What points of view are shared in the message? Which ones are left out? (See page 244.)
☑ 5. What images or sounds catch my attention? (See page 245.)

Medium
☑ 6. What type of media is used to deliver the message? (See page 246.)
☑ 7. What are the strengths and weaknesses of the media format? (See page 247.)

Receiver
☑ 8. Who is the target of the message? (See page 248.)
☑ 9. How might people different from me interpret this message? (See page 249.)

Context
☑ 10. What is the purpose of the message? (See page 250.)
☑ 11. Who controls the transmission of this message? (See page 251.)

Your Turn Read and consider each question in the checklist above. Apply the questions to the next media message you encounter.

Step 4: Assess ongoing skills application.

Of course, the point of learning new skills is to apply them. Tests don't assess application, but you can. After teaching a skill, tell students that you will expect them to use the skill in class. For example, if you have taught students how to communicate in groups, you can provide extra-credit points when you see students use that skill well in class. Also, the *Inquire Student Handbook* provides various evaluation tools, such as the checklist to the left for evaluating media messages.

How can I assess students' projects?

Inquire provides simple but powerful tools for planning and assessing projects. Follow these steps:

Step 1: Set up standards-based goals and objectives.

On *Inquire* pages 356–357, students learn to set goals and objectives for their projects. Use this same approach to define goals and objectives based on the standards that you are teaching. Also note that *Inquire* page 357 suggests that students list or outline the tasks required to complete a project. (Each project covered in the *Student Handbook* begins with guidelines that suggest the necessary steps for completing the work. See *Inquire* page 510 for an example.)

■ The **goal** focuses on the project and the reason for doing it.

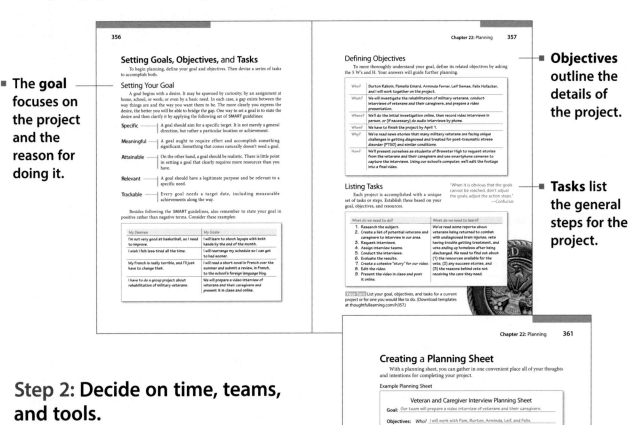

■ **Objectives** outline the details of the project.

■ **Tasks** list the general steps for the project.

Step 2: Decide on time, teams, and tools.

Inquire pages 358–361 help students schedule projects, gather tools, and set up teams. This information, plus the goal and objectives, appears in one place: the planning sheet. Use this sheet to plan any kind of project, from a diorama to a fund-raiser. (Go to thoughtfullearning.com/h361 to download a planning sheet, or copy the sheet on TG page 303.)

Step 3: Assess formatively.

Use the tasks you listed as opportunities for formative assessment throughout the process. For example, when students are making a video, provide feedback as they write scripts, line up actors, rehearse, set up a shooting schedule, and so on. Formative assessment keeps students on schedule and on track.

Step 4: Assign self-assessment.

The planning sheet translates easily into a rubric that students can use to assess their projects before revising them. Students can copy the goal and objectives from the planning sheet to the first column of the rubric sheet. Then they provide written evaluations as well as numerical ratings. These self-evaluations quickly tell students where their projects need to be improved. (Go to thoughtfullearning.com/h417 to download a rubric sheet, or copy the sheet on TG page 304.)

Step 5: Arrange real-world assessments.

When students present their projects, they naturally receive feedback. What do people think of the project? Does it match up to other projects? Does it work? In many ways, the real-world assessment of a project will be more important to the student than any other assessment.

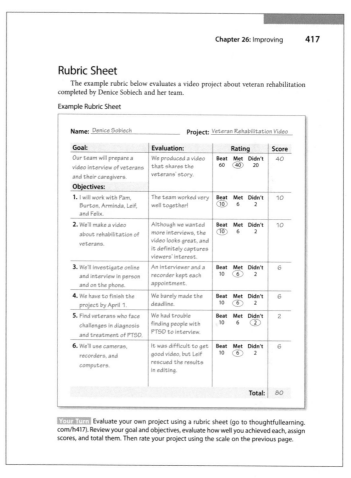

Step 6: Assess summatively.

Once projects are presented, you can assess them using the same rubric that students used for self-assessment. Note that the scale on the rubric produces a total score that can easily be converted to a percentage (superlative is above 100, excellent is 90–99, good is 80–89, average is 70–79, poor is 60–69, and incomplete is 59 and below).

How can I assess collaborative projects?

If you assess only the final project, you'll probably run into a classic problem: high achievers will take over the project from low achievers. The high achievers will feel overworked, and the low achievers will feel excluded. Varied assessment can help address this problem. Follow these steps:

Step 1: Assess the project.

Have students outline the project's goal and objectives, using a planning sheet (see *Inquire* page 361 and TG page 303). Review this document and request changes if the goal and objectives seem either too easy or too challenging. Then use this planning sheet to create a rubric sheet (see *Inquire* page 417 and TG page 304) for scoring the project as a whole.

Step 2: Assess the group and the individuals.

Let students know from the start that they will receive a grade for their teamwork. Outline your own goal and objectives for teams, listing items such as productivity, cooperation, collaboration, problem solving, and conflict resolution. Also let students know they will receive an individual grade for contribution and effort.

Step 3: Assess formatively.

Throughout the process, give students feedback about how well the project is coming together, how well they are working as a team, and how well they are working as individuals. Point out ways to improve. Then have students create an improvement plan like the one on *Inquire* page 421. Go to thoughtfullearning.com/h421 to download a template.

Step 4: Have students self-assess.

At the end of the process, have the group self-assess its project and its group dynamic. Then have individual students self-assess their own contributions.

Step 5: Combine assessments.

Use your assessments and the students' self-assessments to arrive at a final score for each student.

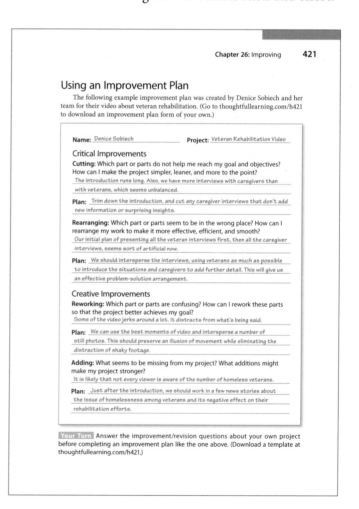

Chapter 26: Improving   **421**

Using an Improvement Plan

The following example improvement plan was created by Denice Sobiech and her team for their video about veteran rehabilitation. (Go to thoughtfullearning.com/h421 to download an improvement plan form of your own.)

Name: Denice Sobiech   **Project:** Veteran Rehabilitation Video

Critical Improvements

Cutting: Which part or parts do not help me reach my goal and objectives? How can I make the project simpler, leaner, and more to the point?
The introduction runs long. Also, we have more interviews with caregivers than with veterans, which seems unbalanced.

Plan: Trim down the introduction, and cut any caregiver interviews that don't add new information or surprising insights.

Rearranging: Which part or parts seem to be in the wrong place? How can I rearrange my work to make it more effective, efficient, and smooth?
Our initial plan of presenting all the veteran interviews first, then all the caregiver interviews, seems sort of artificial now.

Plan: We should intersperse the interviews, using veterans as much as possible to introduce the situations and caregivers to add further detail. This will give us an effective problem-solution arrangement.

Creative Improvements

Reworking: Which part or parts are confusing? How can I rework these parts so that the project better achieves my goal?
Some of the video jerks around a lot. It distracts from what's being said.

Plan: We can use the best moments of video and intersperse a number of still photos. This should preserve an illusion of movement while eliminating the distraction of shaky footage.

Adding: What seems to be missing from my project? What additions might make my project stronger?
It is likely that not every viewer is aware of the number of homeless veterans.

Plan: Just after the introduction, we should work in a few news stories about the issue of homelessness among veterans and its negative effect on their rehabilitation efforts.

Your Turn Answer the improvement/revision questions about your own project before completing an improvement plan like the one above. (Download a template at thoughtfullearning.com/h421.)

Correlations for *Inquire*

We live in a standards-driven world. Even inquiry- and project-based classrooms need to deliver standards-based instruction. This section of the teacher's guide provides an overview of the way that *Inquire* teaches three sets of standards:

In the daily lesson plans, you will also find the specific standards covered in each particular chapter.

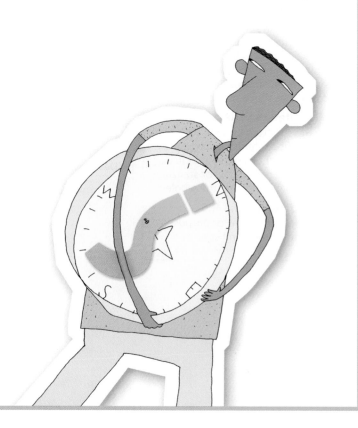

Common Core State Standards

How does *Inquire* teach the ELA Common Core State Standards?

Inquire teaches the college and career readiness standards for reading, writing, listening, speaking, and language. *Inquire* also addresses most of the Common Core ELA standards. For a complete listing, go to thoughtfullearning.com/CCSSELA.

Common Core College and Career Readiness Anchor Standards for Reading	Relevant Chapters from *Inquire*	

Key Ideas and Details
 	
CCSS.ELA-Literacy.CCRA.R.1
Read closely to determine what the text says explicitly and to make logical inferences from it; cite specific textual evidence when writing or speaking to support conclusions drawn from the text.
 	
CCSS.ELA-Literacy.CCRA.R.2
Determine central ideas or themes of a text and analyze their development; summarize the key supporting details and ideas.
 	
CCSS.ELA-Literacy.CCRA.R.3
Analyze how and why individuals, events, or ideas develop and interact over the course of a text.
	Part I
	  7. Building Arguments
	  8. Succeeding in School and College
	  9. Improving Study Skills
	10. Reading to Learn
	12. Writing to Learn
	14. Developing Visual Literacy
	15. Improving Information and Media Literacy
	16. Creating Internet Literacy
	17. Using Social Media
	18. Developing Financial Literacy
		Part II
		23. Conducting Basic Research
		24. Conducting Advanced Research
		
		Part III
		28. Basic Writing Projects
		29. Advanced Writing Projects
		30. Data and Graphing Projects
		33. Performing Projects
		35. Web Projects

Craft and Structure
 	
CCSS.ELA-Literacy.CCRA.R.4
Interpret words and phrases as they are used in a text, including determining technical, connotative, and figurative meanings, and analyze how specific word choices shape meaning or tone.
 	
CCSS.ELA-Literacy.CCRA.R.5
Analyze the structure of texts, including how specific sentences, paragraphs, and larger portions of the text (e.g., a section, chapter, scene, or stanza) relate to each other and the whole.
 	
CCSS.ELA-Literacy.CCRA.R.6
Assess how point of view or purpose shapes the content and style of a text.
	Part I
	  7. Building Arguments
	  9. Improving Study Skills
	10. Reading to Learn
	11. Building Your Vocabulary
	12. Writing to Learn
	13. Taking Exit and Entrance Exams
	14. Developing Visual Literacy
	15. Improving Information and Media Literacy
	16. Creating Internet Literacy
	18. Developing Financial Literacy
	19. Succeeding in the Workplace
		Part II
		21. Questioning
		23. Conducting Basic Research
		24. Conducting Advanced Research
		26. Improving
		
		Part III
		28. Basic Writing Projects
		29. Advanced Writing Projects
		31. Audio-Visual Projects
		32. Design Projects
		33. Performing Projects
		35. Web Projects

CCSS College and Career Readiness Anchor Standards for Reading	Relevant Chapters from *Inquire*	
Integration of Knowledge and Ideas **CCSS.ELA-Literacy.CCRA.R.7** Integrate and evaluate content presented in diverse media and formats, including visually and quantitatively, as well as in words. **CCSS.ELA-Literacy.CCRA.R.8** Delineate and evaluate the argument and specific claims in a text, including the validity of the reasoning as well as the relevance and sufficiency of the evidence. **CCSS.ELA-Literacy.CCRA.R.9** Analyze how two or more texts address similar themes or topics in order to build knowledge or to compare the approaches the authors take.	**Part I** 2. Critical Thinking 3. Creative Thinking 4. Problem Solving 7. Building Arguments 9. Improving Study Skills 10. Reading to Learn 11. Building Your Vocabulary 12. Writing to Learn 13. Taking Exit and Entrance Exams 14. Developing Visual Literacy 15. Improving Information and Media Literacy 16. Creating Internet Literacy 17. Using Social Media	**Part II** 21. Questioning 23. Conducting Basic Research 24. Conducting Advanced Research 26. Improving **Part III** 28. Basic Writing Projects 29. Advanced Writing Projects 30. Data and Graphing Projects 31. Audio-Visual Projects 32. Design Projects 33. Performing Projects 34. Community Projects 35. Web Projects
Range of Reading and Level of Text Complexity **CCSS.ELA-Literacy.CCRA.R.10** Read and comprehend complex literary and informational texts independently and proficiently.	**Part I** 7. Building Arguments 9. Improving Study Skills 10. Reading to Learn 12. Writing to Learn 14. Developing Visual Literacy 15. Improving Information and Media Literacy 16. Creating Internet Literacy	**Part II** 23. Conducting Basic Research 24. Conducting Advanced Research **Part III** 28. Basic Writing Projects 29. Advanced Writing Projects 30. Data and Graphing Projects 31. Audio-Visual Projects 32. Design Projects 33. Performing Projects 34. Community Projects 35. Web Projects

CCSS College and Career Readiness Anchor Standards for Writing	Relevant Chapters from *Inquire*	
Text Types and Purposes **CCSS.ELA-Literacy.CCRA.W.1** Write arguments to support claims in an analysis of substantive topics or texts using valid reasoning and relevant and sufficient evidence. **CCSS.ELA-Literacy.CCRA.W.2** Write informative/explanatory texts to examine and convey complex ideas and information clearly and accurately through the effective selection, organization, and analysis of content. **CCSS.ELA-Literacy.CCRA.W.3** Write narratives to develop real or imagined experiences or events using effective technique, well-chosen details and well-structured event sequences.	**Part I** 2. Critical Thinking 3. Creative Thinking 7. Building Arguments 9. Improving Study Skills 10. Reading to Learn 12. Writing to Learn 13. Taking Exit and Entrance Exams 14. Developing Visual Literacy 15. Improving Information and Media Literacy 16. Creating Internet Literacy	**Part II** 20. Understanding the Inquiry Process 21. Questioning 22. Planning 23. Conducting Basic Research 24. Conducting Advanced Research 25. Creating 26. Improving 27. Presenting **Part III** 28. Basic Writing Projects 29. Advanced Writing Projects 30. Data and Graphing Projects 31. Audio-Visual Projects 32. Design Projects 33. Performing Projects 34. Community Projects 35. Web Projects

CCSS College and Career Readiness Anchor Standards for Writing	Relevant Chapters from *Inquire*	
Production and Distribution of Writing **CCSS.ELA-Literacy.CCRA.W.4** Produce clear and coherent writing in which the development, organization, and style are appropriate to task, purpose, and audience. **CCSS.ELA-Literacy.CCRA.W.5** Develop and strengthen writing as needed by planning, revising, editing, rewriting, or trying a new approach. **CCSS.ELA-Literacy.CCRA.W.6** Use technology, including the Internet, to produce and publish writing and to interact and collaborate with others.	**Part I** 4. Problem Solving 7. Building Arguments 12. Writing to Learn 13. Taking Exit and Entrance Exams 14. Developing Visual Literacy 15. Improving Information and Media Literacy 16. Creating Internet Literacy **Part II** 20. Understanding the Inquiry Process 21. Questioning 22. Planning 23. Conducting Basic Research 24. Conducting Advanced Research 25. Creating 26. Improving 27. Presenting	**Part III** 28. Basic Writing Projects 29. Advanced Writing Projects 30. Data and Graphing Projects 31. Audio-Visual Projects 32. Design Projects 33. Performing Projects 34. Community Projects 35. Web Projects
Research to Build and Present Knowledge **CCSS.ELA-Literacy.CCRA.W.7** Conduct short as well as more sustained research projects based on focused questions, demonstrating understanding of the subject under investigation. **CCSS.ELA-Literacy.CCRA.W.8** Gather relevant information from multiple print and digital sources, assess the credibility and accuracy of each source, and integrate the information while avoiding plagiarism. **CCSS.ELA-Literacy.CCRA.W.9** Draw evidence from literary or informational texts to support analysis, reflection, and research.	**Part I** 4. Problem Solving 7. Building Arguments 9. Improving Study Skills 10. Reading to Learn 12. Writing to Learn 13. Taking Exit and Entrance Exams 14. Developing Visual Literacy 15. Improving Information and Media Literacy 16. Creating Internet Literacy	**Part II** 23. Conducting Basic Research 24. Conducting Advanced Research **Part III** 28. Basic Writing Projects 29. Advanced Writing Projects 30. Data and Graphing Projects 31. Audio-Visual Projects 32. Design Projects 33. Performing Projects 34. Community Projects 35. Web Projects
Range of Writing **CCSS.ELA-Literacy.CCRA.W.10** Write routinely over extended time frames (time for research, reflection, and revision) and shorter time frames (a single sitting or a day or two) for a range of tasks, purposes, and audiences.	**Part I** 2. Critical Thinking 3. Creative Thinking 7. Building Arguments 9. Improving Study Skills 12. Writing to Learn 13. Taking Exit and Entrance Exams 17. Using Social Media **Part II** 21. Questioning 22. Planning 23. Conducting Basic Research 24. Conducting Advanced Research 25. Creating 26. Improving 27. Presenting	**Part III** 28. Basic Writing Projects 29. Advanced Writing Projects 30. Data and Graphing Projects 31. Audio-Visual Projects 32. Design Projects 33. Performing Projects 34. Community Projects 35. Web Projects

CCSS College and Career Readiness Anchor Standards for Speaking and Listening	Relevant Chapters from *Inquire*	
Comprehension and Collaboration **CCSS.ELA-Literacy.CCRA.SL.1** Prepare for and participate effectively in a range of conversations and collaborations with diverse partners, building on others' ideas and expressing their own clearly and persuasively. **CCSS.ELA-Literacy.CCRA.SL.2** Integrate and evaluate information presented in diverse media and formats, including visually, quantitatively, and orally. **CCSS.ELA-Literacy.CCRA.SL.3** Evaluate a speaker's point of view, reasoning, and use of evidence and rhetoric.	**Part I** 1. Overview of 21st Century Skills 4. Problem Solving 5. Communicating 6. Collaborating 14. Developing Visual Literacy 15. Improving Information and Media Literacy 16. Creating Internet Literacy 17. Using Social Media **Part II** 20. Understanding the Inquiry Process 21. Questioning 22. Planning 23. Conducting Basic Research 24. Conducting Advanced Research 26. Improving 27. Presenting	**Part III** 28. Basic Writing Projects 29. Advanced Writing Projects 30. Data and Graphing Projects 31. Audio-Visual Projects 32. Design Projects 33. Performing Projects 34. Community Projects 35. Web Projects
Presentation of Knowledge and Ideas **CCSS.ELA-Literacy.CCRA.SL.4** Present information, findings, and supporting evidence such that listeners can follow the line of reasoning and the organization, development, and style are appropriate to task, purpose, and audience. **CCSS.ELA-Literacy.CCRA.SL.5** Make strategic use of digital media and visual displays of data to express information and enhance understanding of presentations. **CCSS.ELA-Literacy.CCRA.SL.6** Adapt speech to a variety of contexts and communicative tasks, demonstrating command of formal English when indicated or appropriate.	**Part I** 1. Overview of 21st Century Skills 5. Communicating 6. Collaborating 7. Building Arguments 12. Writing to Learn 13. Taking Exit and Entrance Exams 14. Developing Visual Literacy 15. Improving Information and Media Literacy 16. Creating Internet Literacy 17. Using Social Media	**Part II** 20. Understanding the Inquiry Process 21. Questioning 22. Planning 23. Conducting Basic Research 24. Conducting Advanced Research 25. Creating 26. Improving 27. Presenting **Part III** 28. Basic Writing Projects 29. Advanced Writing Projects 30. Data and Graphing Projects 31. Audio-Visual Projects 32. Design Projects 33. Performing Projects 34. Community Projects 35. Web Projects

CCSS College and Career Readiness Anchor Standards for Language	Relevant Chapters from *Inquire*	
Conventions of Standard English **CCSS.ELA-Literacy.CCRA.L.1** Demonstrate command of the conventions of standard English grammar and usage when writing or speaking **CCSS.ELA-Literacy.CCRA.L.2** Demonstrate command of the conventions of standard English capitalization, punctuation, and spelling when writing.	**Part I** 5. Communicating 9. Improving Study Skills 10. Reading to Learn 11. Building Your Vocabulary 12. Writing to Learn 13. Taking Exit and Entrance Exams	**Part II** 26. Improving 27. Presenting **Part III** 28. Basic Writing Projects 29. Advanced Writing Projects 30. Data and Graphing Projects

ELA College and Career Readiness Anchor Standards for Language	Relevant Chapters from *Inquire*	
Knowledge of Language **CCSS.ELA-Literacy.CCRA.L.3** Apply knowledge of language to understand how language functions in different contexts, to make effective choices for meaning or style, and to comprehend more fully when reading or listening.	**Part I** 1. Overview of 21st Century Skills 5. Communicating 6. Collaborating 7. Building Arguments 9. Improving Study Skills 10. Reading to Learn 11. Building Your Vocabulary 12. Writing to Learn 13. Taking Exit and Entrance Exams 17. Using Social Media	**Part II** 23. Conducting Basic Research 24. Conducting Advanced Research 25. Creating 26. Improving 27. Presenting **Part III** 28. Basic Writing Projects 29. Advanced Writing Projects 30. Data and Graphing Projects 31. Audio-Visual Projects 32. Design Projects 33. Performing Projects 34. Community Projects 35. Web Projects
Vocabulary Acquisition and Use **CCSS.ELA-Literacy.CCRA.L.4** Determine or clarify the meaning of unknown and multiple-meaning words and phrases by using context clues, analyzing meaningful word parts, and consulting general and specialized reference materials, as appropriate. **CCSS.ELA-Literacy.CCRA.L.5** Demonstrate understanding of figurative language, word relationships, and nuances in word meanings. **CCSS.ELA-Literacy.CCRA.L.6** Acquire and use accurately a range of general academic and domain-specific words and phrases sufficient for reading, writing, speaking, and listening at the college and career readiness level; demonstrate independence in gathering vocabulary knowledge when encountering an unknown term important to comprehension or expression.	**Part I** 5. Communicating 9. Improving Study Skills 10. Reading to Learn 11. Building Your Vocabulary 12. Writing to Learn 13. Taking Exit and Entrance Exams 15. Improving Information and Media Literacy 16. Creating Internet Literacy 17. Using Social Media 18. Developing Financial Literacy **Part II** 21. Questioning 22. Planning 23. Conducting Basic Research 24. Conducting Advanced Research 25. Creating 26. Improving 27. Presenting	**Part III** 28. Basic Writing Projects 29. Advanced Writing Projects 30. Data and Graphing Projects 31. Audio-Visual Projects 32. Design Projects 33. Performing Projects 34. Community Projects 35. Web Projects

How does *Inquire* teach the Common Core State Standards for math and science?

   Inquire teaches the standards for mathematical practice and for science and engineering practice. These thinking and problem-solving skills help students succeed in math, science, and many other subjects.

Common Core Standards for Mathematical Practice	Relevant Chapters from *Inquire*	
CCSS.Math.Practice.MP1 **Make sense of problems and persevere in solving them.**	**Part I** 1. Overview of 21st Century Skills 2. Critical Thinking 3. Creative Thinking 4. Problem Solving 8. Succeeding in School and College 9. Improving Study Skills 10. Reading to Learn 13. Taking Exit and Entrance Exams 18. Developing Financial Literacy 19. Succeeding in the Workplace	**Part II** 20. Understanding the Inquiry Process 21. Questioning 22. Planning 23. Conducting Basic Research 24. Conducting Advanced Research 25. Creating 26. Improving 27. Presenting **Part III** 29. Advanced Writing Projects 30. Data and Graphing Projects 31. Audio-Visual Projects 32. Design Projects 34. Community Projects 35. Web Projects
CCSS.Math.Practice.MP2 **Reason abstractly and quantitatively.**	**Part I** 2. Critical Thinking 3. Creative Thinking 4. Problem Solving 7. Building Arguments 15. Improving Information and Media Literacy 16. Creating Internet Literacy 18. Developing Financial Literacy 19. Succeeding in the Workplace	**Part II** 21. Questioning 22. Planning 25. Creating 26. Improving **Part III** 30. Data and Graphing Projects 31. Audio-Visual Projects 32. Design Projects 34. Community Projects 35. Web Projects
CCSS.Math.Practice.MP3 **Construct viable arguments and critique the reasoning of others.**	**Part I** 2. Critical Thinking 3. Creative Thinking 4. Problem Solving 5. Communicating 6. Collaborating 7. Building Arguments 10. Reading to Learn 12. Writing to Learn 13. Taking Exit and Entrance Exams 15. Improving Information and Media Literacy 16. Creating Internet Literacy 17. Using Social Media 19. Succeeding in the Workplace	**Part II** 21. Questioning 22. Planning 23. Conducting Basic Research 24. Conducting Advanced Research 25. Creating 26. Improving **Part III** 28. Basic Writing Projects 29. Advanced Writing Projects 30. Data and Graphing Projects 31. Audio-Visual Projects 32. Design Projects 33. Performing Projects 34. Community Projects 35. Web Projects

CCSS Standards for Mathematical Practice	Relevant Chapters from *Inquire*	
CCSS.Math.Practice.MP4 **Model with mathematics.**	**Part I** 2. Critical Thinking 3. Creative Thinking 4. Problem Solving 7. Building Arguments 8. Succeeding in School and College 14. Developing Visual Literacy 15. Improving Information and Media Literacy 18. Developing Financial Literacy 19. Succeeding in the Workplace	**Part II** 22. Planning 23. Conducting Basic Research 24. Conducting Advanced Research 26. Improving **Part III** 29. Advanced Writing Projects 30. Data and Graphing Projects 31. Audio-Visual Projects 32. Design Projects 34. Community Projects 35. Web Projects
CCSS.Math.Practice.MP5 **Use appropriate tools strategically.**	**Part I** 2. Critical Thinking 3. Creative Thinking 4. Problem Solving 7. Building Arguments 8. Succeeding in School and College 9. Improving Study Skills 12. Writing to Learn 14. Developing Visual Literacy 15. Improving Information and Media Literacy 16. Creating Internet Literacy 17. Using Social Media 18. Developing Financial Literacy 19. Succeeding in the Workplace	**Part II** 23. Conducting Basic Research 24. Conducting Advanced Research 25. Creating 26. Improving 27. Presenting **Part III** 28. Basic Writing Projects 29. Advanced Writing Projects 30. Data and Graphing Projects 31. Audio-Visual Projects 32. Design Projects 33. Performing Projects 34. Community Projects 35. Web Projects
CCSS.Math.Practice.MP6 **Attend to precision.**	**Part I** 2. Critical Thinking 4. Problem Solving 7. Building Arguments 8. Succeeding in School and College 9. Improving Study Skills 10. Reading to Learn 12. Writing to Learn 13. Taking Exit and Entrance Exams 15. Improving Information and Media Literacy 16. Creating Internet Literacy 18. Developing Financial Literacy 19. Succeeding in the Workplace	**Part II** 22. Planning 23. Conducting Basic Research 24. Conducting Advanced Research 26. Improving **Part III** 28. Basic Writing Projects 29. Advanced Writing Projects 30. Data and Graphing Projects 31. Audio-Visual Projects 32. Design Projects 33. Performing Projects 34. Community Projects 35. Web Projects
CCSS.Math.Practice.MP7 **Look for and make use of structure.**	**Part I** 2. Critical Thinking 3. Creative Thinking 4. Problem Solving 7. Building Arguments 10. Reading to Learn 13. Taking Exit and Entrance Exams 14. Developing Visual Literacy 15. Improving Information and Media Literacy 16. Creating Internet Literacy 18. Developing Financial Literacy 19. Succeeding in the Workplace	**Part II** 22. Planning 23. Conducting Basic Research 24. Conducting Advanced Research 25. Creating **Part III (All)** ■ Chapters 29–35

CCSS Standards for Mathematical Practice	Relevant Chapters from *Inquire*	
CCSS.Math.Practice.MP8 **Look for and express regularity in repeated reasoning**	**Part I** 2. Critical Thinking 3. Creative Thinking 4. Problem Solving 7. Building Arguments 9. Improving Study Skills 10. Reading to Learn 11. Building Your Vocabulary 12. Writing to Learn 13. Taking Exit and Entrance Exams 15. Improving Information and Media Literacy 16. Creating Internet Literacy 18. Developing Financial Literacy	**Part II** 20. Understanding the Inquiry Process 21. Questioning 22. Planning 23. Conducting Basic Research 24. Conducting Advanced Research 25. Creating 26. Improving 27. Presenting **Part III** 30. Data and Graphing Projects 31. Audio-Visual Projects 32. Design Projects 34. Community Projects 35. Web Projects

CCSS Standards for Science and Engineering Practices	Relevant Chapters from *Inquire*	
CCSS.Science.Practice.SP1 **Asking questions and defining problems**	**Part I** 1. Overview of 21st Century Skills 2. Critical Thinking 3. Creative Thinking 4. Problem Solving 7. Building Arguments 8. Succeeding in School and College 9. Improving Study Skills 10. Reading to Learn 11. Building Your Vocabulary 12. Writing to Learn 13. Taking Exit and Entrance Exams 19. Succeeding in the Workplace	**Part II** 20. Understanding the Inquiry Process 21. Questioning 22. Planning 23. Conducting Basic Research 24. Conducting Advanced Research 25. Creating 26. Improving 27. Presenting **Part III** 28. Basic Writing Projects 29. Advanced Writing Projects 30. Data and Graphing Projects 31. Audio-Visual Projects 32. Design Projects 33. Performing Projects 34. Community Projects 35. Web Projects
CCSS.Science.Practice.SP2 **Developing and using models**	**Part I** 2. Critical Thinking 3. Creative Thinking 4. Problem Solving 7. Building Arguments 14. Developing Visual Literacy 18. Developing Financial Literacy 19. Succeeding in the Workplace **Part II** 20. Understanding Inquiry Process 21. Questioning 22. Planning 23. Conducting Basic Research 24. Conducting Advanced Research 25. Creating 26. Improving 27. Presenting	**Part III** 28. Basic Writing Projects 29. Advanced Writing Projects 30. Data and Graphing Projects 31. Audio-Visual Projects 32. Design Projects 33. Performing Projects 34. Community Projects 35. Web Projects

CCSS Standards for Science and Engineering Practices	Relevant Chapters from *Inquire*	
CCSS.Science.Practice.SP3 **Planning and carrying out investigations**	**Part I** 2. Critical Thinking 3. Creative Thinking 4. Problem Solving 6. Collaborating 7. Building Arguments 9. Improving Study Skills 10. Reading to Learn 12. Writing to Learn 15. Improving Information and Media Literacy 16. Creating Internet Literacy 19. Succeeding in the Workplace	**Part II** 20. Understanding the Inquiry Process 21. Questioning 22. Planning 23. Conducting Basic Research 24. Conducting Advanced Research 25. Creating 26. Improving 27. Presenting **Part III** 28. Basic Writing Projects 29. Advanced Writing Projects 30. Data and Graphing Projects 31. Audio-Visual Projects 32. Design Projects 33. Performing Projects 34. Community Projects 35. Web Projects
CCSS.Science.Practice.SP4 **Analyzing and interpreting data**	**Part I** 2. Critical Thinking 3. Creative Thinking 4. Problem Solving 5. Communicating 7. Building Arguments 8. Succeeding in School and College 9. Improving Study Skills 10. Reading to Learn 11. Building Your Vocabulary 12. Writing to Learn 13. Taking Exit and Entrance Exams 14. Developing Visual Literacy 15. Improving Information and Media Literacy 16. Creating Internet Literacy 18. Developing Financial Literacy	**Part II** 23. Conducting Basic Research 24. Conducting Advanced Research 26. Improving **Part III** 28. Basic Writing Projects 29. Advanced Writing Projects 30. Data and Graphing Projects 31. Audio-Visual Projects 32. Design Projects 33. Performing Projects 34. Community Projects 35. Web Projects
CCSS.Science.Practice.SP5 **Using mathematics and computational thinking**	**Part I** 2. Critical Thinking 3. Creative Thinking 4. Problem Solving 7. Building Arguments 8. Succeeding in School and College 18. Developing Financial Literacy 19. Succeeding in the Workplace	**Part II** 22. Planning 23. Conducting Basic Research 24. Conducting Advanced Research 26. Improving **Part III** 30. Data and Graphing Projects 31. Audio-Visual Projects 32. Design Projects 34. Community Projects 35. Web Projects

CCSS Standards for Science and Engineering Practices	Relevant Chapters from *Inquire*	
CCSS.Science.Practice.SP6 **Constructing explanations and designing solutions**	**Part I** 1. Overview of 21st Century Skills 2. Critical Thinking 3. Creative Thinking 4. Problem Solving 5. Communicating 6. Collaborating 7. Building Arguments 18. Developing Financial Literacy 19. Succeeding in the Workplace	**Part II** 20. Understanding the Inquiry Process 21. Questioning 22. Planning 23. Conducting Basic Research 24. Conducting Advanced Research 25. Creating 26. Improving 27. Presenting **Part III** 28. Basic Writing Projects 29. Advanced Writing Projects 30. Data and Graphing Projects 31. Audio-Visual Projects 32. Design Projects 33. Performing Projects 34. Community Projects 35. Web Projects
CCSS.Science.Practice.SP7 **Engaging in argument from evidence**	**Part I** 2. Critical Thinking 3. Creative Thinking 4. Problem Solving 5. Communicating 6. Collaborating 7. Building Arguments 8. Succeeding in School and College 9. Improving Study Skills 10. Reading to Learn 12. Writing to Learn 13. Taking Exit and Entrance Exams 19. Succeeding in the Workplace	**Part II** 21. Questioning 22. Planning 23. Conducting Basic Research 24. Conducting Advanced Research 25. Creating 26. Improving 27. Presenting **Part III** 28. Basic Writing Projects 29. Advanced Writing Projects 30. Data and Graphing Projects 31. Audio-Visual Projects 32. Design Projects 33. Performing Projects 34. Community Projects 35. Web Projects
CCSS.Science.Practice.SP8 **Obtaining, evaluating, and communicating information**	**Part I** 2. Critical Thinking 3. Creative Thinking 4. Problem Solving 5. Communicating 6. Collaborating 7. Building Arguments 8. Succeeding in School and College 9. Improving Study Skills 10. Reading to Learn 11. Building Your Vocabulary 12. Writing to Learn 13. Taking Exit and Entrance Exams 14. Developing Visual Literacy 15. Improving Information/Media Literacy 16. Creating Internet Literacy 17. Using Social Media 18. Developing Financial Literacy 19. Succeeding in the Workplace	**Part II** 20. Understanding the Inquiry Process 21. Questioning 22. Planning 23. Conducting Basic Research 24. Conducting Advanced Research 25. Creating 26. Improving 27. Presenting **Part III** 28. Basic Writing Projects 29. Advanced Writing Projects 30. Data and Graphing Projects 31. Audio-Visual Projects 32. Design Projects 33. Performing Projects 34. Community Projects 35. Web Projects

Partnership for 21st Century Skills Framework

How does *Inquire* teach 21st century skills?

Inquire teaches the learning, literacy, and life skills advocated by the Partnership for 21st Century Skills. The following tables show how *Inquire* correlates to the framework provided by the Partnership.

Creativity and Innovation	Relevant Chapters from *Inquire*	
Think Creatively ■ Use a wide range of idea-creation techniques (such as brainstorming) ■ Create new and worthwhile ideas (both incremental and radical concepts) ■ Elaborate, refine, analyze, and evaluate ideas in order to improve and maximize creative efforts	**Part I** 3. Creative Thinking 4. Problem Solving 7. Building Arguments 17. Using Social Media 19. Succeeding in the Workplace	**Part II (All)** ■ Chapters 20–28 **Part III (All)** ■ Chapters 29–35
Work Creatively with Others ■ Develop, implement, and communicate new ideas to others effectively ■ Be open and responsive to new and diverse perspectives; incorporate group input and feedback into the work ■ Demonstrate originality and inventiveness in work and understand the real-world limits to adopting new ideas ■ View failure as an opportunity to learn; understand that creativity and innovation is a long-term, cyclical process of small successes and frequent mistakes	**Part I** 3. Creative Thinking 4. Problem Solving 5. Communicating 6. Collaborating 7. Building Arguments 17. Using Social Media 19. Succeeding in the Workplace	**Part II** 22. Planning 26. Improving 27. Presenting **Part III** 31. Audio-Visual Projects 32. Design Projects 33. Performing Projects 34. Community Projects
Implement Innovations ■ Act on creative ideas to make a tangible and useful contribution to the field in which the innovation will occur	**Part I** 3. Creative Thinking 4. Problem Solving 6. Collaborating 19. Succeeding in the Workplace	**Part II (All)** ■ Chapters 20–28 **Part III (All)** ■ Chapters 29–35

Critical Thinking and Problem Solving	Relevant Chapters from *Inquire*	
Reason Effectively and Use Systems Thinking ■ Use various types of reasoning (inductive, deductive, etc.) as appropriate to the situation ■ Analyze how parts of a whole interact with each other to produce overall outcomes in complex systems	**Part I** 2. Critical Thinking 4. Problem Solving 7. Building Arguments 10. Reading to Learn 11. Building Your Vocabulary 13. Taking Exit/Entrance Exams 18. Developing Financial Literacy	**Part II (All)** ■ Chapters 20–28 **Part III (All)** ■ Chapters 29–35
Make Judgments and Decisions ■ Effectively analyze and evaluate evidence, arguments, claims, and beliefs ■ Analyze and evaluate major alternative points of view ■ Synthesize and make connections between information and arguments ■ Interpret information and draw conclusions based on the best analysis ■ Reflect critically on learning experiences and processes	**Part I** 2. Critical Thinking 7. Building Arguments 10. Reading to Learn 12. Writing to Learn 13. Taking Exit/Entrance Exams 14. Developing Visual Literacy 15. Improving Information and Media Literacy	**Part II (All)** ■ Chapters 20–28 **Part III (All)** ■ Chapters 29–35
Solve Problems ■ Solve different kinds of non-familiar problems in both conventional and innovative ways ■ Identify and ask significant questions that clarify various points of view and lead to better solutions	**Part I** 2. Critical Thinking 4. Problem Solving 6. Collaborating	**Part II (All)** ■ Chapters 20–28 **Part III (All)** ■ Chapters 29–35

Communication and Collaboration	Relevant Chapters from *Inquire*	
Communicate Clearly ■ Articulate thoughts and ideas effectively using oral, written, and nonverbal communication skills in a variety of forms and contexts ■ Listen effectively to decipher meaning, including knowledge, values, attitudes, and intentions ■ Use communication for a range of purposes (e.g., to inform, instruct, motivate, and persuade) ■ Utilize multiple media and technologies, and know how to judge their effectiveness *a priori* as well as assess their impact ■ Communicate effectively in diverse environments (including multi-lingual)	**Part I** 5. Communicating 7. Building Arguments 10. Reading to Learn 11. Building Your Vocabulary 12. Writing to Learn 14. Developing Visual Literacy 15. Information/Media Literacy 16. Creating Internet Literacy 17. Using Social Media 18. Financial Literacy 19. Succeeding in Workplace	**Part II** 21. Questioning 22. Planning 23. Conducting Basic Research 24. Conducting Advanced Research 25. Creating 26. Improving 27. Presenting **Part III (All)** ■ Chapters 29–35
Collaborate with Others ■ Demonstrate ability to work with diverse teams ■ Exercise flexibility and willingness to be helpful in making necessary compromises to accomplish a common goal ■ Assume shared responsibility for collaborative work, and value individual contributions made by the team	**Part I** 5. Communicating 6. Collaborating 8. School/College Success 19. Succeeding in the Workplace	**Part II** 22. Planning 23. Basic Research 26. Improving **Part III (All)** ■ Chapters 29–35
Access and Evaluate Information ■ Access information efficiently (time) and effectively (sources) ■ Evaluate information critically and competently	**Part I** 9. Improving Study Skills 10. Reading to Learn 15. Information/Media Literacy 18. Financial Literacy	**Part II** 23. Basic Research 24. Advanced Research **Part III (All)** ■ Chapters 29–35
Use and Manage Information ■ Use information accurately and creatively for the issue or problem at hand ■ Manage flow of information from a variety of sources ■ Apply a fundamental understanding of the ethical/legal issues surrounding the access and use of information	**Part I** 14. Developing Visual Literacy 15. Information/Media Literacy 16. Creating Internet Literacy 17. Using Social Media 18. Financial Literacy	**Part II** 23. Basic Research 24. Advanced Research **Part III (All)** ■ Chapters 29–35

Media Literacy	Relevant Chapters from *Inquire*	
Analyze Media ■ Understand both how and why media messages are constructed, and for what purposes ■ Examine how individuals interpret messages differently, how values and points of view are included or excluded, and how media can influence beliefs ■ Apply a fundamental understanding of the ethical/legal issues surrounding the access and use of media	**Part I** 5. Communicating 7. Building Arguments 14. Developing Visual Literacy 15. Improving Information and Media Literacy 16. Creating Internet Literacy 17. Using Social Media	**Part II** 23. Conducting Basic Research 24. Conducting Advanced Research **Part III (All)** ■ Chapters 29–35
Create Media Products ■ Understand and utilize the most appropriate media-creation tools, characteristics, and conventions ■ Understand utilize appropriate expressions and interpretations in diverse, multi-cultural environments	**Part I** 14. Developing Visual Literacy 15. Information/Media Literacy 16. Creating Internet Literacy 17. Using Social Media	**Part II** 25. Creating 27. Presenting **Part III (All)** ■ Chapters 29–35
Apply Technology Effectively ■ Use technology as a tool to research, organize, evaluate, and communicate information ■ Use digital technologies (computers, PDAs, media players, GPS, etc.), communication/networking tools, and social networks appropriately to access, manage, integrate, evaluate, and create information to successfully function in a knowledge economy ■ Apply an understanding of the ethical/legal issues around the access and use of information technology	**Part I** 8. Succeeding in School and College 9. Improving Study Skills 10. Reading to Learn 12. Writing to Learn 15. Improving Information and Media Literacy 16. Creating Internet Literacy 17. Using Social Media	**Part II** 23. Conducting Basic Research 24. Conducting Advanced Research 25. Creating 27. Presenting **Part III (All)** ■ Chapters 29–35

Life and Career Skills	Relevant Chapters from *Inquire*	
Flexibility and Adaptability ■ Adapt to varied roles, job responsibilities, schedules, and contexts ■ Work effectively in a climate of ambiguity and changing priorities ■ Incorporate feedback effectively ■ Deal positively with praise, setbacks, and criticism ■ Understand, negotiate, and balance diverse views and beliefs to reach workable solutions	**Part I** 2. Critical Thinking 3. Creative Thinking 4. Problem Solving 6. Collaborating 8. Succeeding in High School and College 19. Succeeding in the Workplace	**Part II (All)** ■ Chapters 20–28 **Part III (All)** ■ Chapters 29–35
Initiative and Self-Direction ■ Set goals with tangible and intangible success criteria ■ Balance tactical (short-term) and strategic (long-term) goals efficiently ■ Monitor, define, prioritize, and complete tasks without direct oversight ■ Go beyond basic mastery of skills and/or curriculum to explore and expand one's own learning and opportunities to gain expertise ■ Demonstrate initiative to advance skill levels towards a professional level ■ Demonstrate commitment to learning as a lifelong process ■ Reflect critically on past experiences in order to inform future progress ■ Utilize time and manage workload	**Part I** 1. Overview of 21st Century Skills 2. Critical Thinking 3. Creative Thinking 4. Problem Solving 5. Communicating 6. Collaborating 7. Building Arguments 8. Succeeding in High School and College 19. Succeeding in the Workplace	**Part II (All)** ■ Chapters 20–28 **Part III (All)** ■ Chapters 29–35
Social and Cross-Cultural Skills ■ Know when it is appropriate to listen and when to speak ■ Conduct oneself in a respectable, professional manner ■ Respect cultural differences and work effectively with people from a range of social and cultural backgrounds ■ Respond open-mindedly to different ideas and values ■ Leverage social and cultural differences to create new ideas and increase both innovation and quality of work	**Part I** 4. Problem Solving 5. Communicating 6. Collaborating 7. Building Arguments 8. Succeeding in School and College 17. Using Social Media 19. Succeeding in the Workplace	**Part II (All)** ■ Chapters 20–28 **Part III (All)** ■ Chapters 29–35
Productivity and Accountability ■ Set and meet goals, even in the face of obstacles and competing pressure ■ Prioritize, plan, and manage work to achieve the intended result ■ Work positively and ethically ■ Manage time and projects effectively ■ Multi-task ■ Participate actively, as well as be reliable and punctual ■ Present oneself professionally and with proper etiquette ■ Collaborate and cooperate effectively with teams ■ Respect and appreciate team diversity ■ Be accountable for results	**Part I** 2. Critical Thinking 3. Creative Thinking 4. Problem Solving 5. Communicating 6. Collaborating 8. Succeeding in School and College 18. Developing Financial Literacy 19. Succeeding in the Workplace	**Part II (All)** ■ Chapters 20–28 **Part III (All)** ■ Chapters 29–35
Leadership and Responsibility ■ Use interpersonal and problem-solving skills to influence and guide others toward a goal ■ Leverage strengths of others to accomplish a common goal ■ Inspire others to reach their very best via example and selflessness ■ Demonstrate integrity and ethical behavior in using influence and power ■ Act responsibly with the interests of the larger community in mind	**Part I** 4. Problem Solving 5. Communicating 6. Collaborating 7. Building Arguments 8. Succeeding in School and College 19. Succeeding in the Workplace	**Part II (All)** ■ Chapters 20–28 **Part III (All)** ■ Chapters 29–35

ISTE Correlations

What ISTE standards does *Inquire* cover?

The International Society for Technology in Education has outlined the following standards, which *Inquire* promotes.

1. Creativity and Innovation	Relevant Chapters from *Inquire*	
Students demonstrate creative thinking, construct knowledge, and develop innovative products and processes using technology. Students a. apply existing knowledge to generate new ideas, products, or processes. b. create original works as a means of personal or group expression. c. use models and simulations to explore complex systems and issues. d. identify trends/forecast possibilities.	**Part I** 3. Creative Thinking 4. Problem Solving 5. Communicating 6. Collaborating 7. Building Arguments 8. Succeeding in High School and College 19. Succeeding in the Workplace	**Part II (All)** ■ Chapters 20–28 **Part III (All):** ■ Chapters 29–35

2. Communication and Collaboration	Relevant Chapters from *Inquire*	
Students use digital media and environments to communicate and work collaboratively, including at a distance, to support individual learning and contribute to the learning of others. Students a. interact, collaborate, and publish with peers, experts, or others employing a variety of digital environments/media. b. communicate information and ideas effectively to multiple audiences using a variety of media and formats. c. develop cultural understanding and global awareness by engaging with learners of other cultures. d. contribute to project teams to produce original works or solve problems.	**Part I:** 1. Overview of 21st Century Skills 4. Problem Solving 5. Communicating 6. Collaborating 14. Developing Visual Literacy 15. Improving Information and Media Literacy 16. Creating Internet Literacy 17. Using Social Media 18. Developing Financial Literacy 19. Succeeding in the Workplace	**Part II (All)** ■ Chapters 20–28 **Part III (All):** ■ Chapters 29–35

3. Research and Information Fluency	Relevant Chapters from *Inquire*	
Students apply digital tools to gather, evaluate, and use information. Students a. plan strategies to guide inquiry. b. locate, organize, analyze, evaluate, synthesize, and ethically use information from sources and media. c. evaluate and select information sources and digital tools based on the appropriateness to specific tasks. d. process data and report results.	**Part I** 2. Critical Thinking 3. Creative Thinking 4. Problem Solving 14. Developing Visual Literacy 15. Improving Information and Media Literacy 16. Creating Internet Literacy 17. Using Social Media 18. Developing Financial Literacy 19. Succeeding in the Workplace	**Part II (All)** ■ Chapters 20–28 **Part III (All):** ■ Chapters 29–35

4. Critical Thinking, Problem Solving, and Decision Making	Relevant Chapters from *Inquire*	

Students use critical thinking skills to plan and conduct research, manage projects, solve problems, and make informed decisions using appropriate digital tools and resources. Students
 	
a. identify and define authentic problems and significant questions for investigation.
b. plan and manage activities to develop a solution or complete a project.
c. collect and analyze data to identify solutions and/or make informed decisions.
d. use multiple processes and diverse perspectives to explore alternative solutions.
	Part I
	  2. Critical Thinking
	  4. Problem Solving
	  5. Communicating
	  6. Collaborating
	  7. Building Arguments
	  8. Succeeding in High School and College
	 19. Succeeding in the Workplace
		Part II (All)
		 ■ Chapters 20–28
		Part III (All)
		 ■ Chapters 29–35

5. Digital Citizenship	**Relevant Chapters from *Inquire***	

Students understand human, cultural, and societal issues related to technology and practice legal and ethical behavior. Students
 	
a. advocate and practice safe, legal, and responsible use of information and technology.
b. exhibit a positive attitude toward using technology that supports collaboration, learning, and productivity.
c. demonstrate personal responsibility for lifelong learning.
d. exhibit leadership for digital citizenship.
	Part I
	  4. Problem Solving
	  8. Succeeding in High School and College
	  9. Improving Study Skills
	 10. Reading to Learn
	 12. Writing to Learn
	 14. Developing Visual Literacy
	 15. Improving Information and Media Literacy
	 16. Creating Internet Literacy
	 17. Using Social Media
	 18. Developing Financial Literacy
	 19. Succeeding in the Workplace
		Part II
		 22. Planning
		 23. Conducting Basic Research
		 24. Conducting Advanced Research
		 25. Creating
		 27. Presenting
		
		Part III
		 30. Data and Graphing Projects
		 31. Audio-Visual Projects
		 32. Design Projects
		 34. Community Projects
		 35. Web Projects

6. Technology Operations and Concepts	**Relevant Chapters from *Inquire***	

Students demonstrate a sound understanding of technology concepts, systems, and operations. Students
 	
a. understand and use technology systems.
b. select and use applications effectively and productively.
c. troubleshoot systems and applications.
d. transfer current knowledge to learning of new technologies.
	Part I
	  4. Problem Solving
	  5. Communicating
	  8. Succeeding in School and College
	  9. Improving Study Skills
	 10. Reading to Learn
	 12. Writing to Learn
	 14. Developing Visual Literacy
	 15. Improving Information and Media Literacy
	 16. Creating Internet Literacy
	 17. Using Social Media
	 18. Developing Financial Literacy
	 19. Succeeding in the Workplace
		Part II
		 22. Planning
		 23. Conducting Basic Research
		 24. Conducting Advanced Research
		 25. Creating
		 27. Presenting
		
		Part III
		 30. Data and Graphing Projects
		 31. Audio-Visual Projects
		 32. Design Projects
		 34. Community Projects
		 35. Web Projects

Research and Additional Resources

The *Inquire* program draws its inspiration from many, many sources. The next few pages list the chief ones—books, articles, Web sites, and even live presentations. *Inquire* is truly the product of a diverse community of educators and thinkers.

In addition to these sources, much of the material in *Inquire* was inspired by and field-tested in Ms. Cindy Smith's project-based learning classroom at Karcher School in Burlington, Wisconsin. The authors owe a great debt of gratitude to Ms. Smith and her class of 32 students.

And, of course, *Inquire* arose from the collaborative labors of the talented educators, developers, and designers at Thoughtful Learning.

What resources support *Inquire?*

Inquire was built on a broad base of research into 21st century skills, inquiry, and project-based learning. The authors used the following research materials and suggest them as resources for those who wish to delve deeper.

"Ad Council Home Page." *Adcouncil.org.* Ad Council, 21 Mar. 2011. Web. 24 Mar. 2011. <http://www.adcouncil.org/>

"Admongo Home Page." *Admongo.gov.* Federal Trade Commission, n.d. Web. 24 Mar. 2011. <http://www.admongo.gov/>

Alvarado, Amy E., and Patricia R. Herr. *Inquiry-Based Learning Using Everyday Objects: Hands-On Instructional Strategies That Promote Active Learning in Grades 3-8.* Thousand Oaks, CA: Corwin Press, 2003. Print.

Barell, John. *Problem-Based Learning: An Inquiry Approach,* 2nd Edition. Thousand Oaks, CA: Corwin Press, 2007. Print.

Barell, John. *Why Are School Buses Always Yellow? Teaching for Inquiry, PreK-5.* Thousand Oaks, CA: Corwin Press, 2008. Print.

Bartelmay, Kathy, and Jeff Burch. "Strengthening Literacy Through Science Projects." Coronado Convention Center, Orlando, FL, 18 Nov. 2010. (NCTE Session).

Bellanca, James. *Enriched Learning Projects: A Practical Pathway to 21st Century Skills.* Bloomington, IN: Solution Tree Press, 2010. Print.

Biederbeck, Eric. "Digital Storytelling in the Science and Math Classrooms." Baltimore Convention Center, Baltimore, MD, 5 Nov. 2010. (NMSA Session).

Burmark, Lynell. *Visual Literacy: Learn to See, See to Learn.* Alexandria, VA: ASCD, 2002. Print.

Cecil, Nancy L. *The Art of Inquiry: Questioning Strategies for K-6 Classrooms.* Winnipeg: Peguis Publishers, 1995. Print.

"Comic Creator." *Readwritethink.org.* International Reading Association/NCTE, n.d. Web. 24 Mar. 2011. <http://www.readwritethink.org/files/resources/interactives/comic/>

Cross, Stephanie B. "Project-Based Student-Centered Curriculum in the Standards-Based Classroom." Baltimore Convention Center, Baltimore, MD, 5 Nov. 2010. (NMSA Session).

DiBlasi, Howie. "Ten Projects to Teach Creativity and Problem Solving in Your Classroom." Baltimore Convention Center, Baltimore, MD, 6 Nov. 2010. (NMSA Session).

"DiRT FrontPage." *Digital Research Tools Wiki.* PBWorks, n.d. Web. 24 Mar. 2011. <https://digitalresearchtools.pbworks.com/w/page/ 178 016 72/FrontPage>

Dodd, Julie, and Judy Robinson. "Multimedia Blogging—Strategies for Creating a Community Within the Classroom and Beyond." Coronado Convention Center, Orlando, FL, 18 Nov. 2010. (NCTE Session).

"Duke School Home Page." *DukeSchool.org.* Duke School, n.d. Web. 24 Mar. 2011. <http://www.dukeschool.org/home/home.asp>

"Edutopia Home Page." *Edutopia.org.* The George Lucas Educational Foundation, n.d. Web 24 Mar. 2011. <http://www.edutopia.org/>

Falinski, Joanne, and Lizabeth Fogel. "Living with Digital Natives in Elementary Classrooms: Dual Language Students Construct New and Traditional Literacies Through Digital Storytelling." Coronado Convention Center, Orlando, FL, 20 Nov. 2010. (NCTE Session).

Forsten, Char. "Model Drawing for Middle School." Baltimore Convention Center, Baltimore, MD, 4 Nov. 2010. (NMSA Session).

"Framework for 21st Century Skills." *P 21.org.* Partnership for 21st Century Skills, n.d. Web. 24 March 2011. <http://www.p 21.org/>

Galante, Nichole, et al. "Living, Teaching, and Learning in Online Communities." Coronado Convention Center, Orlando, FL, 19 Nov. 2010. (NCTE Session).

"Games Planet Arcade." U.S. Department of Commerce/National Oceanographic and Atmospheric Administration. 25 June 2010. Web. 24 March 2011. <http://games.noaa.gov/>

Graceffa, Laura. "Collaborative Science Writing: Using Digital Writing to Enhance and Accelerate Learning." Baltimore Convention Center, Baltimore, MD, 5 Nov. 2010. (NMSA Session).

Greenstone, Barbara. "Promoting Literacy with Cartoons, Comics, and Graphic Novels." Baltimore Convention Center, Baltimore, MD, 4 Nov. 2010. (NMSA Session).

Harvey, Stephanie, and Harvey Daniels. *Inquiry Circles in Action: Comprehension & Collaboration.* Portsmouth, NH: Heinemann, 2009. Print.

Haselbauer, Nathan. *The Mammoth Book of New IQ Puzzles.* Philadelphia: Running Press Book Publishers, 2010. Print.

"High Tech High Home Page." *HighTechHigh.org.* High Tech High, n.d. Web. 24 Mar. 2011. <http://www.hightechhigh.org/>

"International Visual Literacy Association Home Page." *Ivla.org.* International Visual Literacy Association, n.d. Web. 24 Mar. 2011. <http://www.ivla.org/>

Kagan, Laurie. "Teaching with the Brain in Mind." Baltimore Convention Center, Baltimore, MD, 5 Nov. 2010. (NMSA Session).

Kuhlthau, Carol C., Leslie K. Maniotes, and Ann K. Caspari. *Guided Inquiry: Learning in the 21st Century.* Westport, CT: Libraries Unlimited, 2007. Print.

Lattimer, Heather, and Diana Combs. "Real World Literacy: Project-Based Learning in the English/Language Arts Classroom." Coronado Convention Center, Orlando, FL, 19 Nov. 2010. (NCTE Session).

Lavine, Alan. "Dominoe 50 Ways." *CogDogRoo.* 3 Oct. 2009. Web. 24 Mar. 2011. <http://cogdogroo. wikispaces.com/Dominoe+ 50+Ways>

Leach, Jennifer, and Dutchess Maye. "Teaching Critical Literacy Skills Using 21st Century Literacy." Coronado Convention Center, Orlando, FL, 19 Nov. 2010. (NCTE Session).

Livingstone, Ian, and Jamie Thomson. *Brain Teasers.* New York: Skyhorse Publishing, 2009. Print.

Melber, Leah M., and Alyce Hunter. *Integrating Language Arts and Social Studies.* Los Angeles: Sage, 2010. Print.

Moline, Steve, and David Drew. "Visual Literacy K-8." *K-8visual.info.* Black Cockatoo Publishing, n.d. Web. 24 Mar. 2011. <http://k-8visual.info>

Murdough, Kathleen, and Jessica Tilton. "Global Issues Multigenre Project: Combining English Literacy with Cultural Literacy." Coronado Convention Center, Orlando, FL, 18 Nov. 2010. (NCTE Session).

Oliver, Bruce. "Top Ten Tips for Teaching and Learning in the 21st Century." Baltimore Convention Center, Baltimore, MD, 4 Nov. 2010. (NMSA Session).

Pellerin, Jenifer, and Meg Petersen. "Composing with Images and Words: Creating a Comics Composing Community with Students." Coronado Convention Center, Orlando, FL, 20 Nov. 2010. (NCTE Session).

"Project-Based Learning for the 21st Century." *Bie.org*. Buck Institute for Education, n.d. Web. 24 Mar. 2011. <http://www.bie.org/>

Roth, LaVonna. "Creating Brains That Reign." Baltimore Convention Center, Baltimore, MD, 4 Nov. 2010. (NMSA Session).

Short, Kathy G., et al. *Learning Together Through Inquiry: From Columbus to Integrated Curriculum.* York, ME: Stenhouse, 1996. Print.

"Standards for Global Learning in the Digital Age." *Iste.org*. International Society for Technology in Education, n.d. Web. 24 Mar. 2011. <http://www.iste.org/standards.aspx>

Steffen, Peggy. "Educational Gaming: New Teaching Strategies." Baltimore Convention Center, Baltimore, MD, 5 Nov. 2010. (NMSA Session).

Sutman, Frank X., Joseph S. Schmuckler, and Joyce D. Woodfield. *The Science Quest: Using Inquiry/Discovery to Enhance Student Learning.* San Francisco: Jossey-Bass, 2008. Print.

Tanner, Lori, and Elaine Wiegert. "Problem-Based Learning: The Good, the Bad, the Challenges, and Where to Begin." Baltimore Convention Center, Baltimore, MD, 6 Nov. 2010. (NMSA Session).

"TeAchnology Home Page." *TeAchnology.com* Teachnology, n.d. Web. 24 Mar. 2011. <http://www.teach-nology.com/>

Thompson, Randy. "Curriculum Development—With the Brain Involved?" Baltimore Convention Center, Baltimore, MD, 6 Nov. 2010. (NMSA Session).

Trilling, Bernie, and Charles Fadel. *21st Century Skills: Learning for Life in Our Times.* San Francisco: Jossey-Bass, 2009. Print.

"Visual Literacy: An E-Learning Tutorial on Visualization for Communication, Engineering and Business." *Visual-Literacy.org*. Universitat St. Galen/Universite De Geneve, n.d. Web. 24 Mar. 2011. <http://www.visual-literacy.org/>

Wheatley, Gail, and Eric Bort. "EdHeads: Activate Your Mind." *Edheads.org*. Ed Heads, n.d. Web. 24 Mar. 2011. <http://www.edheads.org/>

Willingham, Daniel T. "Critical Thinking: Why Is It So Hard to Teach?" *American Educator* Summer 2007: 8- 19. Print.

Wright, Julie. "Visual Literacy in the 21st Century." Coronado Convention Center, Orlando, FL, 18 Nov. 2010. (NCTE Session).

Part I:
Building 21st Century Skills (Lesson Plans)

None of us can guess the future, but we can equip students with the skills to adapt to whatever comes. These 21st century skills—critical and creative thinking, problem solving, communicating, collaborating, and building arguments—are the same skills that 19th century pioneers used. They, too, were venturing into uncharted lands.

The lesson plans on the following pages help you teach these 21st century skills as well as the traditional study skills—understanding media, reading to learn, test taking, building vocabulary, and so on. Each lesson plan includes the following:

- Learning outcomes and standards correlations
- A daily lesson plan
- An extension activity
- A review that can also serve as a chapter quiz
- Minilessons for math, science, social studies, and English

Part I:
Building 21st Century Skills

Chapter 1
Overview of 21st Century Skills

(Inquire pages 3–10)

Forecasters predict that most of today's students will make multiple career changes (perhaps 10 or more) over the span of their working lives. As a result, they should expect to "learn, unlearn, and relearn" many times over. The 21st century skills are meant to prepare students for all of this change. These skills can also make classrooms more stimulating and engaging and help students approach core content critically and thoughtfully. This chapter provides an overview of these skills.

Learning Outcomes
- Preview critical and creative thinking.
- Examine problem solving and the inquiry process.
- Survey communicating and collaborating.
- Examine building arguments.
- Preview using information and media.
- Survey life skills that are developed through inquiry and that foster success in school and the workplace.
- See problem solving as foundational to science and mathematics.

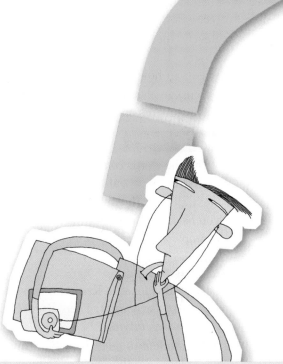

Correlations

Common Core State Standards		
ELA-Literacy.CCRA.SL.1–6	Math.Practice.MP1	Science.Practice.SP1
ELA-Literacy.CCRA.L.3		Science.Practice.SP6

Partnership for 21st Century Skills	
Creativity and Innovation ▪ Think Creatively	**ICT Literacy** ▪ Apply Technology Effectively
Critical Thinking and Problem Solving ▪ Make Judgments and Decisions	**Life and Career Skills** ▪ Initiative and Self-Direction
Communication and Collaboration ▪ Communicate Clearly ▪ Collaborate with Others	▪ Productivity and Accountability ▪ Leadership and Responsibility

International Society for Technology in Education	
1. Creativity and Innovation ▪ Students demonstrate creative thinking, construct knowledge, and develop innovative products and processes using technology.	**4. Critical Thinking, Problem Solving, and Decision Making** ▪ Students use critical thinking skills to plan and conduct research, manage projects, solve problems, and make informed decisions.
2. Communication and Collaboration ▪ Students use digital media and environments to communicate and work collaboratively.	**6. Technology Operations and Concepts** ▪ Students demonstrate a sound understanding of technology.

Lesson Plan: Overview of 21st Century Skills

1. Ask a volunteer to read the introduction on page 3 aloud. In addition, share with students that they will likely make multiple career changes over the course of their working lives. Discuss with them their thoughts and feelings about their world in terms of career opportunities and rapidly changing technology.

2. Review the information on page 4 about the human brain. Ask volunteers to share any facts or observations about the brain not listed in the text. Discuss with students what these facts and myths say about how we learn.

3. Discuss in class the parts of the brain, their function, and the types of thinking explained on page 5. Have students complete the "Your Turn" activity at the bottom of the page.

4. Write the words *convergent* and *divergent* on the board. Ask students to volunteer definitions. Then review the material about critical and creative thinking on page 6.

5. Next, discuss the problem-solving graphic, pointing out how working toward a solution often takes you back and forth between critical and creative thinking. Elaborate on this idea by applying it to an example situation, such as buying a car or planning a meal. Finally, assign the "Your Turn" activity.

6. Display this Charlie Kaufman quotation: "Constantly talking isn't necessarily communicating." Ask students to explain it. Then discuss "Communicating" on page 7, and have students complete the "Your Turn" activity.

7. Ask a student to read "Collaborating" aloud. Inform the class that some of the most engaging workplaces are those where employees collaborate on projects, much like students do in project-based learning environments. Have pairs of students complete the "Your Turn" activity together.

8. Write the words *persuasion* and *argumentation* on the board. Discuss the difference between simple persuasion (one friend convincing others to see a certain movie) and formal argumentation (defending your opinion about a new curfew with logical support). Ask students to volunteer other examples. Review with the class the information about building arguments on the top of page 8.

9. Display and discuss the following statements: *Art class is a waste because I don't like it. / Senator Buzz is a former Eagle Scout, so he deserves your vote.* Point out, with the help of the class, the illogical elements of these statements. Then review "Avoiding Logical Fallacies" on page 8. Ask for volunteers to share what the Net says about some of these fallacies. Discuss the "Your Turn" activity as a class.

10. Point out that at one time, being literate meant being able to read and write. Now the term "literate" applies to other skills as well: information literacy, media literacy, financial literacy, etc. Discuss the information on page 9. Afterward, have students complete the "Your Turn" activity.

11. Review page 10 with students, correlating the 21st century skills with the three parts of the *Inquire* text. Ask students to complete the "Your Turn" activity.

Extension: Overview of 21st Century Skills

Name _____   Date _____

Your Turn Complete the following before/after organizer. First identify the ways in which people learned and worked before the computer age. Then identify the ways in which people have been learning and working since computers became so important in school and the workplace. (Do some research to fill in the chart with pertinent details and information.)

Learning and Careers Before and After Computers

Before	After

Follow-up: Write a brief explanation of the information you gathered in the graphic organizer above.

Review: Overview of 21st Century Skills

Name _____ Date _____

Your Turn Answer the questions below.

1. What fact about the brain do you find the most surprising and why?

   _____

   _____

   _____

2. What are some of the essential differences between critical and creative thinking?

   _____

   _____

   _____

   _____

3. Which of the problem-solving steps below require critical thinking (CT), and which require creative thinking (CR)? Label them accordingly.

   ▪ Analyze the problem. _____   ▪ Critique the solution. _____

   ▪ Brainstorm solutions. _____   ▪ Improve the solution. _____

   ▪ Evaluate solutions. _____   ▪ Implement the solution. _____

   ▪ Innovate the solution. _____

4. Name and define the five parts of a communication situation.

   a. _____   d. _____

   b. _____   e. _____

   c. _____

5. What is a deductive argument?

   _____

   _____

6. To achieve financial literacy, what types of skills do you need? Name two.

   _____

   _____

Reflect: What does this Confucius quote mean to you? "Learning without thought is labor lost."

Science Minilessons: Overview of 21st Century Skills

Critical Thinking

REVIEW "Critical Thinking" (*Inquire* page 6).

RESEARCH "WIFI" quickly on the Internet.

REACT to this topic in four separate ways, providing information or making a comment that uses each of the following critical thought activities:

- Understand (Identify)
- Apply (Diagram)
- Analyze
- Evaluate

SHARE your work with your classmates.

Creative Thinking and Collaborating

Genetics is the science of heredity and variation in living organisms.

INVENT at least two theories that explain some aspect of genetic variation. Write a short explanation of each theory.

SHARE your theories with a partner.

COLLABORATE by fine-tuning the theories you have both devised, finally choosing two that you would be willing to share in a class discussion.

Collaborating and Building Arguments

Working with a partner, **CHOOSE** one of the following topics for building a logical argument.

- Besides water, what is the most important factor in seed germination?
- What is the best way to ripen fruit?
- Which is better—tap water or bottled water?
- Which is better—natural or chemical bug sprays?
- Which is more nutritious—canned, frozen, or fresh vegetables?

RESEARCH your topic briefly.

WRITE the general premise or claim for your argument.

IDENTIFY several facts or details that support your premise.

Literacy Skills

LOCATE a physics-related Web site that interests you. (Consider sites about electricity, fluid mechanics, thermodynamics, energy, acceleration, wave motion, etc.)

DETERMINE the communication situation (*Inquire* page 7) for the site by answering the following questions:

- Sender: Who created the site?
- Message: What is its subject or purpose?
- Medium: What medium is used?
- Receiver: Who is the intended audience?
- Context: When and where was it created?

SHARE information about the site with your classmates.

Math Minilessons: Overview of 21st Century Skills

Your Brain: A User's Guide

REVIEW the myths and facts about the brain on page 4.

DISCUSS with a partner how this information can direct or change your approach to math.

WRITE DOWN three observations.

SHARE them with your classmates.

Your Brain: A User's Guide

CONSIDER the challenges that you face (or faced) with solving quadratic or linear equations in your algebra class.

Then **REVIEW** the different ways that your brain processes information (page 5).

EXPLAIN which of these different brain processes are dominant when you solve challenging algebraic equations.

Problem Solving

Problem solving is at the core of mathematics.

STUDY the problem-solving graphic on page 6.

WORK with a partner to **EXAMINE** how this graphic could be used to plot out the process of solving a math problem.

ADJUST the graphic so that it works for solving this basic mathematical equation:

$34 = 35 + -1x. x =$.

SHARE the adjusted graphic and the math solution with your classmates.

Literacy Skills

In some math classes, such as Probability and Statistics, students may use graphic calculators.

RESEARCH the Web for sites that effectively explain how to use this type of calculator.

IDENTIFY a site that is most helpful.

WRITE DOWN one or two specific features of the site that you really like.

Afterward, **SHARE** the site with your classmates.

Life Skills

One of the life skills listed on page 10 is initiative and self-direction—the ability to take charge of your learning and life, now and for years to come.

With this life skill in mind, **RESEARCH** the Web to learn for yourself about careers in which geometry plays an important role.

Afterward, **SHARE** your findings with your classmates.

DISCUSS the specific applications of geometry in each career.

Social Studies/History Minilessons: Overview of 21st Century Skills

Your Brain: A User's Guide

One of the facts about the brain on page 4 states that modern technology has rewired the way the brain works.

FIND an online article that discusses this phenomenon.

IDENTIFY two things that you learned in the article.

Then **EXPLORE** your thoughts about our "rewired brains" in a 5- to 8-minute freewriting. Consider what this phenomenon says about our society and how we engage with other people.

Afterward, **SHARE** your thoughts with your classmates.

Critical and Creative Thinking

THINK ABOUT some of the explorers and discoverers that you have learned about in a World History class.

CHOOSE one for this activity.

Then **IDENTIFY** and **EXPLAIN** at least two or three critical thinking tasks (measure, organize, etc.) and two or three creative thinking tasks (imagine, improvise, etc.) that this person must have carried out. (See page 6.)

Explorer/Discoverer:

Critical thinking tasks:

Creative thinking tasks:

Your Brain: A User's Guide

If you are taking psychology, you may study *motivation* and *attention*.

Using the Web, **DEFINE** each of these terms.

Also **EXPLAIN** how these attributes help us in our daily lives.

Finally, **IDENTIFY** the part of the brain that controls motivation and attention.

Literacy Skills

SEARCH the Web for helpful resources discussing presidential elections as part of your work in an American Government class or a related course.

LIST two sites that you find especially useful.

IDENTIFY two facts or ideas that you learned from each one.

SHARE your findings with your classmates.

Financial Literacy

RATE your financial literacy by circling the star that identifies your skill level for each category.

Fiscal responsibility
weak ★ ★ ★ ★ ★ strong

Money-management skills
weak ★ ★ ★ ★ ★ strong

Credit and debt management
weak ★ ★ ★ ★ ★ strong

Saving and investing skills
weak ★ ★ ★ ★ ★ strong

Then **COMPLETE** a 5- to 8-minute freewriting, exploring your financial literacy skills.

English Minilessons: Overview of 21st Century Skills

Communicating

LIST two of the most recent pieces of literature (novels, short stories, essay, etc.) that you have read in your English class.

Then **DETERMINE** the five parts of the communication situation (page 7) for each piece. **RECORD** them in this format:

Title: _____

- Sender:
- Message:
- Receiver:
- Medium:
- Context:

Title: _____

- Sender:
- Message:
- Receiver:
- Medium:
- Context:

Building Arguments

CHOOSE a favorite book to review for your classmates.

WRITE a general premise or claim to serve as the main idea for your review. (Be more specific than "This book is really good.")

ADD two points that support your premise.

USE your work as a starting point for a class discussion about the book.

Collaborating

Suppose your class is starting a literary magazine.

BRAINSTORM with one or two classmates a list of questions about how to make such a magazine a reality.

CREATE a master list of questions by combining ideas from the lists of other groups.

CONTINUE planning your magazine as a class.

Literacy Skills

SEARCH the Web for a list of 10 books you should read in high school.

LIST the books on a piece of paper.

PUT a check next to the titles you have read.

COMPARE lists in class and choose one book to read "as a class." Plan a date for discussing the book together.

21st Century Skills in Context

REVIEW the graphic on page 10.

IMAGINE you are working on a research paper, a common writing project in English.

WRITE these three headings across a piece of paper:

    Part I   **Part II**   **Part III**

Then **LIST** the skills or activities covered in each part of *Inquire* that will help you with your work. (For example, "critical thinking" in Part I will be helpful.)

SHARE your lists with your classmates.

Chapter 2
Critical Thinking

(*Inquire* pages 11–28)

One 21st century skill that has received far more attention than any of the others is critical thinking. Any discussion about student readiness for post-secondary education and for the workplace begins with improving their critical-thinking skills. Review the Core Standards for any discipline and you will see imperative after imperative beginning with words such as *apply, determine, interpret, analyze, integrate,* and *delineate*—all elements of critical thinking. Yes, critical thinking is important, and that is why it is featured early and often in *Inquire*.

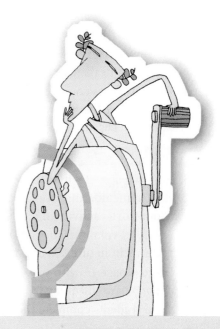

Learning Outcomes
- Understand critical thinking.
- Develop critical-thinking habits.
- Learn specific critical-thinking strategies.
- Practice complex levels of critical thinking.

Correlations

Common Core State Standards		
ELA-Literacy.CCRA.R.1–3	ELA-Literacy.CCRA.W.1–3	Math.Practice.MP1–8
ELA-Literacy.CCRA.R.7–9	ELA-Literacy.CCRA.W.10	Science.Practice.SP1–8

Partnership for 21st Century Skills
Critical Thinking and Problem Solving
■ Reason Effectively and Use Systems Thinking
■ Make Judgments and Decisions

International Society for Technology in Education

4. Critical Thinking, Problem Solving, and Decision Making

a. Identify and define authentic problems and significant questions for investigation.

b. Plan and manage activities to develop a solution or complete a project.

c. Collect and analyze data to identify solutions and/or make informed decisions.

d. Use multiple processes and diverse perspectives to explore alternative solutions.

Lesson Plan: Critical Thinking

Day 1

1. Ask students to react to the following words of Albert Einstein: "The whole of science is nothing more than the refinement of everyday thinking."
2. Then read the chapter introduction on page 11. Connect it to the Einstein quotation.
3. Have volunteers read "Critical Thinking and the Inquiry Process" on page 12. (Point out that Part II of *Inquire* deals with the inquiry process in detail.)
4. Have students complete the "Your Turn" activity (page 12). Ask them to use that information as they answer the following question in a 5- to 8-minute freewriting: *In which course do I do my best thinking?* Discuss these writings in class.

Day 2

5. Review page 13 with your students. Point out that the rest of the chapter addresses each thinking skill (remembering, understanding, etc.) separately. Have students offer their thoughts concerning the "Your Turn" activity in a class discussion.
6. Ask for a volunteer to read page 14. Discuss the "Your Turn" activity as a class. Talk about spiral patterns in nature, as man-made structural elements, and so on.
7. Discuss page 15 with your students. Point out that *mnemonic* comes from the Greek word *mnemonikos*, meaning "mindful."
8. Have students complete the "Your Turn" activity. Ask volunteers to share mnemonics they have made.

Day 3

9. Review the six example graphic organizers for "Understanding" on pages 16–17. **Note:** Graphic organizers such as these can help students analyze topics as well.
10. Give students the choice of which of the four "Your Turn" activities they will complete.
11. Next, discuss pages 18 and 19 with your students. Along with supplying instructions, mention how modeling, illustrating, and imitating are other activities that require the application of ideas or information. Consider some examples of these activities together.
12. Have your students complete the "Your Turn" activity (page 19).

Day 4

13. Have students review the first part of page 20 on their own.
14. Assign pairs of students to complete the "Your Turn" activity. (To simplify, choose two of the four areas to explore.)
15. Discuss pages 22 and 23 with your students. Together, explore how the goals, objectives, and traits established during the planning step, at the beginning of a project, become just as essential during the improving and presenting steps, near the end of a project.
16. When students begin their next class project, assign the "Your Turn" activity at the bottom of page 22. Ask them to use their rubrics to guide their work throughout the project.

Day 5

17. After reviewing page 24, ask students which of these processes or systems they have used. Then have students complete the "Your Turn" activity.
18. Review with your students the engineering design process on page 25.
19. If time remains, discuss page 26 and the "Your Turn" activity as a class.

Extension: Critical Thinking

Name _____   Date _____

Critical thinking often involves asking and answering meaningful questions. As writer Randall VanderMey states, "Questions are like can openers to a critical thinker. He or she uses them to pry into topics." The following scenario and questions reveal how one critical thinker might work toward understanding a new word.

Understand ▪ In Jorge's biology class, his teacher used the word *pandemic* during a discussion. To better understand the word, Jorge asked himself these questions:

- ▪ What is the word's dictionary definition?
- ▪ What idea or word is *pandemic* similar to? Different from?
- ▪ Where did the word come from?
- ▪ Why is it important to know?
- ▪ When would I use this word?

Your Turn Decide on four or five questions that the student in each of the following scenarios could ask. (One sample question is provided for each scenario.)

Analyze ▪ Amika's art teacher displayed an unusual sculpture in class. To analyze it, Amika could ask herself these questions:

- ▪ What is the sculpture's shape?

Create ▪ Theo's group must create a project that connects two courses of study. They have decided to create a humorous play about the history of math. To carefully consider the subject of math, they could ask themselves these questions:

- ▪ What distinguishes math from other courses?

Follow-up: Compare your questions with those of your classmates. How are they alike or different?

Your Turn Search a newspaper, newsmagazine, or news Web site to find a difficult problem to solve. Then answer these questions:

1. Examine the problem by answering the 5 W's and H about it.

2. Analyze the problem by completing a cause-effect chart about it.

3. Create a cluster of possible solutions for the problem.

Review: Critical Thinking

Name _____   Date _____

Your Turn Answer each of the following questions with complete sentences.

1. What does Bloom's Revised Taxonomy show?

   _____

   _____

2. How can this taxonomy help you deepen or sharpen your thinking?

   _____

3. How can a pattern help you remember information?

   _____

   _____

4. What two graphic organizers can help you understand a topic?

   _____

   _____

5. How is a set of instructions like or different from an algorithm?

   _____

   _____

   _____

6. Why is writing a set of instructions a way of applying what you know?

   _____

   _____

7. How can identifying constants and variables help you analyze something?

   _____

   _____

8. Why is a rubric a valuable evaluation tool?

   _____

   _____

Reflect: Complete your own comparison about critical thinking, using this example as a guide:

Critical thinking is like an onion because it forms in layers,
starting with a core of understanding.

Science Minilessons: Critical Thinking

Remembering

Page 14 of *Inquire* reminds you that once you recognize a pattern, such as a spiral, you will begin to see it in many places.

Now **CONSIDER** another common pattern: the wave.

Working with a partner, **LIST** as many examples of this pattern as possible.

COMPARE lists as a class.

Questioning

Suppose you are making a musical instrument as part of a science project.

LIST a series of questions that could initiate your work.

ANSWER at least two or three of the questions after doing some reading and researching.

SHARE what you have learned with your classmates.

Extension: Continue your research if you are interested.

Remembering

FIND a list of the different types of body systems. (The nervous system is an example.)

Then **CREATE** a mnemonic that will help you remember this information.

SHARE your mnemonic with your classmates.

Understanding

READ about Newton's first law of motion online or in a physics book. Consider what the law means and find examples of it in daily life.

Then **CREATE** an original graphic that shows your understanding of the law or some part of it.

SHARE your graphic with your classmates.

Evaluating

Suppose that in an ecology class, you and a partner have been asked to plan a rain garden for your school.

RESEARCH online to learn about rain gardens.

CREATE a rubric for your project, identifying your goal and objectives. (See *Inquire* page 22.)

SHARE the rubric with your classmates.

Math Minilessons: Critical Thinking

Questioning

IMAGINE you've been asked to calculate the square footage of a floor plan, so that the designer knows how much flooring to order.

Working with a partner, **LIST** the questions you would have to answer to provide this information.

COMPARE lists and **DISCUSS** questions with your classmates.

Applying

REVIEW "factoring in pairs," an operation that you learned in algebra.

WORK THROUGH a few expressions until you remember and understand the steps in the process.

DEVELOP a set of instructions for "factoring in pairs."

DEMONSTRATE your instructions for your classmates.

Understanding

IDENTIFY one of Luke Winn's cnnsi.com postings for college basketball in which he relies heavily on formulas as well as statistics. (Here is an example: "Scheduleball: Colorado State, Pitt exploit weaknesses of RPI," September 27, 2012.)

Carefully **ANALYZE** the posting.

SHARE your understanding of the mathematics with your classmate.

Creating

Working with a partner, **PLAN** a statistics project using the scientific method (*Inquire* page 21).

START by forming an interesting and meaningful question to investigate. Here is an example:

> Do the reading habits of parents or guardians have any bearing on the reading habits of students at Rose Grove High School?

Next, **FORM** a hypothesis—a statement that identifies what you expect to discover from your investigation.

Then **CREATE** a questionnaire or survey to gather data.

COMPARE survey questions with another pair of students.

Extension: Continue your investigation.

Creating

RESEARCH digital imaging.

DETERMINE how geometry and/or trigonometry are used in this field.

PREPARE a brief report of your findings.

SUBMIT your report for class review.

Social Studies Minilessons: Critical Thinking

Questioning

CHOOSE one essential of life to explore as it relates to medieval Europe. Consider housing, clothing, entertainment, agriculture, education, work, science, laws, business, or medicine.

LIST six or seven questions that you would like to answer.

FIND answers to at least two of your questions.

SHARE your discoveries with your classmates.

Extension: Continue your research.

Remembering

IMAGINE that in a sociology class you have been studying patterns of self-destruction.

SELECT one of these patterns to explore.

RESEARCH the pattern online or in your textbook.

Then **DESCRIBE** the pattern as a downward spiral.

SHARE your findings with your classmates.

Understanding

IMAGINE that you have been asked to compare the presidential campaigns and elections from two different periods in history for an American Government class.

CONDUCT some initial research concerning the two.

FILL IN a similarities/differences chart or a Venn diagram with what you have discovered so far. (See page 17.)

EXPLAIN your findings in a brief essay.

Extension: **CONTINUE** working on the project.

Analyzing

Consider the amazing success of a company such as Apple, Facebook, or Google.

FORM an understanding of the company through research and discussion.

Then **LIST** some of the constants—factors that the company shares with other companies in a similar business—and some of the variables—factors that set it apart.

SHARE your analysis in a class discussion.

Evaluating

IMAGINE that for an economics class, your assignment is to create a business plan for a small business, such as a bike-rental shop.

Working with a partner or small group, **DECIDE** on a type of start-up business.

PREPARE a rubric including a goal statement and objectives to guide your work. (See page 22.)

SHARE your initial plan with other groups in the class.

Extension: **CONTINUE** working on the project.

Learning Inductively

Suppose in a psychology class you have been asked to form a basic conclusion about motivation in your school.

GATHER a few specifics first by writing a statement or two about the different groups of kids in your school.

THINK about what motivates each group as you form your statements.

Then **FORM** your conclusion based on your statements.

SHARE your conclusion with other classmates.

English Minilessons: Critical Thinking

Questioning

Let's say that you are about to begin reading a novel for class.

LIST at least four or five questions that you would like to have answered in the first part of your reading. For example, "Who is the main character?"

COMPARE your questions with a classmate's and adjust your list if you'd like.

WATCH for answers to your questions as you read.

Remembering

SELECT a mnemonic device that will help you remember the parts of a plot line, the common figures of speech, or some other set of literary terms. (See thoughtfullearning.com/h15 to find links to mnemonic devices and generators.)

CREATE your mnemonic.

SHARE it with your classmates.

Understanding

RESEARCH the differences between Standard English (SE) and nonstandard dialects (NS) on the Web or in a textbook.

CREATE a T-chart in which you highlight the features of SE on one side and the features of NS on the other.

COMPARE charts in class.

Then **COMPOSE** a master chart to display in your classroom.

Understanding

LEARN about the different sentence styles, such as "loose," that allow you to add detail and arrange words for a particular rhythm and effect.

NAME them in a table like the one on the bottom of *Inquire* page 16.

Beneath each sentence type, **PROVIDE** a few details that describe it.

Extension: **WRITE** your own examples of each type.

Analyzing

LEARN about the constants (elements) of a basic pattern of literature: comedy, tragedy, or quest.

Then **IDENTIFY** the constants and any variables (those elements that break the pattern) for a novel or play you have read or are reading.

SHARE your analysis with your classmates for discussion.

Note: A literary piece that deviates from a basic pattern is sometimes classified as irony.

Evaluating

Suppose you and a partner are creating a video script in which you highlight certain events in the life of a favorite author or filmmaker.

WRITE a goal statement and objectives in a basic rubric to guide your work. (See *Inquire* page 22.)

SHARE your initial plan with your classmates.

Extension: **CONTINUE** working on this project.

Chapter 3
Creative Thinking
(*Inquire* pages 29–46)

Creative thinking is really a mind-set, a way of accessing new and different ideas. Science-fiction writer Ray Bradbury said, "Thinking is the enemy of creativity." By that, he probably meant that careful, measured thinking restrains creativity and prevents individuals from unlocking imaginative, divergent thoughts.

When students are developing academic projects or solving problems, they need to complement their critical thinking with plenty of creativity. Creative thinking generates the raw material that they can mold into effective finished products. This chapter provides strategies that students can use to unlock their creativity.

Learning Outcomes
- Understand creative thinking and the inquiry process.
- Appreciate different levels of creative thinking.
- Learn creative-thinking strategies.
- Deepen creative thinking.
- Preview creative-project work.

Correlations

Common Core State Standards

ELA-Literacy.CCRA.W.1–3	ELA-Literacy.CCRA.W.1–3	Math.Practice.MP1
ELA-Literacy.CCRA.R.7–9	ELA-Literacy.CCRA.W.10	Science.Practice.SP1

Partnership for 21st Century Skills

Creativity and Innovation
- Think Creatively
- Work Creatively with Others
- Implement Innovations

Critical Thinking and Problem Solving
- Solve Problems

International Society for Technology in Education

1. Creativity and Innovation
  a. Apply existing knowledge to generate new ideas, products, or processes.
  b. Create original works as a means of personal or group expression.
  c. Use models and simulations to explore complex systems and issues.
  d. Identify trends and forecast possibilities.

Lesson Plan: Creative Thinking

Special Note: This chapter contains many "Your Turn" activities—perhaps too many to assign during a one-week chapter review, but enough to offer your students an excellent choice.

Day 1

1. Ask students if this statement—*Peanut butter tastes like first grade*—reflects a critical or a creative mind at work. Point out that creative thinking often involves making new connections.
2. Ask for a volunteer to read page 29 and the introduction on page 30 aloud. Share a story of creative thinking in action, such as the history of Velcro (details for which can easily be found online).
3. Then discuss the rest of the page and have students complete the "Your Turn" activity.
4. Discuss "Creative-Thinking Strategies" and the "Your Turn" activity on page 31. Consider assigning all or part of "Abundance and Novelty," page 45.

Day 2

5. Discuss pages 32–33 with your students. Have them complete one or both of the "Your Turn" activities, depending on the time available.
6. Discuss pages 34–35 with your students. Point out that each of these imaginative activities can improve their understanding of a topic. Either ask students to complete one or more of the "Your Turn" activities on their own, or work on the "Forced Connections" activity (page 35) together as a class. Ask for student input and write their ideas on the board.

Day 3

7. Discuss pages 36–37 with your students. Have them complete one or more of the "Your Turn" activities, depending on the time available.
8. Discuss pages 38–39 with your students. Either ask them to complete one or more of the "Your Turn" activities on their own, or engage the class in a discussion about a topic you are currently studying. Ask a number of Socratic questions about the topic (page 38) and write students' ideas on the board. Continue the discussion as long as time permits.

Day 4

9. Discuss pages 40–41 with your students. Have students complete one or both of the "Your Turn" activities.

Day 5

10. Discuss pages 42–43 with your students. Have students complete the "Your Turn" activities on both pages.
11. Also discuss page 44. Assign the "Your Turn" activities as homework in order to complete students' preview of creative-project planning.

Extension: Creative Thinking

Name _____   Date _____

Your Turn Think creatively about the common, ordinary paper clip by completing the following activities. You will focus on remembering, understanding, and applying (*Inquire* pages 32-37).

1. Generate your initial thoughts about a paper clip by completing a cluster about it (page 32).

_____

_____

_____

_____

_____

2. Next, think metaphorically about a paper clip by creating a simile, a metaphor, another analogy, and a symbol for it (page 34).

_____

_____

_____

_____

_____

3. Then compose a square-peg question about a paper clip using the sentence formula on page 36. Answer the question in as many ways as you can.

_____

_____

_____

_____

Follow-up: Write freely for 5 to 8 minutes, highlighting the discoveries you have made about paper clips with the three creative strategies above.

_____

_____

_____

_____

Review: Creative Thinking

Name _____ Date _____

Your Turn Answer each of the following questions.

1. What is conceptual blending?

   _____

   _____

2. Write a question that creates an original conceptual blend. Answer it creatively.

   _____

   _____

3. What is role-playing?

   _____

   _____

4. Identify three forms of role-playing.

   _____

   _____

5. What is counterfactual thinking?

   _____

   _____

6. Write one counterfactual question about a paper clip. Then answer it.

   _____

   _____

7. What is SCAMPER?

   _____

   _____

8. Write three questions about a paper clip—one from each of the first three SCAMPER categories.

   _____

   _____

Reflect: How might thinking creatively about a problem help you to solve it?

   _____

Science Minilessons: Creative Thinking

Questioning

GENERATE at least four physics-related questions that interest you. For example, *Why does a bungee jumper feel weightless during a jump? When two similar cars collide head-on, is the impact the same as hitting a solid wall?*

CHOOSE one question and **WRITE** freely for 5 minutes to see what ideas you can generate.

UNDERLINE your most creative thoughts and circle your most critical thoughts.

Extension: **CONTINUE** exploring the question using both creative- and critical-thinking strategies.

Role-Playing

Imagine you've been asked to explain cell respiration to an audience of your choice.

LEARN ABOUT this function online or in a biology textbook.

Then **PREPARE** an interview or press conference about cell respiration, role-playing with one or two classmates.

PRESENT your interview or press conference to an audience.

ASK for feedback and **ANSWER** questions.

Metaphorical Thinking

Hydrofracking is an engineering/mining process used to gain access to oil and natural gas.

RESEARCH this process online.

Then **GENERATE** four metaphorical statements that show your understanding of hydrofracking.

SHARE your statements as part of a class discussion.

Visualization

In a biology class, you have been asked to memorize a list of features; for example, the anatomical features that support photosynthesis in a plant.

CHOOSE a biological concept or list of features and **CREATE** a visual version of it following the four steps on page 33.

SHARE your visualization with your classmates for discussion.

Provocative Thinking

Suppose that in an ecology class, you've been asked to explore the precarious condition of the ocean's coral reefs.

RESEARCH this issue online.

LIST four assumptions about coral reefs that you discovered during your research.

Then **ASK** questions that challenge these assumptions.

SHARE your work during a class discussion.

Reverse Thinking

In a project related to food science, suppose you are exploring effective ways to limit oxidation.

GAIN an understanding of this process through basic research.

Then **CREATE** a reverse-thinking chart about oxidation using the information on page 39 to guide you.

CONSIDER how this creative activity helps you see oxidation in new ways.

Social Studies Minilessons: Creative Thinking

Brainstorming

INITIATE your own *History Detectives* investigation by focusing your attention on some object in your school, classroom, or house. Consider the object's historical value or significance.

CLUSTER your first thoughts about it. (See *Inquire* page 32.)

SELECT one idea in the first cluster, and begin a new cluster that makes an even deeper creative connection to the object's historical significance.

Extension: **CONTINUE** your "historical" thinking about the object.

Using Manipulative Verbs

STUDY the quotation below expressed by a distinguished guest on *Bill Moyer's Journal:*

> "The opposite of poverty is not wealth. It is justice."

APPLY a manipulative verb, either one from *Inquire* page 37 or one of your own choosing, to the quotation.

Then **LIST** at least two or three questions that come to mind.

REPEAT the process with another verb. Finally, **SHARE** your work during a class discussion.

Counterfactual Thinking

Imagine you have been studying the oppression of women in certain Asian countries.

ASK at least four "what if" questions about this topic. (See *Inquire* page 38.)

Then **REACT** to one of the questions by writing freely about it for 5 to 8 minutes.

Afterward, **DETERMINE** what this activity has added to your understanding of the topic.

Using Socratic Questions

Imagine you have been studying the controversial issue of selling the Great Lakes' fresh water.

ANALYZE this issue (or a similar issue) by answering the Socratic questions on *Inquire* page 38. Skip any questions that don't apply to your topic.

Afterward, **DETERMINE** what this activity has added to your understanding of the topic.

Forced Connections

THINK of a historical figure who intrigues you.

CHOOSE an item completely unrelated to this person.

Then **LIST** as many connections as possible between the two. (Set up your list like the ones on *Inquire* page 35.)

IDENTIFY ways in which this activity made you think about the person in a new way.

Perspective Shifting

COMPLETE a perspective-shifting chart about yourself, using the information and example on *Inquire* page 35. Consider the people, places, and events that you have studied in your history or sociology class to compose the "what if" part of your chart.

DISCUSS your work with a partner.

DECIDE what each of you has learned from this activity.

Math Minilessons: Creative Thinking

Metaphorical Thinking

To deepen your understanding of fractions, think metaphorically about them.

CREATE at least four examples of metaphorical thinking about fractions, choosing from similes, metaphors, other analogies, and symbols. (See *Inquire* page 34.)

Then **WRITE FREELY** about the experience. Focus on what your comparisons have taught you about the properties of fractions.

Visualization

There are six trigonometric functions: sine, cosine, tangent, cotangent, secant, and cosecant.

CREATE a visual version of these functions to help you remember them. (See *Inquire* page 33 for the steps.)

Afterward, **SHARE** your visualization with your classmates.

Role-Playing

With one or two partners, **DEVELOP** a scenario that demonstrates a real-life application of geometry.

DECIDE on a profession (construction, robotics, computer graphics, structural engineering, etc.) and a specific task that involves a challenge or problem that can be solved with geometric principles.

PRACTICE and **PRESENT** your scenario to the class.

DISCUSS the results.

Forced Connections

In algebra, your goal is to analyze and solve equations, which, as you know, state that one quantity is equal to another $(x-b) = (a + c)$.

STUDY the basic principles related to equations, either in your textbook or online.

Then **THINK** creatively about these principles by writing as many connections as you can between the term *equation* and a dissimilar object or idea. (See *Inquire* page 35.)

Afterward, **SHARE** your connections with your classmates for discussion.

Using Manipulative Verbs

An empirical probability is determined by dividing the number of times something has happened by the total number of observations. For example:

> Of 100 starting pitchers, 33 pitched at least 150 innings during the past season. The probability that a pitcher will pitch that many innings is 33/100 or .33 or 33%.

USE a manipulative verb (perhaps one of those on *Inquire* page 37) to change the way you look at empirical probability.

LIST at least two or three questions that come to mind as you apply the verb.

REPEAT the process with another verb.

Afterward, **SHARE** your work during a class discussion.

English Minilessons: Creative Thinking

Brainstorming

NAME the most interesting or enlightening nonfiction book you have read within the last year or so.

CLUSTER your thoughts about this book. (See *Inquire* page 32.)

SELECT one idea from your first cluster to use as the starting point for another.

IDENTIFY two discoveries you have made.

Visualization

THINK of a set of grammatical terms that you may have trouble remembering, such as the three cases of nouns or pronouns, or the types of verbals.

CREATE a visual version of the terms to help you remember them, following the guidelines on *Inquire* page 33.

SHARE your visualization with classmates.

Forced Connections

IDENTIFY a memorable character in a novel or short story you have read or are reading.

CHOOSE an item completely unrelated to this character.

Then **LIST** as many connections between them as possible.

CONSIDER how this activity has enriched your understanding of the character.

Conceptual Blending

CONSIDER a form of writing, such as an essay of argumentation, a book review, or a personal commentary.

CREATE a conceptual blend by composing a question that connects this form of writing to something completely different. (See *Inquire* page 34.)

Then **ANSWER** the question as creatively as you can.

REPEAT the process.

Provocative Thinking

WRITE four or five basic assumptions about the value of studying classic literature. (See *Inquire* page 39.) Here is an example assumption:

  Studying classic literature provides a foundation for appreciating modern literature.

Then **ASK** a question that counters each assumption. Here is an example:

  How can we understand and appreciate literature that we have so little in common with?

DISCUSS classic literature, using these assumptions and questions as a starting point.

Square-Pegging

CREATE a square-peg question about *irony, satire, slice of life, etc.*, using the following formula:

  How can _____ _____?

  (literary style or form)   (do something it was not intended to do)

Then **ANSWER** the question in as many ways as you can.

DECIDE how this increases your understanding of the concept.

Chapter 4
Problem Solving

(Inquire pages 47–66)

Students should realize that all of life's experiences, from *choosing what to wear today* to *applying to a prestigious university,* are problems to be solved. And to solve challenging problems, they need to follow a few problem-solving guidelines. Combining critical- and creative-thinking skills and addressing the connection between problem solving and the inquiry process, this chapter provides those guidelines. Students will learn about problem solving in mathematics, science, history, and language.

Learning Outcomes

- Understand the problem-solving process.
- Use critical- and creative-thinking strategies.
- See problem solving as a form of inquiry.
- Review problem solving (inquiry) in mathematics, science, history, and language.

Correlations

Common Core State Standards		
ELA-Literacy.CCRA.R.7–9	ELA-Literacy.CCRA.SL.1–3	Science.Practice.SP1–8
ELA-Literacy.CCRA.W.4–9	Math.Practice.MP1–8	

Partnership for 21st Century Skills

Creativity and Innovation
- Think Creatively
- Work Creatively with Others
- Implement Innovations

Critical Thinking and Problem Solving
- Reason Effectively and Use Systems Thinking
- Make Judgments and Decisions
- Solve Problems

Life and Career Skills
- Flexibility and Adaptability
- Initiative and Self-Direction
- Social and Cross-Cultural Skills
- Productivity and Accountability
- Leadership and Responsibility

International Society for Technology in Education

1. Creativity and Innovation
- Students demonstrate creative thinking, construct knowledge, and develop innovative products and processes.

3. Research and Information Fluency
- Students apply digital tools to gather, evaluate, and use information.

4. Critical Thinking, Problem Solving, and Decision Making
- Students use critical thinking skills to plan and conduct research, manage projects, solve problems, and make informed decisions.

Lesson Plan: Problem Solving

Day 1

1. Introduce this scenario: *The principal has just informed students that the water in the school, and throughout the community, contains high levels of radium. They must stop drinking the water in the school immediately.* Then ask, "What should we do?"
2. Ask students to plan a course of action to address this problem, both in the short term and in the long term.
3. At the end of the class period, discuss the plans students have come up with. Ask them to consider their problem-solving methods and get ready to compare those methods with the approach they will learn about in this chapter during the rest of the week.

Day 2

4. Read and discuss pages 47 and 48 of the chapter and assign the "Your Turn" activity. Have students pick an original topic (not the contaminated-water problem introduced on day 1).
5. Next, read and discuss pages 49 and 50 and assign the "Your Turn" activities.
6. Finally, read and discuss pages 51 and 52. Assign either or both of the "Your Turn" activities as time permits.

Special Note: The remaining pages of the chapter deal with problem solving (inquiry) in specific content areas. Consider asking content-area teachers to cover the appropriate pages.

Day 3

7. Read and discuss page 53. Do the "Your Turn" activity together in class.
8. Review "Scientific Inquiry," pages 54–57. Assign the "Your Turn" activities as time permits.

Day 4

9. Review "Mathematical Inquiry," pages 58–61. Assign both "Your Turn" activities.

Day 5

10. Review "Historical Inquiry," pages 62–63. Assign the "Your Turn" activities as time permits.
11. Review "Language Inquiry," pages 64–65. Assign the "Your Turn" activity.

Extension: Problem Solving

Name _____   Date _____

Your Turn Report on a particular problem and its solution by completing this page. Choose an event or a discovery you have learned about in science, mathematics, history, social studies, or English. (Grant's victory at Vicksburg during the Civil War is an example, as is Pasteur's method of using heat to prevent deadly bacteria from forming in perishable liquids like milk.)

1. Identify the basic components of your chosen event, discovery, etc., by answering these questions:

   - Who? _____

   - What? _____

   - When? _____

   - Where? _____

   - Why? _____

2. Next, analyze the problem in a brief report or by completing a cause-effect chart. (See *Inquire* page 49.)

   _____

   _____

   _____

   _____

   _____

3. Explain the circumstances surrounding the solution to the problem. Also address the solution's impact.

   _____

   _____

   _____

   _____

   _____

Follow-up: Share your findings during a class discussion.

Review: Problem Solving

Name _____   Date _____

Your Turn Answer the following questions.

1. How is creative thinking part of the problem-solving process?

   _____

   _____

   _____

2. Which graphic organizer works well to analyze a problem? Describe it.

   _____

   _____

   _____

3. What role does a trait evaluation play in the problem-solving process?

   _____

   _____

   _____

4. Problem solving is actually a version of which other process?

   _____

   _____

   _____

5. Scientists follow the scientific method to carry out experiments (and solve problems). Name the steps in this method.

   _____

   _____

   _____

Reflect: Consider how both critical and creative thinking are a part of the scientific method.

   _____

   _____

Science Minilessons: Problem Solving

Analyzing a Problem

Controversy exists over parents choosing not to have their children inoculated for contagious childhood diseases.

RESEARCH this controversy online and in print materials.

DISCUSS it with a small group of classmates.

Then **ANALYZE** the issue using a cause-effect chart. (See *Inquire* page 49.)

PROPOSE a reasonable solution to this problem.

Designing an Experiment

Late in the warm season, many inland freshwater lakes suffer from algae blooms.

RESEARCH the issue to learn what, if anything, is being done about it.

Working in a small group, **DESIGN** your own experiment to explore/solve this problem. (See *Inquire* page 55.)

SHARE your experiment design with the other groups for discussion.

Extension: **CARRY OUT** your experiment if possible.

Questioning (Inquiry)

Suppose you are interested in the phenomenon of absolute or perfect pitch. More specifically, you want to know how it is measured.

LIST questions that would get such a project underway.

Then **CONDUCT** some initial research.

IDENTIFY two problems that you would likely face if you were to carry out an experiment that measures absolute pitch.

Scientific Inquiry

In at least some states, vending-machine operators are now required to post the number of calories in soft drinks available for purchase. Suppose you have two questions about this information: (1) How is the calorie count determined? (2) How accurate are the numbers?

USE the scientific method to determine your own calorie count. (See *Inquire* page 54.)

PLAN at least the first three steps.

Extension: **CARRY OUT** your experiment if possible.

Imagining and Planning Solutions

Driving at night is a serious problem for many drivers, especially when it is snowing or raining.

CLUSTER possible solutions to this problem. (See *Inquire* page 50.)

COMPARE clusters with a classmate.

DECIDE together on the best solution.

Then **CHECK** online to see what science and engineering experts are doing about this problem.

Designing an Experiment

Suppose you are interested in astronomy, especially in meteor showers.

RESEARCH meteor showers online.

INVESTIGATE specifically how you can track them.

DESIGN an experiment and carry it out. (See *Inquire* page 55.)

REFLECT on how well the problem-solving method worked for you.

Math Minilessons: Problem Solving

Mathematical Inquiry

INITIATE a statistical analysis related to some aspect of your community's law enforcement, social services, public service, etc.

START by identifying something to analyze—such as statistics about the number of parking tickets written or the number of bus fares purchased during a period of time, and what those statistics reveal.

WORK THROUGH the first two or three steps of the inquiry process about your topic.

Extension: **CONTINUE** with your analysis if it interests you.

Mathematical Problem Solving

A skydiver planned the highest and fastest free fall in history—a 23-mile dive. A news article reported that the speed of the skydiver's fall would be 690 miles per hour, breaking the sound barrier.

READ about this attempt online.

Then **USE** mathematical inquiry and problem solving to determine how researchers may have arrived at this speed. (See *Inquire* pages 58–59 and 61.)

REPORT your findings in class.

Estimating

Imagine you are a cross-country runner, and your best time on your home course is 16:30. The record time is 15:20, and the length of the course is 5,000 meters.

ESTIMATE the following:

- How fast you run in miles per hour
- How fast the record holder runs in miles per hour
- The difference between your running speeds
- How much you would have to increase your speed in miles per hour to (a) match the record and (b) beat it by 12 seconds

Mathematical Problem Solving

CREATE a word problem related to a specific subject you are studying in math class.

APPLY mathematical problem solving/inquiry to solve the word problem.

SET UP your word problem in the same way the problem on *Inquire* page 61 is presented.

Afterward, **EXCHANGE** your work with a partner and discuss each other's problem-solving methods.

Mathematical Inquiry

In a calculus class, you've learned how to find the next number in a sequence. **IMAGINE** you must teach this operation to other students.

REVIEW the operation until you feel that you understand it well.

CREATE one or two demonstration sequences.

USE mathematical problem solving/inquiry to identify the next number in each sequence. (See *Inquire* pages 58–59 and 61.)

DEMONSTRATE the process in class.

Social Studies Minilessons: Problem Solving

Historical Inquiry

The Battle of Hastings is one of the most important battles in British history.

EXPLORE the following question: Why was this battle so significant?

RESEARCH the question online and in textbooks.

DISCUSS your initial findings with your classmates.

Historical Inquiry

James Garfield was the second of four presidents to be assassinated. He was shot by Charles J. Guiteau.

EXPLORE the following question: What were Guiteau's motives for shooting Garfield?

RESEARCH the question, tapping into primary sources if possible.

DISCUSS your initial findings with your classmates.

Imagining and Planning Solutions

Abandoned vehicles have become a blight on the urban landscape. Municipalities are running out of ways to deal with them.

BRAINSTORM possible solutions to this problem in a cluster (see *Inquire* page 50). Work with a partner or in a small group.

SELECT one or two solutions that seem the most promising.

SHARE these solutions in a class discussion about the problem.

Extension: **CHECK** online to see what you can find out about this problem.

Problem Solving in Action

You have been studying the phenomenon of social media and how addicting it can be. A recent report says that even the media themselves are addicted to social media. Could this be a problem?

ANALYZE this problem or situation using a cause-effect chart. (See *Inquire* page 49.)

LIST possible solutions to this problem.

SHARE your work in a class discussion about the problem.

Inquiry into Society

Amtrak is the national rail service in the United States. It is also known as the National Railroad Passenger Corporation.

RESEARCH this service, perhaps starting with a government Web site.

IDENTIFY one or two problems that this service is experiencing and any proposed solutions.

DISCUSS your initial findings with your classmates.

Problem Solving as Inquiry

Here's your challenge: Your aunt wants to invest in four green companies that seem like solid, safe choices. Since you are taking an economics course, she would like your advice.

DETERMINE what options are available.

LEARN ABOUT and **ANALYZE** these options.

PREPARE a brief report that identifies your recommendations.

English Minilessons: Problem Solving

Analyzing the Problem

IMAGINE that you have a lot of trouble understanding the literary term *irony*. Although you have a vague understanding of the word, you would feel more confident if you understood it more fully.

RESEARCH the term online or in your textbook. Then **IDENTIFY** the different types of irony in a line diagram.

USE the diagram as a guide when you are analyzing literature.

The Reading Process

Narrative of the Life of Frederick Douglass is the famous memoir of Frederick Douglass, a former slave. While this book is certainly enlightening, it presents a reading challenge for its unfamiliar writing style.

USE the reading process (*Inquire* page 64) to help you read chapter 1 of the memoir.

In addition, **EXPLORE** your thoughts and feelings in a reading log before, during, and after your reading.

Note: You can find this book online.

The Writing Process

You can't complete a piece of writing in one quick draft and expect it to reflect your best thinking. Instead, you must approach writing as a process that cannot be rushed.

PLAN a personal response to chapter 1 of Douglass's memoir using *Inquire* page 65 as a guide.

SHARE your response with your classmates.

Questioning

Suppose your literature class will be watching a film version of a novel or play that you have just read.

FORM a list of questions that come to mind before you view the film.

USE your list as a guide while you view the film, and later as you discuss it in class.

Imagining and Planning Solutions

You have been assigned to analyze one of the main characters in a well-known piece of British literature (your choice).

BRAINSTORM for writing ideas by clustering your thoughts about the character of your choice.

IDENTIFY the one or two ideas that have the most potential.

WRITE freely about either or both of these ideas to see what you can discover.

Analyzing the Problem

Suppose that an English tutor has noted that your essay should be more formal in tone and style. But you're not sure how a formal style differs, exactly, from the informal style you have used.

ANALYZE this problem by researching formal and informal writing online or in a textbook.

LIST the basic characteristics of each style, perhaps using an appropriate graphic organizer.

USE your list as a guide during writing projects.

Chapter 5
Communicating

(*Inquire* pages 67–82)

When you commute to work, you go from your home to your business. You physically shift from one place to another. When thoughts commute from brain to brain, we call the process communicating. Just as there are many vehicles for commuting, there are many media for communicating. This chapter focuses on speaking and listening, though later chapters cover writing and reading, creating graphs and visuals, performing and designing, and many other ways to help ideas commute.

Learning Outcomes

- Understand the communication situation.
- Learn about active listening.
- Read faces and body language.
- Understand speaking in different settings.
- Overcome stage fright.

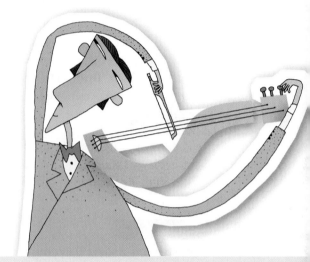

Correlations

Common Core State Standards		
ELA-Literacy.CCRA.SL.1–6	ELA-Literacy.CCRA.L.3–6	Science.Practice.SP4
ELA-Literacy.CCRA.L.1–2	Math.Practice.MP3	Science.Practice.SP6–8

Partnership for 21st Century Skills	

Communication and Collaboration
■ Communicate Clearly
  • Articulate thoughts using oral, written, and nonverbal communication skills.
  • Listen effectively.
	• Use communication for a range of purposes.
	• Utilize multiple media and technologies.

International Society for Technology in Education	
Communication and Collaboration **a.** Interact, collaborate, and publish with peers, experts, or others.	**b.** Communicate information to multiple audiences. **c.** Contribute to project teams.

Lesson Plan: Communicating

Day 1

1. As a class, discuss *speaking versus talking* and *listening versus hearing*. What distinctions between these activities do your students know about or realize? (*Speaking* suggests planning and preparation more than *talking* does; *listening* suggests focus and engagement more than *hearing* does.)
2. Mention the current perception that speaking has become a "lost art." Talk about why speaking matters.
3. Read aloud the chapter introduction and "Understanding the Communication Situation" on pages 67 and 68. Together, name a few famous communications, either written or spoken, and choose one or two to analyze, perhaps beginning with the Emancipation Proclamation.
4. Discuss the "Your Turn" activity with students. Ask them to identify their most deliberate and formal communication experiences.

Day 2

5. Read aloud and discuss "Listening Actively" on page 69. Assign the "Your Turn" activity.
6. Next, review "Listening to Words," page 70, with your students. Assign the "Your Turn" activity, asking students to address one of the scenarios presented. Allow volunteers to share their analyses.
7. Finally, review "Listening to Voice" on page 71. Assign the "Your Turn" activity if time permits.

Day 3

8. Have students review "Reading Faces" and "Reading Body Language," pages 72–73, and complete the "Your Turn" activities.
9. Read and discuss "Speaking," page 74. Have students complete the "Your Turn" activity, and ask for volunteers to read their sample sentences.

Day 4

10. Read and discuss "Speaking One-on-One," page 75. Assign the "Your Turn" activity, asking students to create their charts and add to them throughout the semester.
11. Read and discuss "Speaking in a Group," page 76. Include the "Your Turn" activity in your discussion.
12. Read and discuss "Speaking to an Audience," page 77. Include the "Your Turn" activity in your discussion.

Day 5

13. Review "Parts of a Speech," page 78. Point out the importance of carefully preparing and practicing any speech, especially one given in front of a large audience.
14. Assign the "Your Turn" activity on page 79, which directs pairs of students to discuss the guidelines for overcoming stage fright.
15. Assign the "Your Turn" activity on page 80, which introduces students to the glossary of listening and speaking terms.

Extension: Communicating

Name _____　　Date _____

Your Turn Identify the five basic components of each of the following communication situations. (See *Inquire* page 68.) Some research will be required.

1. Sojourner Truth's "Ain't I a Woman?" speech

- ▪ Sender: _____

- ▪ Message: _____

- ▪ Medium: _____

- ▪ Receiver: _____

- ▪ Context: _____

2. Chief Joseph's "I Will Fight No More Forever" speech

- ▪ Sender: _____

- ▪ Message: _____

- ▪ Medium: _____

- ▪ Receiver: _____

- ▪ Context: _____

3. Winston Churchill's "We Shall Fight on the Beaches" speech

- ▪ Sender: _____

- ▪ Message: _____

- ▪ Medium: _____

- ▪ Receiver: _____

- ▪ Context: _____

4. Cesar Chavez's "What Is the Worth of a Man or a Woman?" speech

- ▪ Sender: _____

- ▪ Message: _____

- ▪ Medium: _____

- ▪ Receiver: _____

- ▪ Context: _____

Follow-up: Select one passage to memorize from one of the speeches mentioned above. Then share the passage with your classmates and explain why you chose it.

Review: Communicating

Name _____   Date _____

Your Turn Answer the following questions.

1. Define the following components of a communication situation.

   ▪ Sender: _____

   ▪ Medium: _____

   ▪ Context: _____

2. If you are listening at the analytical level, what types of responses might you make? (Name two.)

   _____

   _____

3. What are the main characteristics of semiformal and formal communication situations?

   ▪ Semiformal: _____

   ▪ Formal: _____

4. When speaking in a group, why should you start sentences with "I" instead of "You"?

   _____

   _____

5. As a speaker, how can you engage a large audience?

   _____

   _____

6. When dealing with stage fright, what does it mean to "get into a wholesome mental space"?

   _____

   _____

7. Define *inflection*.

   _____

   _____

Reflect: What two things can you do to improve your listening skills? What two things can you do to improve your speaking skills in a small-group discussion?

   _____

   _____

Science Minilessons: Communicating

Listening to Words

GO to "The Vertical Farm Project" online.

LISTEN carefully to one of Dr. Dickson Despommier's video presentations.

Then **IDENTIFY** the basic components of the presentation. (See *Inquire* page 70.)

1. Subject:
2. Main point:
3. Support:
4. Purpose:
5. Implication:
6. Outcome

Listening to Words

GO to "High School Science" on YouTube.

VIEW a video related to something you are studying in your science class.

IDENTIFY the basic components of the presentation. (See *Inquire* page 70.)

1. Subject:
2. Main point:
3. Support:
4. Purpose:
5. Implication:
6. Outcome

Listening to Voice

GO to the *MythBusters* site online.

SELECT one of the science videos to watch.

LISTEN to the speakers carefully.

IDENTIFY what each person's voice reveals about these components of the communication situation: the sender/speaker, the message being conveyed, the receiver/audience, and the context.

SHARE your discoveries with your classmates.

Speaking One-on-One

TEAM UP with a partner for an interview.

Individually **RESEARCH** the following topic (or one of your own choosing): the spreading Antarctic ice.

DECIDE on a role (interviewer/interviewee) and **PREPARE** for the interview. (See *Inquire* page 75.)

CARRY OUT the interview.

Extension: **ASK** your classmates to critique the interview.

Speaking in a Group

PREPARE for a small-group discussion on the use of compressed natural gas to fuel cars and trucks.

RESEARCH this subject online.

REVIEW the tips on *Inquire* page 76.

CARRY OUT your group discussion.

Speaking to an Audience

INFORM a specific audience, perhaps elementary students, about the UV index posted in the weather section of your local newspaper.

RESEARCH this index online.

PREPARE your speech, writing it word for word or using note cards. (See *Inquire* page 78.)

Extension: **PRESENT** the speech to an audience. (See *Inquire* page 77.)

Math Minilessons: Communicating

Understanding the Communication Situation

LISTEN to an online speech about mathematics, such as Timothy Gower's "The Importance of Mathematics." (You may choose to listen to part of a speech if it is very long.)

IDENTIFY the basic components of the speech's communication situation and **LIST** its main points. (See *Inquire* pages 68 and 78.)

SHARE what you have learned with your classmates.

Listening to Words

GO to "High School Science" on YouTube.

RECOMMEND to your classmates a video related to something you are studying in math.

WATCH the video with your classmates.

Together, **IDENTIFY** the components of the presentation listed here. (See *Inquire* page 70.)

1. Subject:
2. Main point:
3. Support:
4. Purpose:
5. Implication:
6. Outcome:

Listening Actively

REVIEW the chart on *Inquire* page 69.

TEAM UP with a partner to have a conversation about math.

BEGIN the conversation by completing this sentence: "The most important (*challenging, interesting, useful, etc.*) thing I have learned recently in math is . . ."

Your partner **CONTINUES** the conversation with a comment at the remembering level.

You **ADD** an appropriate comment at the understanding level.

ALTERNATE comments through each level of thinking.

Afterward, **DISCUSS** the conversation.

Extension: **SWITCH** roles and repeat the process.

Speaking to an Audience

FIND a practical application, either in everyday life or in the workplace, for something you are studying in math class.

RESEARCH this application.

PLAN a presentation of information about this application for your classmates.

WRITE OUT the introduction for your presentation. (See *Inquire* page 78.)

Extension: **CONTINUE** working until you are ready to give your presentation.

Speaking to a Group

FIND a certain sports statistic (*on-base percentage in baseball, passing rating in football, etc.*) that intrigues you.

LEARN what the statistic represents and how it is calculated.

REVIEW the speaking tips on *Inquire* page 76.

SHARE what you have learned with the members of a small group.

Social Studies Minilessons: Communicating

Understanding the Communication Situation

NAME a great speech in American history.

RESEARCH and **READ** the speech.

IDENTIFY its basic components.

- Sender/Source:
- Audience:
- Message:
- Context:
- Medium:

Then **EXPLAIN** in a paragraph or brief essay why this is a great speech.

Listening to Words

REVIEW "Listening to Words" on *Inquire* page 70.

VIEW part or all of a presidential/political speech on video, perhaps a Democratic or Republican National Convention speech.

IDENTIFY the main parts of the message.

1. Subject:
2. Main point:
3. Support:
4. Purpose:
5. Implication:
6. Outcome:

Speaking in a Group

PREPARE for a small-group discussion on the following topic: *Do vice presidents really matter?*

RESEARCH the topic online and in a textbook.

REVIEW the speaking tips on *Inquire* page 76.

CARRY OUT the discussion.

Afterward, **WRITE FREELY** for 5 to 8 minutes about the experience, exploring the quality of the discussion.

Levels of Formality

LEARN ABOUT a contemporary social issue, such as the use of race in college admissions.

REVIEW *Inquire* page 74.

DISCUSS the issue with a classmate using informal or semiformal language.

Then **DISCUSS** the same issue with a different classmate using formal language.

Afterward, **CONSIDER** how the level of formality affected the discussion.

Parts of a Speech

REVIEW your history textbook for a specific person, place, event, or idea that interests you.

LEARN more about the topic online or in history texts.

Then **WRITE** an introduction (see *Inquire* page 78) that could serve as the starting point for a speech or an essay about this topic.

SHARE the introduction with your classmates for discussion.

Extension: **CONTINUE** developing a speech or essay about your topic.

Impromptu

PICK a topic out of a hat. (The topics will be familiar subjects you have studied in class.)

SPEAK for 3 to 5 minutes about the topic in front of a small group of students or in front of the whole class.

BE AWARE of your voice—what it reveals about your approach (lighthearted, serious, confused, sarcastic, etc.), your personality, your understanding, and so on. (See *Inquire* page 71.)

Afterward, **ASSESS** your performance.

English Minilessons: Communicating

Understanding the Communication Situation

VIEW the online video of James Geary's speech "Metaphorically Speaking."

IDENTIFY the speech's communication situation.

- Sender/Source:
- Message:
- Medium:
- Audience:
- Context:

Afterward, **EXPLAIN** in a paragraph what you learned from this speech.

COMPARE explanations with your classmates.

Listening Actively

REVIEW the chart on *Inquire* page 69.

TEAM UP with a partner to have a conversation about literature.

BEGIN the conversation by completing this sentence: "In [name of essay, novel, etc.] the most important point [theme] is . . ."

CONTINUE the conversation with your partner, alternating responses until you have moved through all the levels of thinking, beginning with *remembering*.

Afterward, **DISCUSS** the conversation.

Extension: **SWITCH** roles, having your partner complete the sentence, and repeat the process.

Levels of Formality

THINK of a memorable character in a piece of literature that you have recently read.

Then **DEVELOP** a brief script in which this character uses a level of language that is completely "out of character" for him or her.

PREPARE and **PRESENT** your script to the class.

DISCUSS how the "new way of talking" changes the character and why.

Speaking in a Group

RESEARCH the origins of language online— why we speak, how we started, why languages vary, etc.—for a group discussion.

REVIEW the speaking tips on *Inquire* page 76.

HOLD a small-group discussion on the topic.

Afterward, **WRITE FREELY** about the experience, exploring the quality of the discussion.

Parts of a Speech

CHOOSE a literary or language topic that interests you—perhaps an author, a character, a type of literature, a linguistic device, etc. (Review your class notebook for ideas.)

LEARN more about the topic online or in texts.

Then **WRITE** an introduction (see *Inquire* page 78) that could serve as the starting point for a speech or an essay about this topic.

SHARE your work in a class discussion.

Extension: **CONTINUE** developing a speech or essay about your topic.

Reading Faces and Body Language

VIEW an interview, a speech, a scene from a television show, a famous movie clip, etc.

As you watch, **NOTE** the facial expressions and body language of the speakers or actors. (See *Inquire* pages 72 and 73.)

Afterward, **SHARE** what you learned with your classmates.

Chapter 6
Collaborating
(Inquire pages 83–94)

In the traditional classroom, a teacher usually stood behind a podium and lectured to a classroom of students. The students, in turn, sat in their desks and listened passively. What that approach lacked, of course, was meaningful interaction between class members, an essential element of the learning process. Contemporary educators recognize the value of collaborating, so they regularly assign group work. And business leaders like the idea because it prepares students for the workplace. This chapter provides strategies that will help students work in groups.

Learning Outcomes

- Understand the basics of collaboration.
- Learn about collaborative strategies.
- Understand the rules for conducting formal meetings.
- Review online collaborative options.
- Learn about using netiquette.

Correlations

Common Core State Standards		
ELA-Literacy.CCRA.SL.1–6	Math.Practice.MP3	Science.Practice.SP3
ELA-Literacy.CCRA.L.3		Science.Practice.SP6–8

Partnership for 21st Century Skills

Communication and Collaboration
- Collaborate with Others
  - Demonstrate ability to work effectively and respectfully with diverse teams.
- Exercise flexibility and willingness to be helpful.
- Assume shared responsibility for collaborative work.

International Society for Technology in Education

2. **Communication and Collaboration**
   a. Interact, collaborate, and publish with peers, experts, or others.
   b. Develop cultural understanding and global awareness by engaging with learners of other cultures.
   c. Contribute to project teams.

Lesson Plan: Collaborating

Day 1

1. To open your discussion of this chapter, have students react to this quote: "The secret is to gang up on the problem, rather than each other" (Thomas Stallkamp). Then read the introduction on page 83.
2. Read and discuss "Understanding Collaboration" (page 84). Pay special attention to "Respect, Trust, and Goal Setting" since they are so important to effective group work. Assign the "Your Turn" activity.
3. Read "Using Strategies in Groups" and include the "Your Turn" activities in the discussion (page 85).

Day 2

4. Read and discuss "Understanding the Situation" (page 86) and assign the "Your Turn" activity.
5. Then go over "Brainstorming Ideas" on page 87. Assign the "Your Turn" activity, working with the class as they complete it together. Afterward, discuss the results of students' brainstorming.

Day 3

6. Have groups of three students read and discuss "Making Decisions" and the "Your Turn" activity on the top of page 88.
7. As a class, discuss the introduction to page 89, "Planning." Ask students to work individually on the accompanying "Your Turn" activity.
8. Then work through "Delegating," assigning the "Your Turn" activity as an outside-of-class extension activity. Next, continue with "Monitoring Progress," asking students to complete the first part of the "Your Turn" activity—planning the project.

Day 4

9. Have students review *Robert's Rules* on page 90. Then ask them the following questions:
   - What is your first reaction to these rules?
   - Have you ever used them? If so, under what circumstances?
   - How does this approach help or hamper group discussions?
10. Discuss the formats for meeting agendas and minutes on page 91.
11. Have students observe a formal meeting, either in person or electronically. Ask them to pay careful attention to the participants' conduct. Discuss students' experiences in class.

Day 5

12. Read and discuss "Collaborating Online" on page 92 and assign the "Your Turn" activity.
13. Have students review the tips on page 93 for using netiquette. Then discuss the "Your Turn" questions as a class, adding these:
    - What poor netiquette have you experienced?
    - Have you used poor netiquette yourself?

Extra: Have small groups find an example of online student collaboration and report their findings to the rest of the class.

Extension: Collaborating

Name _____   Date _____

Your Turn With the help of two or three classmates, analyze a famous collaborative effort by answering the questions below. Use effective group strategies to complete your work.

1. Name the situation (drafting the Constitution, planning the 1851 World's Fair in London, etc.):

   _____

   _____

2. Review the 5 W's and H of the situation. (See *Inquire* page 86.)

   ▪ Who? _____

   ▪ What? _____

   ▪ Where? _____

   ▪ When? _____

   ▪ Why? _____

   ▪ How? _____

3. Explore the leadership strategies. (See *Inquire* page 85.)

   ▪ Who was the leader? _____

   _____

   ▪ What leadership strategies did he or she employ? _____

   _____

4. Explore the group member strategies. (See *Inquire* page 85.)

   ▪ What stands out about some or all of the group members? _____

   _____

   ▪ Which strategies did these group members use? _____

   _____

5. Consider the decision making. (See *Inquire* page 87.)

   ▪ How did the group come to its decision/decisions? _____

   _____

   ▪ Was this a smooth or a rough process? Explain. _____

   _____

Follow-up: Prepare a brief report of your analysis to share with the class for discussion.

Review: Collaborating

Name _____   Date _____

Your Turn Answer each of the following questions.

1. Collaboration is a form of which process? Explain.

   _____

   _____

2. Name three strategies a leader can employ in a group situation.

   a. _____

   b. _____

   c. _____

3. What are the key parts of a collaboration situation?

   a. _____

   b. _____

   c. _____

   d. _____

4. Which of the following is good advice for resolving a conflict?

   a. Always assume the other person is right.   d. Look for weaknesses and pounce.

   b. Always assume the other person is wrong.   e. Ask the teacher to resolve all conflicts.

   c. Allow both sides to calmly explain.   f. Ignore all conflicts and keep smiling.

5. Name two ways to collaborate online.

   a. _____

   b. _____

6. What is netiquette?

   _____

   _____

Reflect: Why is collaborating such an important skill to master? What information in this chapter will be the most helpful to you?

   _____

   _____

Science Minilessons: Collaborating

Understanding Collaboration

LEARN how collaboration has been used in the area of science you are studying (chemistry, physics, biology, etc.).

CONSIDER general work in the area, significant breakthroughs, award-winning research, etc.

PREPARE a brief report about what you learn and share it with your classmates.

Understanding the Situation

An outbreak of fungal meningitis occurred in the United States in the fall of 2012. It is just one of many deadly outbreaks of contagious diseases that has occurred over time.

In a team of three students, **PREPARE** a brief presentation about an outbreak of a contagious disease.

To get started, **REFER** to *Inquire* pages 85–86 for help.

Planning

In a team of three students, **CREATE** a plan for a presentation about some aspect of weather forecasting (pollen counts, extended forecasts, etc.).

FOLLOW the planning process outlined on *Inquire* page 89.

Extension: **CARRY OUT** the plan and make your presentation.

Brainstorming Ideas

In a team of four or five students, **FOLLOW** the brainstorming tips on *Inquire* page 87 to address a question/problem/controversial issue supplied by your instructor. *Example:* Why is less ice forming in the North Pole and more ice forming in the South Pole?

REPORT on your group work—what you accomplished, what went well, and what didn't go so well.

Extension: **CONTINUE** exploring the topic.

Making Group Decisions

Your instructor will supply you with a specific career or occupation related to your science class. (Some of your classmates will receive other choices.)

LEARN ABOUT the training needed, opportunities, the career's importance, etc.

Then **TEAM UP** with three classmates who have learned about different careers.

Next, **DISCUSS** the choices to determine which career seems to have the most potential.

USE the strategies on *Inquire* page 88 to resolve any conflicts.

Collaborating Online

USE one of the online opportunities listed on *Inquire* page 92 to collaborate (*discuss, explore, research, etc.*) on a science topic you are studying.

FOLLOW the tips for netiquette on *Inquire* page 93.

KEEP the collaboration going as long as you can.

Afterward, **REPORT** on the experience to your classmates.

Math Minilessons: Collaborating

Using Strategies in Groups

TEAM UP with two or three classmates for a review before your next exam.

REVIEW the information on *Inquire* page 85 about group strategies.

Then **SELECT** a leader and begin your review.

RESPOND and **REACT** dynamically by energizing, focusing, inquiring, and so on.

Later, **DISCUSS** the effectiveness of the group review.

Brainstorming Ideas

In a team of four or five students, **FOLLOW** the brainstorming tips on *Inquire* page 87 to address a question/problem/issue supplied by your instructor. *Example:* How do you solve absolute value equations?

REPORT on your group work—what you accomplished, what went well, and what didn't go so well.

Extension: **CONTINUE** exploring the topic.

Resolving Conflicts

USE statistics to determine the chances that someone in your classroom is the same height as you (or another problem supplied by your instructor).

Then **TEAM UP** with two or three classmates to compare approaches and answers.

DECIDE on the best approach, using conflict resolution as needed. (See *Inquire* page 88.)

Planning

Suppose that your group (three to five members) has been assigned to plan an after-school math tutorial service.

INITIATE your planning by identifying the following: (See *Inquire* page 89.)

- Define the goal.
- Write objectives.
- List tasks.
- Schedule time.
- Outline the team.
- List tools.

SHARE plans with the other groups.

DECIDE together on the best plan to follow.

Discussing/Debating in Large Groups

TEAM UP with a large group of students to **DEBATE/DISCUSS** the following topic.

Resolved: Mathematics is essentially an individual intellectual activity rather than a group activity.

DIVIDE into two groups, asking one group to **PLAN** to argue for the position, and the other to oppose the position.

CARRY OUT the debate/discussion using *Inquire* pages 560–563 as a guide.

Collaborating Online

USE one of the online opportunities listed on *Inquire* page 92 to collaborate (*discuss, explore, research,* etc.) on a topic you are studying in mathematics.

FOLLOW the tips for netiquette on *Inquire* page 93.

KEEP the collaboration going as long as you can.

Afterward, **REPORT** on the experience to your classmates.

Social Studies Minilessons: Collaborating

Understanding the Situation

FORM a team of four students to discuss funeral customs in different cultures (or another topic provided by your instructor).

IDENTIFY the parts of this communication situation: (See *Inquire* page 86.)

- Members
- Issue or problem
- Medium
- Context

PLAN your discussion following the directives on *Inquire* page 89—define a goal, write objectives, etc. **CARRY OUT** your discussion.

Understanding the Situation

RESEARCH an important meeting between two governments, two empires, two countries, etc.

IDENTIFY the parts of this communication situation: (See *Inquire* page 86.)

- Members
- Issue or problem
- Medium
- Context

Extension: **TEAM UP** with a group of classmates to re-create the meeting.

Using Strategies in Groups

FORM a team of four or five students to discuss the concept of consumer confidence—what it means, why it is measured, how it is measured, its significance, etc.

First **RESEARCH** the topic individually.

Then **SELECT** a leader and a recorder and begin your discussion.

USE the information on *Inquire* page 85 as a discussion guide.

Answering the 5 W's and H

IDENTIFY an important group decision related to the temperance movement, women's suffrage, civil rights, etc.

Then **ANSWER** the 5 W's and H about the decision: (See *Inquire* page 86.)

- Who?
- When?
- What?
- Why?
- Where?
- How?

Extension: **CONTINUE** your research of the decision.

Resolving Conflicts

RESEARCH the actions taken to strip Lance Armstrong of his cycling crowns (or another topic).

Then **GATHER** in groups to discuss the topic as well as the issue of performance-enhancing drugs in cycling.

CONSIDER all sides of the issue and **FORM** an opinion about the actions taken against Armstrong.

USE the strategies on *Inquire* page 88 to resolve any conflicts.

Collaborating Online

USE one of the online opportunities listed on *Inquire* page 92 to collaborate on (*discuss, explore, research, etc.*) a topic about a government you are studying.

FOLLOW the tips for netiquette on *Inquire* page 93.

KEEP the collaboration going as long as you can.

Afterward, **REPORT** on the experience to your classmates.

English Minilessons: Collaborating

Answering the 5 W's and H

SELECT a memorable discussion/conversation involving three or more characters in a piece of fiction or nonfiction.

ANSWER the 5 W's and H about the discussion:

- Who?
- What?
- Where?
- When?
- Why?
- How?

SHARE the discussion and your answers about it with your classmates.

Planning

As a team (four to six members), **SELECT** a memorable scene from an important piece of literature.

CREATE a plan to reenact the scene: (See *Inquire* page 89.)

- Define a goal.
- Write objectives.
- List tasks.
- Schedule time.
- Outline the team.
- List tools.

Extension: **CARRY OUT** the reenactment.

Discussing/Debating in Large Groups

TEAM UP with a large group of students to **DEBATE/DISCUSS** the following topic.

Resolved: In today's world, writing is more important than ever before.

DIVIDE into two groups, asking one group to **PLAN** to argue for the position, and the other to oppose the position.

CARRY OUT the debate/discussion using *Inquire* pages 560–563 as a guide.

Resolving Conflicts

LEARN ABOUT using fair language in communication. (*Fair language* deals with how to address ethnicity, age, disabilities, the sexes, and so on.)

Then **TEAM UP** with four or five classmates to discuss the issue.

LIST five essential points about using fair language. (See *Inquire* page 88 to resolve conflicts.)

SHARE and discuss lists with the other groups.

Collaborating Online

MAINTAIN a blog while reading the next novel assigned in your literature class.

EXPLORE your thoughts about the story line, the main characters, the setting, and/or the author.

ASK classmates to comment on your postings.

Collaborating Online

REVIEW "Collaboration Opportunities" on *Inquire* page 92.

RESEARCH one of the online-collaboration types that could enhance your writing experience.

SHARE what you have learned with your classmates—how it works, how it can be used for writing, how it can be helpful, etc.

Extension: **ACT** on what you've learned.

Chapter 7
Building Arguments

(*Inquire* pages 95–114)

Building logical arguments has been a cornerstone of education since classical times. Aristotle ensured that. While argumentation has always been held as an important skill, it has taken on special importance today, as evidenced by its prominent position in the Common Core State Standards. This emphasis is understandable, because to develop an argument, a student must employ essential 21st century skills such as critical and creative thinking, problem solving, and communicating. This chapter covers all aspects of argumentation.

Learning Outcomes
- Learn about logic.
- Use deduction and induction.
- Understand the basic elements and rules.
- Argue mathematically.
- Build strong arguments.
- Avoid logical fallacies.

Correlations

Common Core State Standards

ELA-Literacy.CCRA.R.1–6	ELA-Literacy.CCRA.SL.4–6	Math.Practice.MP2–8
ELA-Literacy.CCRA.R.7–10	ELA-Literacy.CCRA.L.3	Science.Practice.SP1–8
CCSS.ELA-Literacy.CCRA.W.1–10		

Partnership for 21st Century Skills

Creativity and Innovation
- Think Creatively

Critical Thinking and Problem Solving
- Reason Effectively and Use Systems Thinking
- Make Judgments and Decisions
- Solve Problems

Communication and Collaboration
- Collaborate with Others

Information Literacy
- Use and Manage Information

Media Literacy
- Analyze Media

International Society for Technology in Education

1. **Creativity and Innovation**
   a. Apply existing knowledge to generate new ideas, products, or processes.
3. **Research and Information Fluency**
   b. Locate, organize, analyze, evaluate, synthesize, and ethically use information from a variety of sources and media.

4. **Critical Thinking, Problem Solving, and Decision Making**
   a. Identify and define authentic problems and significant questions for investigation.
   c. Collect and analyze data to identify solutions and/or make informed decisions.

Lesson Plan: Building Arguments

Day 1

1. Share these definitions of argument: (1) a discussion in which disagreement is expressed, (2) a quarrel, and (3) a course of reasoning aimed at demonstrating truth or falsehood. Ask students which definition of argument will probably be addressed here.
2. Read and discuss the chapter introduction on page 95.
3. Ask for a volunteer to read the top half of "Understanding Logic" on page 96. Have students complete the "Your Turn" and activity.
4. Discuss "Separating Fact from Opinion" on page 96. Ask students what it means to prove something objectively. Have students complete the "Your Turn" and share their results with the class.

Day 2

5. Read and discuss "Deductive Arguments" on page 97 and have students complete the "Your Turn" activity. (Students should create their own syllogisms.) Continue with the rest of the page.
6. Ask for a volunteer to read "Understanding the Basic Elements" on page 98 and have students complete the "Your Turn" activity. Ask for volunteers to share their work.
7. As time permits, review "Understanding Logical Rules" on pages 99–100. Have students complete the "Your Turn" activity at the bottom of page 100.

Special Note: Consider asking a math instructor or an accomplished math student to assist with presenting the material on page 101, which shows how the rules of logic work in geometric proofs.

Day 3

8. Read and discuss "Building Strong Arguments" on page 102, which provides a step-by-step process for students to follow.
9. Ask for a volunteer to "Consider the situation" on page 103 and have students complete the "Your Turn." Have a few students share their examples.
10. Continue with "Clarify your thinking," including the "Your Turn" activity.
11. Read and discuss "Constructing a Claim" and "Collecting Evidence" on page 104. Assign the "Your Turn" activity on the bottom of the page.

Day 4

12. Read and discuss "Considering Key Objections" on page 105 and have students complete both "Your Turn" activities. Ask for volunteers to share their work for discussion.
13. Read and discuss the top half of "Crafting Your Argument" on page 106. Make the first "Your Turn" activity part of your discussion.
14. After reviewing "Using Persuasive Appeals," have students consider the "Your Turn" activity. Ask pairs of students to share their thoughts about making an emotional connection in their argument.

Day 5

13. Review "Using Socratic Questions to Examine Arguments" on page 107 with students and have them complete the "Your Turn" activity.
14. During the remaining part of the class period, discuss "Avoiding Logical Fallacies," starting on page 108. There is too much here to cover during the time you have remaining, so consider having students address this material in three parts (108–109, 110, and 111–112), starting this day with 108–109.

Extension: Building Arguments

Name _____   Date _____

Your Turn Read the following argumentative speech by Susan B. Anthony delivered in 1873, after her arrest for casting an illegal vote. (Refer to a dictionary for any unfamiliar words.)

On Women's Right to Vote

Friends and fellow citizens: I stand before you tonight under indictment for the alleged crime of having voted at the last presidential election, without having a lawful right to vote. It shall be my work this evening to prove to you that in thus voting, I not only committed no crime, but, instead, simply exercised my citizen's rights, guaranteed to me and all United States citizens by the National Constitution, beyond the power of any state to deny.

The preamble of the Federal Constitution says:

"We, the people of the United States, in order to from a more perfect union, establish justice, insure domestic tranquility, provide for the common defense, promote the general welfare, and secure the blessings of liberty to ourselves and our posterity, do ordain and establish this Constitution for the United States of America."

It was we, the people; not we, the white male citizens; nor yet we, the male citizens; but we, the whole people, who formed the Union. And we formed it, not to give the blessings of liberty, but to secure them; not to the half of ourselves and the half to our posterity, but to the whole people—women as well as men. And it is a downright mockery to talk to women of their enjoyment of the blessings of liberty while they are denied the use of the only means of securing them provided by this democratic-republican government—the ballot.

For any state to make sex a qualification that must ever result in the disfranchisement of one entire half of the people, is to pass a bill of attainder, or an ex post facto law, and is therefore a violation of the supreme law of the land. By it the blessings of liberty are forever withheld from women and their female posterity.

To them this government has no just powers derived from the consent of the governed. To them this government is not a democracy. It is not a republic. It is an odious aristocracy; a hateful oligarchy of sex; the most hateful aristocracy ever established on the face of the globe; an oligarchy of wealth, where the rich govern the poor. An oligarchy of learning, where the educated govern the ignorant, or even an oligarchy of race, where the Saxon rules the African, might be endured, but this oligarchy of sex, which makes father, brothers, husband, sons, the oligarchs over the mother and sisters, the wife and daughters, of every household—which ordains all men sovereigns, all women subjects, carries dissension, discord, and rebellion into every home of the nation.

Webster, Worcester, and Bouvier all define a citizen to be a person in the United States, entitled to vote and hold office.

The only question left to be settled now is: Are women persons? And I hardly believe any of our opponents will have the hardihood to say they are not. Being persons, then, women are citizens; and no state has a right to make any law, or to enforce any old law, that shall abridge their privileges or immunities. Hence, every discrimination against women in the constitutions and laws of the several states is today null and void, precisely as is every one against Negroes.

Follow-up: In small groups or as a class, discuss the following: *What is Anthony's main claim? What evidence does she present to defend her claim? Does she address any key objections? If so, how? How does she conclude her argument?*

Review: Building Arguments

Name _____ Date _____

Your Turn Answer the following questions.

1. What is the different between a deductive and an inductive argument?

   _____

   _____

2. What are three basic elements of an argument, and how would you define each one?

   a. _____

   b. _____

   c. _____

3. What is a mathematical proof?

   _____

   _____

4. What is the claim in an argument?

   _____

   _____

5. What are two types of supporting evidence identified in the chapter?

   a. _____

   b. _____

6. What does it mean to answer an objection?

   _____

   _____

7. What are logical fallacies?

   _____

   _____

8. What is a *non sequitur*?

   _____

   _____

Reflect: Why is it important to use logic when developing an argument?

Science Minilessons: Building Arguments

Deductive Arguments

CREATE a brief deductive argument (syllogism) related to one of the topics you are studying in your science class. Here is an example: (Also see page 97.)

General Principle — Greenhouse gases trap heat in the atmosphere.

Burning fossil fuels creates greenhouse gases.

Specific Conclusion — Burning fossil fuels traps heat in the atmosphere.

SHARE your syllogism with your classmates and have them **CHECK** it for logic.

Understanding the Basic Elements

CREATE your own argument, beginning with a premise related to a topic that you have studied in your science class.

ADD another premise and at least one inference drawn from the premises.

Then **REACH** a conclusion derived from your premise.

Here is an example: (Also see pages 98–100.)

Premise 1: The phantom shiner is one of many freshwater fish that has become extinct.

Premise 2: Pollution caused by urbanization is a major cause of the disappearance of freshwater species.

Inference: Pollution likely contributed to the extinction of the phantom shiner.

Conclusion: Better pollution control on inland lakes is needed to maintain the various freshwater species of fish.

SHARE your work with your classmates and have them **CHECK** it for logic.

Inductive Arguments

CREATE a brief inductive argument related to the topic you used in the previous minilesson. Here is an example: (Also see page 97.)

Specific Case — Automobiles emit greenhouse gases.

Oil and natural-gas furnaces emit greenhouse gases.

Leaky natural gas supply pipes underground emit greenhouse gases.

Automobiles, oil and gas furnaces, and leaky natural gas lines leak greenhouse gases.

General Principle — The increase in greenhouse gases in the atmosphere comes from many sources.

SHARE your inductive argument with your classmates and have them **CHECK** it for logic.

Consider the Situation

SELECT a science-related issue (one with some controversy attached to it) that you could argue for or against.

ANALYZE the communication situation for such an argument by answering these questions: (Also see page 103.)

- As sender of the message, what role do I have?
- What is the purpose of my argument?
- What medium am I using for my argument (*speech, essay, letter,* etc.)?
- Who is my audience? What do I expect from them?
- When and where will the argument be received?

Extension: **CONTINUE** developing your argument, using pages 103–106 to guide you.

Math Minilessons: Building Arguments

Understanding Logic

On page 96 you learned that "in its most basic form, logic refers to the way that words connect to make meaning."

SELECT an important word or concept related to your class. (The word *linear* in algebra is an example.)

Then **IDENTIFY** three basic ways that this word carries meaning by providing the following:

- Definitions
- Semantics
- Syntax

SHARE your work with your classmates for discussion.

Separating Fact from Opinion

WRITE a series of 10–12 fact and opinion statements related to the material that will be covered on your next test. (See page 96.)

USE these statements as part of your test review while working with a partner.

READ ALOUD each statement and **ASK** your partner if it is a fact or opinion.

DISCUSS each statement as needed.

Then **SWITCH** roles.

Deductive Arguments

CREATE a brief deductive argument (syllogism) related to one of the topics you are studying in your math class. Here is a very basic example: (Also see page 97.)

General Principle | In an algebraic expression, a value that can be changed or varied is called a variable.

In the expression 27 + x, x is a variable.

Specific Conclusion | Thus, the value of x can be changed or varied.

SHARE your syllogism with your classmates and have them **CHECK** it for logic.

Arguing Mathematically
(Solving Proofs)

USE the two-column method to solve the following proof (or one provided by your instructor):

Given: ABCD is a parallelogram.

Prove: AB and DC are equal in length.

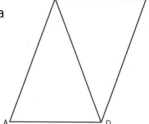

TEAM UP with a partner to discuss your finished proofs.

Avoiding Logical Fallacies

WRITE four different math-related logical fallacies. (See pages 108–112.)

Then **TEAM UP** with a classmate to discuss the work.

EXPLAIN the illogic in each one of your classmate's examples and then **SWITCH** roles.

Social Studies Minilessons: Building Arguments

Understanding Logic

On page 96 you learned that "in its most basic form, logic refers to the way that words connect to make meaning."

SELECT an important word or concept related to your history, sociology, psychology, or economics class. (The word *marginalize* in sociology is an example.)

Then **IDENTIFY** three basic ways that this word carries meaning by providing the following:

- Definitions
- Syntax
- Semantics

SHARE your work with your classmates for discussion.

Deductive Arguments

CREATE a brief deductive argument (syllogism) related to one of the topics you are studying in your history class. Here is an example: (Also see page 97.)

General Principle	All dictators are absolute rulers.
	Adolph Hitler and Josef Stalin were dictators.
Specific Conclusion	Adolph Hitler and Josef Stalin were absolute rulers.

SHARE your syllogism with your classmates and have them check it for logic.

Extension: **CREATE** an inductive argument related to the same topic. (See page 97.)

Understanding the Elements

CREATE your own argument, beginning with a premise related to a topic that you have studied in your history, sociology, or psychology class.

ADD another premise and at least one inference drawn from the premises.

Then **REACH** a conclusion derived from your premise.

Here is an example: (Also see page 98.)

Premise 1: Major General U. S. Grant lead Union troops to victories at Shiloh, Vicksburg, and Chattanooga.

Premise 2: Afterward, Lincoln promoted Grant to lieutenant general in charge of the entire Union Army.

Inference: Lincoln needed Grant's proven leadership abilities.

Conclusion: If Grant had not succeeded at Shiloh, Vicksburg, and Chattanooga, the Civil War could have taken a different course.

SHARE your work with your classmates and have them **CHECK** it for logic.

Consider the Situation

SELECT an economics-related issue (one with some controversy attached to it) that you could argue for or against. *Examples:* Equal pay for equal work, the role that small business plays in an economy, the relationship between tax breaks and improved earning. (Also check with your instructor for ideas.)

ANALYZE the communication situation for such an argument by answering these questions: (Also see page 103.)

- As sender of the message, what role do I have?
- What is the purpose of my argument?
- What medium am I using for my argument (*speech, essay, letter,* etc.)?
- Who is my audience? What do I expect from them?
- When and where will the argument be received?

Extension: **CONTINUE** developing your argument as time permits, referring to pages 103–106 as you go along.

English Minilessons: Building Arguments

Separating Fact from Opinion

CONSIDER the last piece of fiction or nonfiction that you read in class.

WRITE a series of 10–12 statements about the text, making sure to include both facts and opinions. (See page 96.)

Working with a partner, **READ** each statement and **ASK** your partner if it is a fact or opinion.

DISCUSS each statement; then **SWITCH** roles.

Inference Rules

REVIEW the nine inference rules on page 100.

Then **WRITE** your own examples for four different patterns on this page.

SELECT topics related to grammar or composition for your examples.

Here are two examples:

1. Modus Ponens
   - If *grow* is an action verb, then *shrink* is an action verb.
   - *Grow* is an action verb.
   - Therefore, *shrink* is an action verb.
2. Modus Tollens
   - If the verb is plural, the subject is plural.
   - The verb is not plural.
   - Therefore, the subject is not plural.

EXCHANGE your work with a partner, and **CHECK** the logic in each other's examples.

Considering Key Objections

FIND an essay, editorial, or letter to the editor in which the writer considers key objections to his or her position. (See page 105.)

Carefully **ANALYZE** this portion of the text.

THEN prepare a brief report that explains the writer's approach to the objections.

SHARE your report with your classmates.

Understanding the Basic Elements

CREATE your own argument, beginning with a premise related to a concept that you have studied in your literature or composition class.

ADD another premise and at least one inference drawn from the premises.

Then **REACH** a conclusion derived from your premise.

Here is an example: (Also see page 98.)

Premise 1: Classic quests focus on the challenges of a young hero who leaves home in search of fame and fortune and experiences a glorious return.

Premise 2: In the classic quest "Jason and the Golden Fleece," Jason is a young hero who leaves home in search of the Golden Fleece, which he eventually returns with.

Inference: Jason must have experienced challenges on his quest.

Conclusion: Jason's quest brought him fame and fortune.

SHARE your work with your classmates and have them **CHECK** it for logic.

Analyzing an Argument

Carefully **READ** a current essay, editorial, or commentary from an online source. (For seniors, consider something like Neil Postman's "My Graduation Speech." Everyone could also consider essays by Anna Quindlen or some other contemporary commentator. Ask your instructor for suggestions.)

Then **IDENTIFY** the following parts in the text: *the main claim, examples of supporting evidence, any counters or concessions to opposing points of view, and the confirmation of the claim.*

DISCUSS your work with your classmates.

Chapter 8
Succeeding in School and College

(*Inquire* pages 115–126)

Truly successful people rely on good habits. They know how to set short-term and long-term goals, manage time, and complete their work. Equally important, they know how to manage stress and enjoy a balanced life. And they remain life-long learners. This chapter prepares students to take charge of their own assignments and life goals, including preparing for and applying to college.

Learning Outcomes
- Develop good habits.
- Set goals and manage time.
- Complete assignments.
- Manage stress.
- Search for and apply to colleges.
- Apply for financial aid.

Correlations

Common Core State Standards

ELA-Literacy.CCRA.R.1–3	Math.Practice.MP4–6	Science.Practice.SP4–5
Math.Practice.MP1	Science.Practice.SP1	Science.Practice.SP7–8

Partnership for 21st Century Skills

Creativity and Innovation
- Work Creatively with Others

Critical Thinking and Problem Solving
- Make Judgments and Decisions

Communication and Collaboration
- Communicate Clearly
- Collaborate with Others

Information Literacy
- Use and Manage Information

Life and Career Skills
- Flexibility and Adaptability
- Initiative and Self-Direction
- Social and Cross-Cultural Skills
- Productivity and Accountability
- Leadership and Responsibility

International Society for Technology in Education

2. Communication and Collaboration
- Students use digital media and environments to communicate and work collaboratively.

3. Research and Information Fluency
- Students apply digital tools to gather, evaluate, and use information.

4. Critical Thinking, Problem Solving, and Decision Making
- Students use critical thinking skills to plan and conduct research, manage projects, solve problems, and make informed decisions using appropriate digital tools and resources.

Lesson Plan:
Succeeding in School and College

Day 1

1. Have students write for 10–15 minutes about either the goals of a person who inspires them or something they hope to achieve with their own lives.

2. Ask volunteers to share what they wrote about and to relate those goals to the "alive," "connected," and "learning" jobs of the brain, as described on page 116.

3. Turn conversation to the "10 Critical Habits of Learning" on that same page, and ask class members to reveal how well they would score themselves in the "Your Turn" there.

4. Turn student attention to the "Living a Colorful Life" section on page 117, and lead a brief discussion of its contents.

5. As homework, assign students to read the "Matching Education to Life Goals" section of that page and to write a journal entry about their own life goals and educational needs. Tell them that a copy of this journal entry will be collected at the beginning of the next day.

Day 2

6. Gather student journal entries and briefly discuss education and life goals.

7. Read and discuss "Setting Goals" (page 118) and have students do the "Your Turn," to be collected at the end of class.

8. Assign "Managing Time" (page 119) as homework reading, with the "Your Turn" exercise to be collected at the beginning of the next day.

Day 3

9. After gathering homework, briefly review "Completing Assignments" on page 120.

10. Next, read aloud the introductory paragraph of "Managing Stress" on page 121. Ask volunteers to provide examples of situations that have brought them beneficial eustress.

11. Next, provide an example of something that has brought you distress and how you coped with it. Ask student volunteers to share examples as well.

12. Review the five "Stress-Management Techniques" listed on page 121. Remind students to refer to this list of techniques when facing distress in the future.

13. Assign "Searching for Colleges" and "Applying to Colleges" (pages 122–123) as homework.

Day 4

14. As a class, review again "Matching Education to Life Goals" on page 117. Ask students to share their life goals and what education will be needed to meet them.

15. Discuss "Searching for Colleges" and "Applying to Colleges" (pages 122–123) in relation to those goals.

Day 5

16. If possible, have a counselor or other expert speak in class about the college application process and financial aid application.

17. As a chapter review, have students complete the "School-Success Activities" (pages 125–126) either in class or as homework.

18. Consider providing future class sessions for students to prepare college application materials.

Extension: Succeeding in School and College

Name _____   Date _____

Your Turn Use the following checklist whenever you prepare for a new assignment.

1. Understand the assignment. List what you are supposed to do:

_____

_____

2. List the due date:

_____

3. Review the grading process. Explain how the assignment will be graded:

_____

_____

4. List any help options:

_____

_____

5. Divide your time. List steps and target dates:

_____

_____

6. Collect the materials and tools you need. Note them here:

_____

_____

7. Choose a place to work. List your planned work space:

_____

_____

8. Note any problem areas and whom you will ask about them:

_____

_____

Review: Succeeding in School and College

Name _____ Date _____

Your Turn Answer the following questions to review your understanding of this chapter.

1. Which of the following is your brain's first job, second job, and third job? (Number them 1, 2, and 3, respectively.)

   Connected _____   Learning _____   Alive _____

2. What are three critical habits for learning (of ten shared in the chapter)?

   1. _____   2. _____   3. _____

3. Finish each of the following sentence starters in your own words:

   Hourly time management means . . . _____

   _____

   Daily time management means . . . _____

   _____

   Weekly time management means . . . _____

   _____

4. In terms of the chapter's advice for completing assignments, what is your greatest strength? Your greatest weakness?

   _____

   _____

   _____

5. List three of the chapter's five techniques for stress management:

   1. _____   2. _____   3. _____

6. Does your intended career require any training beyond high school? Explain your educational goals below and how you intend to achieve them.

   _____

   _____

   _____

Science Minilessons:
Succeeding in School and College

Science Schools

MAKE a list of different fields of science.

CHOOSE one field to focus on.

INVESTIGATE colleges specializing in that field.

RANK the schools according to their reputation.

CHECK the entrance requirements for the top five schools on your list.

SHARE your findings with classmates.

Stress Test

REVIEW the information about stress, eustress, and stress-management techniques outlined in this chapter.

SEARCH the Web for essays about research into the benefits and detriments of stress on human beings.

SHARE particularly interesting details with your classmates.

Rocket Scientists

INVESTIGATE the thousands of different careers of individuals at NASA.

CHOOSE one career at NASA that would suit your interests.

CREATE a list of long-term goals to reach that goal.

SHARE your information and proposed plan with your classmates.

Math Minilessons:
Succeeding in School and College

Time Is Money

CHOOSE a university that offers at least one math degree.

SELECT a degree from its math offerings.

CALCULATE the total number of semester hours needed to complete that degree.

CALCULATE the total tuition and fees involved. Add estimated book expenses.

DETERMINE a cost-per-hour ratio.

Adding Up to Success

PREVIEW your next math unit.

SET a personal goal for that unit.

LIST the tasks you must finish to achieve that goal.

CREATE a weekly planner to break down your time and track your progress.

FOLLOW THROUGH with your plan.

EVALUATE how well you achieved your goal.

EZ as π

LIST the ways your time is used each week: Sleeping, school, work, movies, and so on.

CALCULATE the hours you spend in each category for a year (including weekends and holidays).

MAKE a pie chart showing how your time is spent. Also **PREDICT** your time use at ages 25, 50, and 75.

Social Studies Minilessons: Succeeding in School and College

Family History

INVESTIGATE your family history (or the family history of a hero of yours).

LIST the occupations held by members of each generation.

DESCRIBE briefly the role education played in each person's career.

CHOOSE a person whose career matches your desires and **MAKE** a plan to achieve that goal.

Military Option

INVESTIGATE the role of military careers in a civilization you have studied in class.

COMPARE that role to the part military careers play in our own civilization.

INTERVIEW a family member or family friend with military experience.

DISCUSS with classmates various options for military careers.

Rainbows from the Past

REVIEW "Living a Full-Color Life" on page 117.

CHOOSE a time and place you have studied in history or read about.

DESCRIBE how people in that time and place divided their time among the items on the "Living a Full-Color Life" spectrum.

English Minilessons: Succeeding in School and College

Bad Example

IDENTIFY a character from fiction whose life choices led to trouble.

MAP those choices on a time line.

IMAGINE the character had chosen differently at any point.

DESCRIBE a likely course of events from the changed decision.

DISCUSS your change and its consequences with your classmates.

Stress the Positive

REMEMBER a time when you felt a lot of stress before a test or other performance.

JOURNAL about how that stress made you feel and how it affected your performance.

RECALL a time when the opposite was true. (For example, if you journaled about eustress helping, recall when distress hurt.)

EXPLAIN which of the stress-management techniques are your favorites.

College and Career Prep

INVESTIGATE career options for a person with an English degree.

CHOOSE one career and compare its projected annual income to the cost of the degree.

EXPLAIN to family and friends what you have learned.

Chapter 9
Improving Study Skills

(*Inquire* pages 127–140)

There may be many predictors of success for your students—both now and in the future. Natural aptitude, prior knowledge, and exposure to varied learning experiences are contributing factors. Another factor that must be considered is engagement. Students who connect with their coursework learn it and succeed. Students who have strong study habits such as taking meaningful notes, maintaining a learning log, and preparing for tests are engaged. This chapter addresses these three study skills.

Learning Outcomes
- Learn note-taking strategies.
- Use a learning log.
- Understand assessment.
- Employ test-taking skills.
- Review objective test strategies.
- Understand responding to prompts.

Correlations

Common Core State Standards

ELA-Literacy.CCRA.R.1–10	Math.Practice.MP1	Science.Practice.SP1
ELA-Literacy.CCRA.W.1–3	Math.Practice.MP5–6	Science.Practice.SP3–4
ELA-Literacy.CCRA.W.7–10	Math.Practice.MP8	Science.Practice.SP7–8
ELA-Literacy.CCRA.L.1–6		

Partnership for 21st Century Skills

Critical Thinking and Problem Solving
- Make Judgments and Decisions
- Solve Problems

Information Literacy
- Access and Evaluate Information

Media Literacy
- Analyze Media

Life and Career Skills
- Productivity and Accountability

International Society for Technology in Education

3. Research and Information Fluency
- Students apply digital tools to gather, evaluate, and use information.

4. Critical Thinking, Problem Solving, and Decision Making
- Students use critical thinking skills to plan and conduct research, manage projects, solve problems, and make informed decisions using appropriate digital tools and resources.

Lesson Plans: Improving Study Skills

Day 1

1. Ask students to paraphrase one of these quotations: (The idea in both quotations is that people create their own success.)

"If your ship doesn't come in, swim out to meet it."
—Jonathan Winters

"Opportunity is missed by most people because it is dressed in overalls and looks like work."
—Thomas Edison

Point out that students will succeed as learners by using strong study skills.

2. Ask for a volunteer(s) to read the introduction (page 127) and "Taking Classroom Notes" (pages 128–129).
3. Have students complete the "Your Turn" activity.

Extension: If time permits, have students take notes while viewing an online talk or discussion. ("CNN—vertical farming—a farm on every rooftop—Earth 2100" on YouTube would work well.) Afterward, have them compare their efforts. (Otherwise, have students complete this activity on their own or at another time.)

Day 2

4. Review with students "Using a Learning Log" on pages 130–131. Have them pay special attention to the strategies and sample entry. Then ask students to complete the "Your Turn" activity. Afterward, ask for volunteers to share their writing.
5. Read and discuss "Understanding Assessments and Tests" on page 132. Make the "Your Turn" activities part of the discussion.
6. Have a volunteer read aloud "Improving Test-Taking Skills" on page 133. Then have students complete the "Your Turn" activity. Afterward, ask for volunteers to share their writing.

Day 3

7. Have students review "Answering Objective Questions" on pages 134–135. Then have them complete the "Your Turn" activities. Afterward, have them share their work.
8. Provide students with a copy of an old objective exam for analysis. Have students point out trends, tips, trouble spots, and so on in the questions.

Day 4

9. Ask for a volunteer to read aloud the top half of "Responding to Prompts" on page 136. Then have students complete the first "Your Turn" activity.
10. For additional practice, have them complete "Analyzing a Prompt" on page 140.
11. Discuss the "Purpose Words" at the bottom of page 136. Make the "Your Turn" activity part of your discussion.
12. Read and discuss "Planning and Writing a Response" and "Sample Response" on pages 137–138.
13. Have students complete "Planning Your Response" on page 140.

Day 5

14. Implement the "Your Turn" activity on 137. (Students will need 45 minutes to complete their work.)

Extension: Improving Study Skills

Name _____   Date _____

Your turn Complete a learning-log entry for the video that you viewed on Day 1 or Day 2 of this unit. Follow the directions below to complete this writing.

Subject of This Entry: _____

- Summarize what was covered in the presentation.

- Predict what this topic/issue will lead to.

- Ask "what if?" or "why?" about this topic/issue.

- Argue for or against the ideas discussed in the presentation.

Follow-up: In your responses above, underline a few ideas that surprise you, deepen your understanding of the topic, prompt you to continue your research, and so on.

Review: Improving Study Skills

Name _____ Date _____

Your Turn Answer each of the following questions.

1. Why is the two-column format effective for note taking?

   _____

   _____

2. When taking notes, you are instructed to "listen for signal words." What are "signal words"?

   _____

   _____

3. You are also instructed to "record references." What are "references"?

   _____

   _____

4. How can writing in a learning log enhance your note taking?

   _____

   _____

5. What is the difference between formative and summative assessment?

   _____

   _____

6. What tip presented in the "During" section of "Using Test-Taking Skills" seems the most critical to you, and why?

   _____

   _____

7. Writing prompts usually contain "purpose words." What are "purpose words"?

   _____

   _____

8. What is an essential difference between a regular writing assignment and responding to a prompt?

   _____

   _____

Reflect: How would you rate your study habits on a scale of 1 (weak) to 5 (strong), and why?

Science Minilessons: Improving Study Skills

Note Taking: Digital Options

Effective note taking is essential in any science class because there are so many terms and concepts to learn.

CONSIDER digital notes using an application such as Evernote or Catch.

INVESTIGATE one or both sites.

USE a digital application for an extended period of time.

REPORT on the experience with your classmates.

Using a Learning Log

INVESTIGATE an interesting topic related to your science class. (*Example:* In a tech class, training roaches instead of robots for engineering applications would interest people.)

RESEARCH the topic (preferably a video presentation), taking notes as needed.

WRITE a learning log entry, exploring what you have learned. (See pages 130–131.)

SHARE in class what you have learned.

Responding to Prompts

Carefully **REVIEW** "Responding to Prompts" on pages 136–137.

Then **DEVELOP** a writing prompt about the topic that you explored in the last minilesson or about a topic related to your science coursework.

PLAN a response to the prompt by (1) forming a thesis statement for the response and (2) listing ideas to support the thesis.

Math Minilessons: Improving Study Skills

Taking Classroom Notes

SERVE as the designated note taker in your math class.

In this role, **TAKE** notes for yourself and for anyone who is absent during the week.

FOLLOW the format described on pages 128–129 for your notes.

BE SURE that your notes are neat, clear, and thorough.

"Dialogging"

TEAM UP with a partner in your math class.

Then, for the next unit, **DISCUSS** your work in a series of learning logs.

ALTERNATE writings, each responding to the other and adding new ideas and thoughts.

CONTINUE in this fashion, back and forth, until the completion of the unit.

Afterward, **DISCUSS** the value of the experience.

Self-Assessment

ASSESS your understanding of the concepts in a unit by doing the following: (See page 139.)

- Review your notes and learning log entries.
- Check the quality of your work on assignments.
- Discuss the unit with a learning partner.
- Quiz yourself.

Afterward, **CONSIDER** the value of your self-assessment.

Social Studies Minilessons: Improving Study Skills

Taking Classroom Notes

REVIEW "Taking Classroom Notes" on pages 128–129.

Then **TAKE** notes during a unit of study in your class.

Periodically **COMPARE** notes with a partner, discussing the similarities and differences in your notes.

CONTINUE in this fashion throughout the unit.

Afterward, **CONSIDER** the value of this process.

Using a Learning Log

INVESTIGATE an interesting topic related to your social studies class. (Examples: In Economics, explore direct sale of fresh produce to people.)

RESEARCH the topic using one or two reliable sources, taking notes as needed. (Use a video presentation if at all possible.)

WRITE a learning-log entry, exploring what you have learned. (See pages 130–131.)

SHARE what you have learned.

Responding to Prompts

REVIEW your notes and learning log entries for a unit you have just completed.

Then **CREATE** a thoughtful writing prompt based on your understanding of the topic.

PLAN a response to the prompt by (1) forming a thesis statement and (2) listing ideas that could support this statement.

Extension: **WRITE** the response within a designated time period.

English Minilessons: Improving Study Skills

Taking Classroom Notes

SEARCH online (perhaps on YouTube) for a video presentation of a grammatical or writing concept.

TAKE notes during the presentation using page 128 as a guide.

Also **WRITE** at least one learning log entry exploring your thoughts and feelings about the presentation.

Extension: **TEACH** the concept to your classmates.

Using a Learning Log

KEEP a learning log during your next writing assignment.

EXPLORE your progress (or lack of it) at different points during the writing process.

Afterward, **REVIEW** your learning log, identifying aspects of your work that went well or not so well.

USE your review as a self-improvement guide for your next writing assignment.

Responding to Prompts

REVIEW your notes and learning-log entries for a piece of literature you have just completed.

CREATE a writing prompt based on some element of the text (characterization, plot, setting, or theme).

PLAN a response by (1) forming a thesis statement and (2) listing ideas that could support this statement.

Extension: **WRITE** the complete response within a designated time.

Chapter 10
Reading to Learn

(Inquire pages 141–158)

The ability to read critically is a skill that all students need to master. The Common Core State Standards give special attention to this skill with standards for fiction and nonfiction in English/language arts and for nonfiction in science and social studies. The standards specifically emphasize determining what a text says and citing textual evidence. This chapter provides strategies that will help students carry out a close reading of nonfiction, fiction, and poetry.

Learning Outcomes
- Use key reading strategies.
- Read nonfiction effectively.
- Read fiction effectively.
- Read poetry effectively.

Correlations

Common Core State Standards

ELA-Literacy.CCRA.R.1–10	Math.Practice.MP1	Science.Practice.SP1
ELA-Literacy.CCRA.W.1–3	Math.Practice.MP3	Science.Practice.SP3–4
ELA-Literacy.CCRA.W.7–9	Math.Practice.MP6–8	Science.Practice.SP7–8
ELA-Literacy.CCRA.L.1–6		

Partnership for 21st Century Skills

Critical Thinking and Problem Solving
- Reason Effectively and Use Systems Thinking
- Make Judgments and Decisions

Communication and Collaboration
- Communicate Clearly
  - Use communication for a range of purposes.

Information Literacy
- Access and Evaluate Information

Media Literacy
- Analyze Media
  - Understand both how and why media messages are constructed, and for what purposes.

ICT Literacy
- Apply Technology Effectively
  - Use technology as a tool to research, organize, evaluate, and communicate information.

International Society for Technology in Education

2. Communication and Collaboration
  - **d.** Contribute to project teams to produce original works or solve problems.

3. Research and Information Fluency
  - **a.** Plan strategies to guide inquiry.
  - **b.** Locate, organize, analyze, evaluate, synthesize, and ethically use information from sources and media.
  - **c.** Evaluate and select information sources and digital tools based on the appropriateness to specific tasks.
  - **d.** Process data and report results.

4. Critical Thinking, Problem Solving, and Decision Making
  - **c.** Collect and analyze data to identify solutions and/or make informed decisions.

5. Digital Citizenship
  - **a.** Advocate and practice safe, legal, and responsible use of information and technology.

6. Technology Operations and Concepts
  - **a.** Understand and use technology systems.
  - **d.** Transfer current knowledge to learning of new technologies.

Lesson Plan: Reading to Learn

Day 1

1. Ask students to explain the following quotation: "Think before you speak. Read before you think" (Fran Lebowitz). Then have students rate on a scale of 1 to 5 the level of importance that reading plays in their lives, with a 1 representing very little importance and 5 representing extreme importance. Ask them to defend their rating. (Point out that the Common Core State Standards places a great deal of emphasis on reading.)

2. Have a volunteer read the introduction on page 141 and continue with another volunteer reading "Reading Actively" on page 142. After each tip is read, ask students if it is something that they typically do. Have students compete the "Your Turn" activity.

3. Then read and discuss "Using Reading Strategies" on page 143. Have students complete the first "Your Turn" activity before you discuss the second half of the page.

Day 2

4. Have a volunteer read aloud "Taking Reading Notes" on page 144. Then ask students to complete the "Your Turn" activity. If they don't have a textbook to use for this activity, then supply them with a text. (You could extend this activity by having the students write a brief learning-log entry about the page.)

5. Read and discuss "Annotating a Text" on page 145. If you want students to complete the "Your Turn" activity in class, then supply them with a text to read and annotate. Also discuss the value of this strategy.

Day 3

6. Read and discuss "Reading Nonfiction" on pages 146–147. Have students complete the "Your Turn" activity. Afterward, ask for a few volunteers to read aloud their paragraphs. Note the similarities and differences in their writing.

7. Have students review "Nonfiction Glossary" on pages 148–149. Assign each student to find out at least one additional piece of information for one or two of the terms to share with the class.

Day 4

8. Read and discuss "Reading Fiction" on pages 150–151. Have students complete the "Your Turn" activity. (They should focus on the "During" and "After" tips.) Afterward, ask for a few volunteers to share their reflections for discussion.

9. Have students review "Fiction Glossary" on pages 152–153. Assign each student to find out at least one additional piece of information for one or two of the terms to share with the class.

Day 5

10. Read and discuss "Reading Poetry" on pages 154–155. Have students complete the "Your Turn" activity for "Fire and Ice," "Sonnet – To Science," or "One's-Self I Sing." (Students should reflect on the poem in a journal entry, or create a new poem inspired by the original.) Afterward, ask for a few volunteers to share their reflections or poems for discussion.

11. Have students review "Poetry Glossary" on pages 156–157. Assign each student to find out at least one additional piece of information for one or two of the terms to share with the class.

Extension: Reading to Learn

Name _____   Date _____

Your Turn Read "Homeless" by Anna Quindlen or an article supplied by your instructor, following the directions below. (You can find "Homeless" online.)

1. Consider the communication situation. (See page 142.)

   ▪ **Sender:** Who wrote this? _____

   _____

   ▪ **Message:** What main point do you think will be made? _____

   _____

   ▪ **Medium:** How is this message presented? _____

   _____

   ▪ **Receiver:** Who do you think is the intended audience? _____

   _____

   ▪ **Context:** When and where was this written? _____

   _____

2. Use the KWL strategy to help connect with the text. (See page 143.)

   Topic: _____

   Know   **W**ant to know   **L**earned

3. Take notes as you read and annotate the text, if you can make a copy of it. (See pages 144–145.)

Follow-up: Summarize your thoughts about the reading.

_____

_____

_____

_____

_____

Review: Reading to Learn

Name _____ Date _____

Your Turn Answer each of the following questions.

1. How do you analyze the communication situation before you read?

   _____

   _____

2. What value is there in making predictions about the reading?

   _____

   _____

3. What is the purpose of the SQ3R strategy? What do the letters and number stand for?

   _____

   _____

4. Will your reading in your science and social studies class be nonfiction or fiction? Why?

   _____

   _____

5. What are four types of meaning that can be found in a poem? What is "meant" by each one?

   a. _____

   b. _____

   c. _____

   d. _____

6. How would you define each of the following terms?

   ■ Analogy _____

   ■ Paradox _____

   ■ Genre _____

   ■ Suspense _____

   ■ Alliteration _____

   ■ Free verse _____

Reflect: What type of reading challenges you the most—nonfiction, fiction, or poetry? Explain your choice.

_____

_____

Science Minilesson: Reading to Learn

Reading Actively

LOCATE a science-related news story in an online or print newspaper.

READ the story, jotting down names, details, notes, impressions, and even quick drawings as you go along.

SPEAK while you read, pronouncing difficult words and stating ideas that you want to remember or ones that surprise or confuse you.

Afterward, **CONSIDER** how your active participation affected your reading.

Using the Reading Strategies

CHOOSE one or more of the following reading strategies to complete your next reading assignment in your science class: (See pages 143–145.)

- KWL
- SQ3R
- Note taking
- Annotating

Afterward, **REFLECT** on your reading experience using the strategies.

Reading Nonfiction

FIND a timely science article to read. (See "http://esciencenews.com" for ideas.)

Carefully **READ** the article, using page 146 as your guide.

SUMMARIZE the text upon completion of your reading.

SHARE your summary with your classmates for discussion.

Math Minilesson: Reading to Learn

Using SQ3R

REVIEW "Reading with SQ3R" on page 143.

Then **APPLY** this strategy to the next chapter in your math textbook.

Afterward, **REFLECT** on the value of using this strategy, noting to what extent it helps you connect with the new information and concepts.

Extension: **CONTINUE** to apply this strategy until it becomes second nature to you.

Annotating a Text

MAKE a copy of two or three pages that you are currently working on in class.

ANNOTATE these pages in the following ways:

- Write notes in the margins.
- Underline important ideas.
- Circle new words.
- Draw lines to connect ideas.
- Use numbers to sort ideas.

Afterward, **REFLECT** on the value of annotating.

Reading Nonfiction

READ the book review by Andrew Strickland of the movie *A Beautiful Mind* (or another such text).

USE the plan on page 146 as your reading guide.

SUMMARIZE the text upon completion of your reading.

SHARE your summary with your classmates for discussion.

Social Studies Minilessons: Reading to Learn

Using KWL

REVIEW "Reading with KWL" on page 143.

Then **APPLY** this strategy to the next article or essay that you are assigned to read.

Afterward, **REFLECT** on the value of using this strategy, noting to what extent it helps you connect with the new information and concepts.

Extension: **CONTINUE** to apply this strategy until it becomes second nature to you.

Reading Nonfiction

FIND online an obituary of a president or presidential candidate to read.

USE the plan on page 146 as your reading guide.

SUMMARIZE the text upon completion of your reading.

SHARE your summary with your classmates for discussion.

Nonfiction Glossary

The writing forms listed below are associated with current events, politics, social trends, and so on.

DEFINE each of them.

- Editorial
- Letter to the Editor
- Personal Commentary
- Satire

Extension: **READ** an example of one of these forms, using "Tips for Active Reading" on page 142 as a guide.

English Minilessons: Reading to Learn

Reading Fiction

For your next fiction reading assignment, **COMPLETE** the "Before . . ." directions on page 150.

Upon completion, **DISCUSS** each part with your classmates.

Extension: **CONTINUE** your reading using the "During . . ." and "After . . ." directions as a guide (minus the formal literary analysis).

Reading Poetry

CHOOSE a poem in your literature anthology to read.

COMPLETE the "Before . . ." and "During . . ." directions on page 154.

Extension: As time permits, **CONTINUE** your reading and analysis by completing the "After . . ." directions.

Fiction and Poetry Glossaries

On pages 152–153 or 156–157, **IDENTIFY** one or two writing techniques that interest you.

LEARN as much as you can about the technique, such as . . .

- what it means,
- why it is used,
- where it is used (strong examples), and
- how to create original versions.

PRESENT your findings to your classmates.

Chapter 11
Building Your Vocabulary

(*Inquire* pages 159–178)

As you probably know, there is a direct link between regular reading and improved vocabulary. Reading, especially if it is varied, exposes students to many new words, and if they apply the right strategies, many of these words will become part of their working vocabulary. And as students build their vocabulary, they improve their reading, thinking, and communicating abilities. Simply put, words pack a lot of power in learning, and in life. This chapter provides a series of word-building strategies that students can apply in reading and learning situations.

Learning Outcomes

- Use a vocabulary notebook.
- Understand context clues.
- Learn about dictionaries and thesauruses.
- Understand word parts.
- Study common prefixes, roots, and suffixes.

Correlations

Common Core State Standards		
ELA-Literacy.CCRA.R.4–6	Math.Practice.MP8	Science.Practice.SP8
ELA-Literacy.CCRA.R.7–9	Science.Practice.SP1	
ELA-Literacy.CCRA.L.1–6	Science.Practice.SP4	

Partnership for 21st Century Skills
Communication and Collaboration
▪ Communicate Clearly

Lesson Plan: Building Your Vocabulary

1. Display this quotation: "You do yourself a grave disservice if you read around the words you don't know. . . ." (Charles Harrington Elster). Ask students what it means to "read around words" and to what extent they do it. Then display this quote by Elster: "For me, reading has always been not only a quest for pleasure and enlightenment but also a word-hunting expedition, a lexical safari." Ask students if they are unsure of any words in this quotation and if there are ways to figure out what they mean. Then ask them to explain the quotation.

2. Ask for a volunteer to read aloud the chapter introduction on page 159. Then review "Keeping a Vocabulary Notebook" on page 160 with them. Have students complete the "Your Turn" activity for two new words in any one of their classes. Have a few students share their entries. *Extension:* Have them include two new words for other classes.

3. Review "Using Context" on page 161 with your students. Have them complete the "Your Turn" activity on that page.

4. Provide students with a passage (online or in print) to read in class. Have them list four or five words that are new to them. Ask them to define these words using context clues and then compare their definitions with those in a dictionary.

5. Review "Using a Dictionary" on pages 162–163 with your students. Also review an online dictionary so they can see the similarities and differences between the print and electronic versions.

6. Read and discuss "Using a Thesaurus" on page 164. Have students complete the "Your Turn" activity. *Extension:* Have students write a brief description of something that is vivid in their minds (a scary movie, a concert they've attended, an accident, etc.). Ask them next to underline a few words that could be more specific and find fitting synonyms in a thesaurus.

7. Review "Understanding Word Parts" on page 165 with your students. Have students complete the "Your Turn" activity.

8. Then review "Prefixes, Roots, and Suffixes" on pages 166–177 with students so they know how to use these pages. Ask students to offer challenging words in their different classes for analysis using this glossary.

9. Assign "Word Builders" on page 178. Have students share their new words, including meanings and origins (how they were put together).

10. Then assign "Analyze the Parts" on page 178. Time permitting, have students share their analyses.

Extension: Building Your Vocabulary

Name _____   Date _____

Your Turn Carefully read the following passage and define the underlined words using context clues. Afterward, compare your definitions with those in a dictionary.

The passage that follows comes from an address presented by Frederick Douglass in which he discusses John Brown's assault on Harper's Ferry, West Virginia. Douglass wrote this address in 1881. (Jon Brown made his assault in 1859.)

Viewed thus broadly our subject is worthy of thoughtful and <u>dispassionate</u> consideration. It invites the study of the poet, scholar, philosopher, and statesman. What the masters in natural science have done for man in the physical world, the masters of social science may yet do for him in the moral world. Science now tells us when storms are in the sky, and when and where their violence will be most felt. Why may we not yet know with equal certainty when storms are in the moral sky, and how to avoid their <u>desolating</u> force? But I can invite you to no such <u>profound</u> discussions. I am not the man, nor is this the occasion for such philosophical enquiry. Mine is the world of grateful memory of an old friend; to tell you what I knew of him—what I knew of his inner life—of what he did and what he attempted, and thus if possible to make the <u>mainspring</u> of his actions <u>manifest</u> and thereby give you a clearer view of his character and services.

- Dispassionate: _____

  _____

- Desolating: _____

  _____

- Profound: _____

  _____

- Mainspring: _____

  _____

- Manifest: _____

  _____

Follow-up: Reread the passage. It should be easier for you to understand after your word study. *Extension:* What synonyms, if any, could Douglass have used for the underlined words?

_____

_____

_____

Review: Building Your Vocabulary

Name _____   Date _____

Your Turn Answer each of the following questions.

1. When keeping a vocabulary notebook, what are three types of information that you could include for each entry?

   a. _____   b. _____   c. _____

2. What does it mean to study a word in context?

   _____

   _____

3. Which of the following is not a context clue?
   a. a definition   **c.** tone   **e.** antonyms
   b. synonyms   **d.** word length

4. A dictionary provides the etymology of a word. What does the etymology indicate?

   _____

   _____

5. A dictionary also provides the inflected forms of a word. What are inflected forms?

   _____

   _____

6. When would you use a thesaurus?

   _____

   _____

7. How does a prefix differ from a suffix?

   _____

   _____

8. Refer to the glossary of prefixes, roots, and suffixes to see what you can learn about the following words:
   - diameter
   - geothermal
   - ornithology
   - fraction

Reflect: Is there one course in which the vocabulary truly challenges you? If so, why? How might the strategies in this chapter help?

Science Minilessons: Building Your Vocabulary

Using Context

IDENTIFY three unfamiliar words in the chapter you are currently reading in your science text.

COPY the sentences or passages containing these words.

Then **DEFINE** each word based on clues provided in the sentences. (See page 161.)

COMPARE your definitions with those in a dictionary.

Extension: **CONTINUE** this practice on a regular basis to become familiar with using context.

Using a Dictionary

LIST three key words related to your science class. (They could be from the previous minilesson.)

STUDY each one in a print or electronic dictionary.

Then **IDENTIFY** the following features:

- Syllabication
- Pronunciation
- First definition
- Etymology
- Variants (if provided)
- Inflected forms (if provided)

SHARE your word study with your classmates.

Understanding Word Parts

REVIEW the glossary of prefixes, roots, and suffixes on pages 166–177.

LIST four science-related words from any part of the glossary.

LEARN what you can about each by studying its parts; then **REFER** to a dictionary for more information.

SHARE what you have learned with your classmates.

Math Minilessons: Building Your Vocabulary

Using Context

MAKE a copy of an online article that has some connection to the math you are studying. (For example, in Statistics you could use an article discussing baseball or football stats.)

As you read the article, **UNDERLINE** and **LIST** any words that are new to you.

DEFINE each of these words using context clues.

COMPARE your definitions with a dictionary's.

SHARE your word study with your classmates.

Using a Dictionary

LIST three key words related to the unit you are studying in math class.

STUDY each word in a dictionary.

Then **IDENTIFY** the following features:

- Syllabication
- Pronunciation
- First definition
- Etymology
- Variants (if provided)
- Inflected forms (if provided)

SHARE your word study with your classmates.

Understanding Word Parts

REVIEW the glossary of prefixes, roots, and suffixes on page 166–177.

LIST four math-related words from any part of the glossary.

LEARN what you can about each by studying its parts; then **REFER** to a dictionary for more information.

SHARE what you have learned with your classmates.

Social Studies Minilessons: Building Your Vocabulary

Understanding Word Parts

REVIEW the glossary of prefixes, roots, and suffixes on page 166–177.

LIST four social studies- or history-related words from any part of the glossary.

LEARN what you can about each word by studying its word parts. **REFER** to a dictionary for more information.

SHARE what you have learned with classmates.

Using a Thesaurus

FIND online or in your textbook a speech made by a famous American.

SELECT part of the speech to copy on your own paper.

CIRCLE a few words to substitute or change.

CONSULT a thesaurus for suitable replacements.

Then **READ** this part of the speech with your synonyms included.

Using Context

IDENTIFY four unfamiliar words in a text related to your course. (The text could be an article, an essay, a chapter, a Web site, and so on.)

WRITE DOWN the sentences (or brief passages) that contain these words, and **UNDERLINE** the words.

Then **DEFINE** the words using context clues. (See page 161.)

COMPARE your definitions with those in a dictionary.

English Minilessons: Building Your Vocabulary

Understanding Word Parts

REVIEW the literary terms on pages 152–153.

LIST four of them for a word study.

LEARN what you can about each word, using the glossary on pages 166–177.

REFER to a dictionary to learn about each word's etymology, variants, labels, and/or examples.

SHARE your word study with your classmates.

Using a Thesaurus

REREAD a piece of writing that you have already completed or are currently working on.

CIRCLE any words that you may have overused as well as words that seem too general.

FIND replacements in a thesaurus. (See page 164.)

Then **REREAD** your text with the new words to see if they have improved the piece.

Using Context

IDENTIFY four unfamiliar words in a text (novel, short story, essay) that you are reading for class.

WRITE DOWN the sentences (or brief passages) that contain these words, and **UNDERLINE** the words.

Then **DEFINE** the words using context clues. (See page 161.)

COMPARE your definitions with those in a dictionary.

SHARE your word study with your classmates.

Chapter 12
Writing to Learn

(*Inquire* pages 179–202)

Thinking and writing work in tandem. You write to think more effectively, and you think to write more effectively. Thinking and writing help students learn and understand. In that way, regular writing helps students do their best in all of their courses—by improving their thinking. This chapter emphasizes writing as a learning tool but also addresses writing to inquire and writing to share via the writing process. You'll also find a guide to the conventions and a glossary of writing terms.

Learning Outcomes

- Understand writing as a learning tool.
- Use writing to assist in the inquiry process.
- Develop writing using the writing process.
- Apply the basic conventions.
- Use a writing glossary.

Correlations

Common Core State Standards

ELA-Literacy.CCRA.R.1–10	ELA-Literacy.CCRA.L.1–6	Science.Practice.SP1
ELA-Literacy.CCRA.W.1–10	Math.Practice.MP3	Science.Practice.SP3–4
ELA-Literacy.CCRA.SL.4–6	Math.Practice.MP5–6	Science.Practice.SP7–8

Partnership for 21st Century Skills

Communication and Collaboration
- Communicate Clearly
  - Articulate thoughts using oral, written, and nonverbal communication skills.
  - Use communication for a range of purposes.
  - Utilize multiple media and technologies.

Information Literacy
- Access and Evaluate Information

ICT Literacy
- Apply Technology Effectively
  - Use technology as a tool to research, organize, evaluate, and communicate information.

International Society for Technology in Education

2. Communication and Collaboration
  d. Contribute to project teams to produce original works or solve problems.

3. Research and Information Fluency
  a. Plan strategies to guide inquiry.
  b. Locate, organize, analyze, evaluate, synthesize, and ethically use information from sources and media.
  c. Evaluate and select information sources and digital tools based on the appropriateness to specific tasks.
  d. Process data and report results.

4. Critical Thinking, Problem Solving, and Decision Making
  c. Collect and analyze data to identify solutions and/or make informed decisions.

5. Digital Citizenship
  a. Advocate and practice safe, legal, and responsible use of information and technology.

6. Technology Operations and Concepts
  a. Understand and use technology systems.
  d. Transfer current knowledge to learning of new technologies

Lesson Plan: Writing to Learn

Day 1

1. Display these three reasons to write and discuss each one:
   - Writing to Learn
   - Writing to Inquire
   - Writing to Share

   Writing to learn is ungraded and carried out to help students learn. *Writing to inquire* focuses on writing to deepen students' understanding of a topic. And *writing to share* deals with the traditional concept of developing essays, articles, and reports for evaluation.

2. Then ask for a volunteer to read aloud the introduction on page 179.

3. Review with students "Writing to Learn" on pages 180–181. Then have students complete the "Your Turn" activity on page 181.

4. Time permitting, review with students "Graphic Organizers" on pages 182–183. Have students complete the "Your Turn" activity.

Day 2

5. Read and discuss "Questioning" on page 184. Have students complete the "Your Turn" activity. Then review "Planning" on page 184 and have students complete the "Your Turn" activity.

6. Read and discuss "Researching and Creating" on page 185. Make the first "Your Turn" activity part of the discussion. Then discuss "Improving" on the same page and have students complete the "Your Turn" activity.

Day 3

7. Review "Using the Writing Process" on page 186 with the students. Make the "Your Turn" activity part of your discussion.

8. Pages 187–190 provide a closer look at each step in the writing process. Give students time to study these pages and complete the "Your Turn" activities.

9. If time permits, assign "Processing Your Writing" on page 202. Ask students to share their responses.

Day 4

10. "Applying Basic Conventions" on pages 191–196 serves as a basic editing and proofreading guide. Give students time to study these pages and complete the "Your Turn" activities.

11. Assign "Following Conventions" on page 202. Ask students to share their responses to this activity.

Day 5

12. Inform students that pages 197–201 provide a handy reference to terms and concepts related to writing. Ask students to review this section and identify terms that are new to them. Discuss these terms as a class. Or ask students to present one new term to the class after briefly researching it online.

Extension: Writing to Learn

Name _____   Date _____

Your Turn Learn online about an important individual in social studies, science, technology, or mathematics. A few possibilities are provided for you here:

Social Studies/History
James Garfield
Charles J. Guiteau
Clarina Nichols
Matthew Brady
Mary McLeod Bethune

Science
Stephen Hawking
Ben Carson
Susan Solomon
Lori B. Garver
Jonas Salk

Technology
Paul Winchell
Alexander Graham Bell
Marissa Mayer
Steven Jobs
Mark Zuckerberg

Mathematics
Archimedes
Al-Khwarizmi
Isaac Newton
Amalie Emmy Noether
Benjamin Banneker

Dialogue

Create a dialogue between you and this person in which you explore important experiences in this person's life and work. Keep the conversation going as long as you can. (Not everything that the other person says has to be completely accurate.)

Note: Set up your conversation in an interview format to make it easy to follow. (See *Inquire* pages 75, 385, and 558–559.)

Follow-up: Reflect on this writing-to-learn activity. Did it help you clarify or deepen your understanding of the person? Explain.

Review: Writing to Learn

Name _____ Date _____

Your Turn Answer each of the following questions.

1. How do writing-to-learn activities help you?

   _____

2. What is meant by these two writing-to-learn activities?

   ▪ Mind mapping is _____

   ▪ Nutshelling is _____

3. Which graphic organizer would you use to consider pros and cons and other two-part structures?

   _____

4. Questioning is an important part of the inquiry process. What type of questions require creative responses? And what type require metaphysical (highly abstract) responses?

   _____

   _____

5. In the writing process, how does revising differ from editing? Explain your answer.

   _____

   _____

6. What is a thesis? (See "Prewriting.")

   _____

   _____

7. When you revise, what are three "global traits" that you should consider?

   _____

8. When should you use "amount" versus "number"? (See "Usage Rules" starting on page 192.)

   _____

9. What is a comma splice, and how do you correct one? (See "Sentence Error Rules" on page 196.)

   _____

   _____

10. What is the meaning of the following writing term?

    ▪ Jargon _____

Science Minilessons: Writing to Learn

Mind Mapping

CREATE a mind map (see page 180) about a topic from your last science class.

In the center of a piece of paper, **WRITE** the topic discussed during the class period.

Then **RECORD** as many connections and associations around it as you can. (Push yourself.)

Afterward, **IDENTIFY** at least one discovery that you made during your mapping.

Cause-Effect Chart

A lot of science involves analyzing causes and effects of a particular phenomenon.

SELECT one of the following topics (or a topic of your own choosing) to analyze in a cause-effect chart. (See page 182.)

- Oxidation
- Algae blooms
- Autism
- Black holes

SHARE your chart with your classmates for discussion.

Questioning

CHOOSE a topic that you are currently studying in your science class.

WRITE a series of questions about this topic using the questions on page 184 as a guide. (Write one example for each type of question.) **FORM** an answer to each of your questions.

REFLECT on this work. Consider whether or not it clarified and deepened your thinking on the topic.

Math Minilessons: Writing to Learn

First Thoughts and Summarizing

At the start of your next math class, **RECORD** your first thoughts about the topic or concept that will be discussed. (See page 180.)

At the conclusion of the class, **SUMMARIZE** the class work for that day. (Consider the relevancy of your first thoughts.)

REPEAT this process for subsequent classes.

After an extended period, **DETERMINE** whether or not these two writing-to-learn activities improved your learning.

Venn Diagram

Working with a classmate, **IDENTIFY** a valuable use of a Venn diagram or another type of comparison/contrast chart in your math class. (See page 183.) *Example:* Comparing different types of numbers in algebra.

CARRY OUT your comparison and contrast with the graphic organizer.

Afterward, **DISCUSS** your work with classmates. *Extension:* **CONSIDER** the other graphic organizers on pages 182–183 for different applications during the year.

Questioning

CHOOSE a concept or operation that you are currently studying in your math class.

WRITE a series of questions about this concept using the questions on page 184 as a guide. (Write one example for each type of question.) Then **FORM** an answer to each of your questions.

REFLECT on this work. Consider whether or not it clarified and deepened your thinking on the concept.

Social Studies Minilessons: Writing to Learn

Correspondence

Corresponding is a writing-to-learn activity in which you craft a letter or email message to someone related to your course work.

SELECT an important person related to the unit you are studying to correspond with.

CHECK online to learn more about the person.

Then **WRITE** your letter or message, exploring the person's beliefs and actions.

DISCUSS your letter with your classmates. (Send your letter if the person is alive and well.)

T-Bar

SELECT a significant piece of legislation, a court decision, or a political choice that you would like to analyze.

CHECK online to learn about the pros and cons of the topic.

FILL IN a T-bar with the appropriate pros and cons.

Then **REFLECT** on your work. Consider whether or not using this graphic organizer clarified and deepened your thinking on the topic.

Questioning

CHOOSE an important topic that you are studying.

WRITE a series of questions about this topic using the questions on page 184 as a guide. (Write one example for each type of question.) Then **FORM** an answer to each of your questions.

Afterward, **WRITE** briefly about your work. Consider whether or not the questions and answers helped you better understand the topic.

Extension: **USE** questioning like this regularly to become more thoughtfully involved in your studies.

English Minilessons: Writing to Learn

Predicting

As you read your next piece of literature, **PREDICT** what you think will happen next and why. (See page 181.) **MAKE** your predictions at regular intervals during your reading.

Afterward, **REFLECT** on your predicting. Consider whether or not this activity aided in your reading and how so.

5 W's and H Chart

As part of a review, **ANSWER** the 5 W's and H questions about an essay, short story, or novel you have read. (See page 183.)

COMPARE your chart with a classmate's chart.

WORK OUT any differences in your answers.

Extension: For another type of text review, **COMPLETE** a time line (See page 183).

Applying Basic Conventions

Working with a partner, **SELECT** four challenging rules for punctuation, usage, mechanics, or sentences. (See pages 191–196.)

PLAN how you can teach the rules to your class, focusing on the following: statement of the rule, tips for understanding it, examples, and quick practice.

TAKE TURNS presenting the rule. (Presentations should be brief—5 minutes or so.)

Chapter 13
Taking Exit and Entrance Exams

(Inquire pages 203–216)

Education has increasingly become defined by exams—none more so than exit and entrance exams. High school students and instructors know their importance and devote a great deal of time in preparing for them. Of course, the best preparation for students is becoming thoroughly engaged in coursework throughout the year. No other single strategy comes close to matching that. But students who know how to take different exams also improve their scores. This chapter provides strategies for doing so.

Learning Outcomes

- Learn how to prepare for exams.
- Understand how to answer objective questions.
- Learn how to answer reading-comprehension questions.
- Understand writing on demand.
- Know how to respond to documents.

Correlations

Common Core State Standards		
ELA-Literacy.CCRA.R.4–9	Math.Practice.MP1	Science.Practice.SP1
ELA-Literacy.CCRA.W.1–10	Math.Practice.MP3	Science.Practice.SP4
ELA-Literacy.CCRA.SL.4–6	Math.Practice.MP6–8	Science.Practice.SP7–8
ELA-Literacy.CCRA.L.1–6		

Partnership for 21st Century Skills

Critical Thinking and Problem Solving
- Make Judgments and Decisions
- Solve Problems

Information Literacy
- Access and Evaluate Information

Media Literacy
- Analyze Media

Life and Career Skills
- Productivity and Accountability

International Society for Technology in Education

3. Research and Information Fluency
- Students apply digital tools to gather, evaluate, and use information.

4. Critical Thinking, Problem Solving, and Decision Making
- Students use critical thinking skills to plan and conduct research, manage projects, solve problems, and make informed decisions using appropriate digital tools and resources.

Lesson Plan: Taking Exit and Entrance Exams

Day 1

1. In a 3-minute quick write, have students respond to the following quotation: "The greatest barrier to success is the fear of failure" (Sven Goran Eriksson). Ask for volunteers to share their responses. Then ask students how this quotation could serve as inspiration for test taking.

2. Ask for a volunteer to read aloud the chapter introduction on page 203. If possible, share sample exit and entrance exams with students.

3. Then have students create a cluster or mind map with "exams" as the nucleus word. (See page 180.) This activity should help them connect with the information in the chapter that follows.

4. Review with students "Preparing for Exams" on page 204. Time permitting, ask students to identify the three most important keys (after the first two in the list).

Day 2

5. Read and discuss "Understanding Question Types" on page 205. Make the "Your Turn" activity part of your discussion.

6. Have students review "Answering Objective Questions" on pages 206–207 and complete the two "Your Turn" activities. *Note:* To complete the "Your Turn" activity on page 206 students will need a recent test or two to review.

Day 3

7. Read and discuss "Answering Comprehension Questions" on pages 208–209 and have students complete the "Your Turn" activity. (If possible, have additional reading-comprehension questions for students to review.)

8. Read and discuss "Answering Revision Questions" on pages 210–211 and have students complete the "Your Turn" activity. (If possible, have additional revising questions for students to review.)

Day 4

9. Ask for a volunteer to read aloud "Writing on Demand" on page 212. Have students complete the "Your Turn" activity.

10. Read and discuss "Responding to Prompts" on page 213.

11. Time permitting, have students plan for and write the introduction for a response to one of the prompts on page 212. (Their plan should include their thesis statement and a list of key supporting points.) Give students a specified time limit (perhaps 12 minutes) to simulate an on-demand writing environment.

Day 5

12. Read and discuss "Responding to Documents" on pages 214–215. As the introduction on page 214 indicates, the information on these pages reflects what might appear on an AP-level exam. If needed, substitute a different example for class discussion.

13. Make the "Your Turn" activity on page 214 part of your discussion if it seems too challenging for students to complete on their own.

14. Time permitting, assign "Questioning Questions" on page 216.

Extension: Taking Exit and Entrance Exams

Name _____   Date _____

Your Turn Have students follow the steps below to plan and write a response to one of the following prompts or a prompt that you provide.

Prompt #1: The American school year is considerably shorter than the school year in most other countries. As a result, some experts say that a lot of time is wasted each fall reviewing what students may have forgotten over the summer. Write a persuasive essay defining or refuting the idea of a twelve-month school year.

Prompt #2: "Power should always be distrusted, in whatever hands it is placed" (Sir William Jones). In a personal essay, discuss the truth of these words, providing supporting examples from personal experience, literature, film, history, and/or current events.

1. Complete a STRAP analysis of the prompt (3–5 minutes).

   - Subject: _____

   - Type: _____

   - Role: _____

   - Audience: _____

   - Purpose: _____

2. Plan the response by writing a thesis statement and creating a brief list of supporting points (5–10 minutes).

   - Thesis statement: _____

   - Supporting points:

     – _____

     _____

     _____

     – _____

     _____

     _____

     – _____

     _____

     _____

3. Write your response (30 minutes). *Remember:* Include a beginning, a middle, and an ending.

Follow-up: Reflect on your performance: Were you able to complete your writing on time? Did it include all three parts? Did you have time to check your work for clarity before the time was up?

Review: Taking Exit and Entrance Exams

Name _____ Date _____

Your Turn Answer each of the following questions:

1. What does it mean to use "multimodal study forms"?

   _____

   _____

2. Why is it important to eat breakfast for taking an exam?

   _____

   _____

3. What is not a basic type of test question?
   a. essay questions   **d.** short-answer questions
   b. objective questions   **e.** none of the above
   c. indirect questions

4. In multiple-choice questions, why must you pay careful attention to "negations"?

   _____

5. What do the articles "a" and "an" indicate in fill-in-the-blank questions?

   _____

   _____

6. What is an "inference question"?

   _____

   _____

7. What is a writing prompt?

   _____

8. What is the purpose of the STRAP questions?

   _____

9. What should you include in the middle part of a response?

   _____

   _____

Reflect: What part of this chapter will prove especially helpful to you and why?

Science Minilessons: Taking Exit and Entrance Exams

Understanding Basic Questions

REVIEW a sample exam provided by your instructor.

NAME the different types of questions on the exam (see page 205) and **IDENTIFY** any questions that may contain any challenging features.

NOTE at least two or three specific strategies in the chapter that would help you take this exam.

DISCUSS your thoughts with your classmates.

Answering Objective Questions

CREATE a set of four questions—multiple-choice, true or false, fill-in-the-blank, and matching—about a unit you are currently studying.

KEEP the challenges for each type of question in mind. (See pages 206–207.)

EXCHANGE questions with a partner and **ANSWER** each other's questions.

Writing on Demand

REVIEW your class notes for important terms and concepts you are studying.

Next, **WRITE** a prompt for an important topic. The prompt should provide background information before stating the specific writing task. (See page 212.)

EXCHANGE prompts with a classmate and **ANALYZE** each other's prompt using the STRAP questions.

Then **PLAN** a response. (Your plan should include a thesis statement and a list of supporting points.)

Math Minilessons: Taking Exit and Entrance Exams

Entrance Exams

RESEARCH the math portion of sample college entrance exams. (Check online.)

WRITE DOWN at least five things that you learned during your research. (Consider the types of questions, the topics covered, special challenges, preparation, and so on.)

PREPARE a brief report of your findings.

DISCUSS your report with your classmates.

Answering Objective Questions

CREATE a set of multiple-choice questions about a unit you are currently studying.

WRITE at least four questions. Keep the challenges for that type of question in mind as you write. (See pages 206.)

EXCHANGE questions with a partner and **ANSWER** each other's questions.

Writing on Demand

REVIEW your class notes for important terms and concepts you are studying.

Next, **WRITE** a prompt for an important topic. The prompt should provide background information before stating the specific writing task. (See page 212.)

EXCHANGE prompts with a classmate and **ANALYZE** each other's prompt using the STRAP questions.

Then **PLAN** a response. (Your plan should include a thesis statement and a list of supporting points.).

Social Studies Minilesson: Taking Exit and Entrance Exams

Answering Objective Questions

CREATE a set of at least eight true or false questions about a unit you are currently studying.

KEEP the challenges for this type of question in mind as you write. (See page 206.)

EXCHANGE questions with a partner and **ANSWER** each other's questions.

Tip: **USE** your Q&A as part of a unit review.

Writing on Demand

REVIEW your class notes for important terms and concepts and **WRITE** a prompt for one.

PROVIDE background information before stating the specific writing task. (See page 212.)

EXCHANGE prompts with a classmate and **ANALYZE** them using the STRAP questions.

PLAN a response. (Your plan should include a thesis statement and a list of supporting points.)

Responding to Documents

With a partner, **IDENTIFY** two documents—passages from essays, articles, or speeches; film clips; photographs; charts—that relate to a major topic you have covered in class.

FORM a writing prompt based on the topic and the two documents. (See page 214.)

EXCHANGE prompts with another group and **ANALYZE** each other's prompt using the STRAP questions.

Then **PLAN** a response. (Your plan should include a thesis statement and a list of supporting points.)

English Minilessons: Taking Exit and Entrance Exams

Answering Objective Questions

CREATE at least 5 fill-in-the-blank or matching questions about a unit you are studying.

KEEP the challenges for these types of questions in mind as you write. (See page 207.)

EXCHANGE questions with a partner and **ANSWER** each other's questions.

Tip: **USE** your Q&A as part of a unit review.

Answering Revision Questions

FIND online a paragraph of least 6 or 7 sentences about a topic that interests you.

Then **COPY** the paragraph on your own paper but include a few revising errors, such as the ones included in the passage on page 211.

FORM questions based on those errors.

Then **EXCHANGE** work with a partner and **ANSWER** each other's questions.

Writing on Demand

WRITE a prompt for an important literary topic you have studied.

PROVIDE background information before stating the specific writing task. (See page 212.)

EXCHANGE prompts with a classmate and **ANALYZE** each other's prompt using the STRAP questions.

Then **PLAN** a response. (Your plan should include a thesis statement and a list of supporting points.)

Chapter 14
Developing Visual Literacy
(*Inquire* pages 217–236)

In discussing the importance of visual literacy, one expert explains it as "the ability to read *and* write visual information." Students must become critical readers of visual information because they are exposed to so much data packaged in a wide variety of graphics. A review of any current textbook, periodical, or Web site will attest to the explosion of visuals. Students should also become skilled writers or developers of visual information by learning how to use the many electronic design tools available to them. This chapter focuses primarily on reading visuals; chapters in Part III focus on developing them.

Learning Outcomes
- Understand visual literacy.
- Understand the elements of visual art.
- Learn about the principles of design.
- Learn about color and symbols.
- Understand page design.
- Learn about information graphics (graphs, tables, etc.).

Correlations

Common Core State Standards

ELA-Literacy.CCRA.R.1–10	Math.Practice.MP4–5	Science.Practice.SP4
ELA-Literacy.CCRA.W.1–9	Math.Practice.MP7	Science.Practice.SP8
ELA-Literacy.CCRA.SL.1–6	Science.Practice.SP2	

Partnership for 21st Century Skills

Critical Thinking and Problem Solving
- Reason Effectively and Use Systems Thinking
  - Use various types of reasoning
  - Analyze how parts of a whole interact with each other
- Make Judgments and Decisions
  - Effectively analyze and evaluate evidence
  - Analyze and evaluate major alternative points of view
  - Interpret information and draw conclusions

Communicating and Collaborating
- Access and Evaluate Information
  - Access information efficiently (time) and effectively (sources)
  - Evaluate information critically and competently

- Use and Manage Information
  - Manage the flow of information from a variety of sources
  - Apply a fundamental understanding of the ethical/legal issues surrounding the access and use of information

Media Literacy
- Analyze Media
  - Understand how and why media messages are constructed
  - Examine how individuals interpret messages differently, how values and points of view are included or excluded, and how media can influence beliefs and behaviors

International Society for Technology in Education

3. Research and Information Fluency
- **c.** Evaluate and select information sources and digital tools based on the appropriateness to specific tasks.
- **d.** Process data and report results.

Lesson Plans: Developing Visual Literacy

Day 1

1. Have students page through *Inquire* and locate examples of visual information that interest them. Ask for volunteers to explain their choices.
2. Have a volunteer read aloud the chapter introduction on page 217.
3. Then review as a class "Introduction to Visual Literacy" on page 218. (Make note of the definition of visual literacy in the second paragraph.)
4. Discuss the first and third "Your Turn" activities on page 218 as a class. Then ask students to complete the second activity on their own.

Day 2

5. Review as a class "Understanding What You See" on page 219 and have students complete the "Your Turn" activity.
6. Review "Interpreting What You See" on page 220 and have students complete the "Your Turn" activity.
7. Review "Evaluating What You See" on page 221 and have students complete the first "Your Turn" activity if time permits. Otherwise, assign it as homework. (Consider the second activity for another time.)

Day 3

8. Ask a student to read aloud "Understanding the Elements of Visual Art" on page 222. Assign the "Your Turn" activity as homework.
9. Have another student read aloud "Understanding the Principles of Design" on page 223. Assign the "Your Turn" activity as homework.
10. Discuss with students "A Closer Look at Colors" on page 224. Make the "Your Turn" activity part of your discussion.

Day 4

11. Discuss with students "Understanding Symbols" on page 225. Assign the "Your Turn" activity as homework.
12. Discuss "Understanding Page Design" on pages 226–227 with students. Make the "Your Turn" activity on page 226 part of your discussion. Assign the "Your Turn" activity on page 227 as homework, but only if students have a recent writing assignment to work with.

Day 5

13. Point out to students that "Understanding Information Graphics" on pages 228–234 will help students read graphics. Chapters in Part III of *Inquire* provide guidelines for creating these graphics.
14. Have students read and complete the activities in this section on their own, or have small groups of students study and present a particular section to the rest of the class. (The presentations could spill over into the next week.)

Extension: Developing Visual Literacy

Name _____   Date _____

Your Turn Find an image in one of your textbooks or online that truly enlightens, surprises, or amuses you. If possible, make a copy of the image to attach to this activity. Then explore your understanding, interpretation, and evaluation of the image below. (Use the questions to prompt your thinking. Also see *Inquire* pages 219–221.)

1. **Understanding What You See** (*What are the main features in the image? Where are your eyes drawn? What else contributes to the image—symbols, lighting, etc.)?*

   _____

   _____

   _____

   _____

   _____

   _____

2. **Interpreting What You See** (*What is the subject of the image, and how is this subject portrayed? What type of image is it—painting, sculpture, photograph, etc.? How do you interpret or explain the image? Who created it?*)

   _____

   _____

   _____

   _____

   _____

   _____

3. **Evaluating What You See** (*Does it distort anything? Does it communicate the subject in an effective way? Does the image look professional or homemade?*)

   _____

   _____

   _____

   _____

   _____

Follow-up: Share your image and analysis with your classmates. Determine if they share similar or different feelings about it.

Review: Developing Visual Literacy

Name _____   Date _____

Your Turn Answer the following questions about the chapter.

1. What is visual literacy?

   _____

   _____

   _____

2. How does an individual's "perception cloud" affect his or her ability to interpret an image?

   _____

   _____

   _____

3. What is not an element of visual art?
   - **a.** lines
   - **b.** shapes
   - **c.** reflections
   - **d.** space
   - **e.** textures
   - **f.** colors

4. What does it mean for an image to be in balance?

   _____

   _____

   _____

5. What is meant by the connotative, or secondary, meaning of a symbol?

   _____

   _____

   _____

6. Which of the following points identify principles of page design?
   - **a.** contrast
   - **b.** thoughts
   - **c.** alignment
   - **d.** revising
   - **e.** pictures
   - **f.** both a and c

7. Which of the graphics presented on pages 228–234 do you find the most interesting, and why?

   _____

   _____

   _____

Science Minilessons: Developing Visual Literacy

Understanding What You See

LOCATE an image (photograph, illustration, etc.) related to a science topic.

ANALYZE the image using the first five steps on page 219 as a guide.

Then, **WRITE** a brief report, summarizing your analysis.

ATTACH a copy of the image with your report.

Extension: **EXPAND** your analysis by answering the questions on pages 220 and 221.

Understanding the Elements of Visual Art

IDENTIFY a striking photograph in your science textbook or a science-related periodical.

Carefully **INSPECT** the photograph for the six elements described on page 222 in *Inquire*. **RECORD** your thoughts and feelings as you go along.

ORGANIZE your thoughts for a classroom presentation.

Then **PRESENT** your finding to your classmates.

A Closer Look at Colors

REVIEW the information on color on page 224 in *Inquire*.

Also **CHECK** online for more information, especially in terms of the use of color in different settings.

Then **DETERMINE** which colors you would use in the following departments in a new science/technology company:

- an entrance and lobby
- a brainstorming area
- a testing lab
- an employee lounge

SHARE your thoughts with your classmates.

Understanding Symbols

IDENTIFY two or three important symbols related to science, medicine, technology, etc.

ANALYZE each symbol by answering the questions on page 225.

ORGANIZE your thoughts in a brief report (a paragraph for two) for each symbol.

PUBLISH your work on a class Web site.

Understanding Information Graphics

FIND two graphics (graphs, charts, tables, diagrams, etc.) addressing the same science-related topic (perhaps one graphic in your textbook and another one on a Web site).

USE the appropriate tips or guidelines from pages 228–234 in *Inquire* to read each graphic.

Then **DETERMINE** their similarities and differences.

SHARE your findings with your classmates.

Extension: **COMPARE/CONTRAST** the two graphics in an essay. (See *Inquire* pages 460–462.)

Math Minilessons: Developing Visual Literacy

Understanding the Principles of Design

REVIEW "Understanding the Principles of Design" on page 223 in *Inquire*.

Then **LOCATE** an image (photograph, illustration, etc.) that contains some interesting shapes, angles, etc.

ANALYZE the image using the principles listed on page 223 as a guide.

Then **APPLY** at least one geometric principle to your analysis.

COMPILE your analysis in a brief report (a paragraph or two). **ATTACH** a copy of the image to your report.

Line Graphs and Scatter Plots

STUDY "Line Graphs and Scatter Plots" on page 228 in *Inquire*.

FIND an interesting/informative line graph or scatter plot online.

ANALYZE the graph using the tips or guidelines on page 228 as a guide.

Then **REVIEW** the math applied in the graph.

SHARE the graphic and your analysis in a group discussion. (Display or provide individual copies of the graph.)

Bar Graphs and Pie Charts

STUDY "Bar Graphs" on page 229 and "Pie Charts" on page 230 in *Inquire*.

FIND an interesting bar graph or pie chart online.

ANALYZE the graphic following the appropriate guidelines.

Then **REVIEW** the math applied in the graphic.

PRESENT your analysis to the class. (Display or provide individual copies of the graphic.)

Bubble Charts

REVIEW "Bubble Charts" on page 231.

LOCATE an interesting/informative bubble chart online or in a textbook.

ANALYZE the chart using page 231 in *Inquire* as a guide.

Then **REVIEW** the math applied in the chart.

COMPILE your analysis in a brief report (a paragraph or two). **ATTACH** a copy of the chart to your report.

Types of Graphics

LOCATE "A Periodic Table of Visualization Methods" online.

REVIEW the variety of graphics presented on this site.

SELECT one that has a mathematical element and is not included in *Inquire* on page 228–234.

ANALYZE the graphic for its message, design, math, etc.

SHARE the graphic and your analysis with your class.

Social Studies Minilessons: Developing Visual Literacy

Understanding What You See

LOCATE an image (photograph, illustration, etc.) online related to a topic you have been studying.

STUDY it using the first five steps on page 219 as a guide.

Then, **WRITE** a brief report, summarizing your understanding of the image. **ATTACH** a copy of the image with your report.

Extension: **EXPAND** your analysis of the image by answering the questions on pages 220 and 221.

Understanding the Elements of Visual Art

IDENTIFY a striking photograph in your social studies or history textbook.

Carefully **INSPECT** the photograph for the six elements described on page 222 in *Inquire*.

RECORD your observations for each element.

Then **PRESENT** your observations to a small group of your classmates.

Understanding the Principles of Design

REVIEW "Understanding the Principles of Design" on page 223 in *Inquire*.

FIND online or in a textbook a painting of a famous historical event.

RESEARCH the event.

Then **ANALYZE** the painting using the principles on page 223 as a guide.

DISCUSS the painting and your analysis with a partner.

Extension: **PREPARE** a written analysis of the painting for publication.

Understanding Symbols

IDENTIFY two or three important symbols related to economics, government, politics, etc.

ANALYZE each symbol by answering the questions on page 225.

COMPILE your thoughts in a paragraph or two for each symbol.

PUBLISH your analyses on a class Web site.

Understanding Information Graphics

LOCATE online a funny or satiric graphic related to current events, politics, etc.

MAKE a copy of the graphic and **ANALYZE** it.

SHARE your work with your classmates.

Extension: **CREATE** your own funny or satiric graphic. (See "Graphing Outside the Box" on page 236.)

English Minilessons: Developing Visual Literacy

Understanding Page Design

FIND a page (or two-page spread) from one of your textbooks.

ANALYZE its design using the information on pages 226–227 in *Inquire* as a guide.

TAKE notes as you go along, recording your observations of design elements, typography, etc.

COMPILE a brief written analysis from your notes. If possible, **ATTACH** a copy of the page with your analysis.

Understanding Page Design of an Original Text

LOCATE online an original text (important document, newspaper article, novel, etc.) from history.

ANALYZE a page or two of the document using the information on pages 226–227 in *Inquire* as a guide.

TAKE notes as you go along, recording your observations of design elements, typography, etc.

COMPILE a brief analysis, paying particular attention to the similarities and differences between the design of the document and current design theory.

Understanding Information Graphics

SEARCH a composition or language text (in print or online) for a useful chart or diagram—perhaps a grammar chart or a chart of frequently misused words.

Carefully **REVIEW** it for its value, clarity, etc.

Then **PRESENT** a brief report of the chart to your classmates.

DISPLAY a copy of the chart as you make your presentation.

Word Clouds

FIND a word cloud online or in a textbook.

READ it using the information on page 231 in *Inquire* as a guide.

Then **PRESENT** a brief report of the visual to a small group of classmates.

DISPLAY a copy of the word cloud as you make your presentation.

Extension: **CONSIDER** additional words that could be added to the word cloud.

Reviewing Graphic Novels

RESEARCH graphic novels online.

Then **ANALYZE** a sample spread or two from a graphic novel, using the information in the chapter as a general guide.

COMPILE your thoughts in a brief writing.

DISCUSS your analysis with your classmates for discussion.

DISPLAY the sample pages during your discussion.

Chapter 15
Improving Information and Media Literacy

(*Inquire* pages 237–256)

Citizenship in the 21st century requires awareness of how media messages are constructed to achieve particular aims with particular audiences. This chapter prepares students to evaluate the messages they encounter in various media and to produce their own media messages.

Learning Outcomes
- Understand key concepts of media literacy.
- Evaluate media messages.
- Create media.
- Understand media literacy terms.

Correlations

Common Core State Standards

ELA-Literacy.CCRA.R.1–10	ELA-Literacy.CCRA.L.4–6	Science.Practice.SP3–4
ELA-Literacy.CCRA.W.1–9	Math.Practice.MP2–8	Science.Practice.SP8
ELA-Literacy.CCRA.SL.1–6		

Partnership for 21st Century Skills

Critical Thinking and Problem Solving
- Reason Effectively and Use Systems Thinking
- Make Judgments and Decisions
- Solve Problems

Communication and Collaboration
- Communicate Clearly

Information Literacy
- Access and Evaluate Information
- Use and Manage Information

Media Literacy
- Analyze Media
- Create Media Products

Information and Communication Technologies Literacy
- Apply Technology Effectively

Life and Career Skills
- Social and Cross-Cultural Skills
- Productivity and Accountability
- Leadership and Responsibility

International Society for Technology in Education

2. Communication and Collaboration
- **c.** Develop cultural understanding and global awareness by engaging with learners of other cultures.
- **d.** Contribute to project teams to produce original works or solve problems.

3. Research and Information Fluency
- **a.** Plan strategies to guide inquiry.
- **b.** Locate, organize, analyze, evaluate, synthesize, and ethically use information from a variety of sources and media.
- **c.** Evaluate and select information sources and digital tools based on the appropriateness to specific tasks.

4. Critical Thinking, Problem Solving, and Decision Making
- **c.** Collect and analyze data to identify solutions and/or make informed decisions.

5. Digital Citizenship
- **a.** Advocate and practice safe, legal, and responsible use of information and technology.
- **b.** Exhibit a positive attitude toward using technology that supports collaboration, learning, and productivity.
- **c.** Demonstrate personal responsibility for lifelong learning.
- **d.** Exhibit leadership for digital citizenship.

6. Technology Operations and Concepts
- **a.** Understand and use technology systems.
- **b.** Select and use applications effectively and productively.
- **d.** Transfer current knowledge to learning of new technologies.

Lesson Plan: Improving Information and Media Literacy

1. Briefly review *Inquire* page 237 in class, focusing on the "You will learn . . ." bullet points.
2. Read page 238 in class and discuss the first part of the "Your Turn."
3. Read and discuss page 239 in class.
4. Give students class time to work in small groups to consider the second part of the "Your Turn" on page 238 and prepare a short statement about the "Your Turn" on page 239.
5. Assign pages 240–245 as homework reading.

6. Discuss pages 240–245 in class.
7. Provide class time for students to read pages 246–251.
8. Have students complete that reading and the extension activity as homework.

9. Choose students to share the results of their extension activity.
10. Lead class discussions of those examples.

11. Read and discuss pages 252–253 in class.
12. Point students to the glossary on page 254.
13. Assign students to choose one information and media literacy activity from pages 255–256 and begin working on it as homework. Announce that this homework will be due at the beginning of class on Monday.

14. If possible, arrange computer time or library time for students to work on their assignments.

Extension: Improving Information and Media Literacy

Name _____   Date _____

Your Turn Choose an example of a news or commercial message in print or online and answer the following questions about it. Share the example and your answers in class.

1. Who created the source? What do you know about their reliability?

    _____

2. What is the basic message?

    _____

3. How fair and logical is the message? What bias or logical fallacies does it contain?

    _____

    _____

4. What information is stressed? What information is left out?

    _____

    _____

5. How does the medium itself affect your understanding of and disposition toward the message?

    _____

    _____

6. Who is the target of the message? How can you tell?

    _____

    _____

7. How do you react to the message? How might someone react differently?

    _____

    _____

8. What is the purpose of the message? How effective is the message at that purpose?

    _____

    _____

9. Who controls transmission of the message?

    _____

Review: Improving Information and Media Literacy

Name _____   Date _____

Your Turn Answer the following questions to check your information and media literacy.

1. Which of the following are media literacy abilities?
   - **a.** create communication
   - **b.** analyze communication
   - **c.** access communication
   - **d.** evaluate communication
   - **e.** all of the above
   - **f.** none of the above

2. Which of the following is NOT a key concept of media literacy?
   - **a.** Different media use special techniques.
   - **b.** Many people today can create media.
   - **c.** Media messages are constructed.
   - **d.** Different people interpret media differently.
   - **e.** All media sources are equally valid.
   - **f.** Media messages share a point of view.

3. Write a short definition for each of the following:

   Fact: _____

   Opinion: _____

   Claim: _____

4. Rank the following from fastest delivery to slowest delivery.

   ____ TV   ____ Book   ____ Magazine   ____ Blog

5. Rank the following from most reliable to least reliable.

   ____ Microblog   ____ Newspaper   ____ Academic journal   ____ Movie

6. Name and explain one way of detecting bias in a message.

   _____

   _____

7. Explain how different people might interpret a message differently.

   _____

   _____

8. List one way you could use social media to spread your own message.

   _____

   _____

Science Minilessons: Improving Information and Media Literacy

Message from Mars

INVESTIGATE the idea that the Internet now extends to Mars.

CONSIDER how communication is affected by distance between Mars and Earth.

IMAGINE that you are one of the first settlers on Mars.

WRITE a short essay describing your communication with Earth.

Computer Bugs

CONSIDER Robert Pirsig's observation that different cities have different personalities.

DISCUSS with classmates how a city is like and different from a living organism.

CONSIDER next the group organization of an anthill or other insect hive.

DISCUSS ways in which social media is like and unlike hive communication.

Now and Then

WATCH a popular movie or television show from the 1950s or 1960s, depicting the world at that time.

NOTE differences in media technology and presentation between that time and the present.

REFLECT on ways modern media technology affect our understanding of the world.

Math Minilessons: Improving Information and Media Literacy

Math Messaging

VISIT Twitter.com or another favorite social-media site.

SEARCH for "mathematics" or another math-related term.

FOLLOW links to any interesting news in the resulting messages.

BOOKMARK one of those news stories.

SHARE with classmates what you have learned.

Math Catch

ARRANGE with a classmate or a friend to play a game of "Math Tag."

CHOOSE one person to go first.

HAVE that player send an unsolved equation by text message to the other.

HAVE the other player respond with the solution and a new unsolved equation.

KEEP playing until someone "drops the ball" by incorrectly responding.

Math Media

SEARCH for an article that uses mathematics, perhaps to discuss economics, population, or science.

ANALYZE the article, focusing on sender, message, medium, receiver, and context.

EXPLAIN how mathematics helps the sender achieve the purpose, and **IDENTIFY** any distortions.

SHARE your analysis with classmates.

Social Studies Minilessons: Improving Information and Media Literacy

A Social Snapshot

VISIT your favorite social-media service.

SEARCH for messages about Japan on that service.

RECORD a dozen of the most interesting messages.

INVESTIGATE further the subject of one.

SHARE your discoveries in class.

Fair and Balanced

CHOOSE a controversial subject currently being debated in the media.

FIND at least one message on all sides of the argument.

ANALYZE the fairness and completeness of each message.

EXPLAIN your analysis to classmates.

The View Out Your Window

INVESTIGATE the demographics in the United States of public access to social media.

CONSIDER aspects such as region, age, and income level.

DISCUSS with classmates how these differences might determine what messages are available to a person and how access might shape the person's opinions.

English Minilessons: Improving Information and Media Literacy

Two Views of Local News

WATCH a TV news program from a nearby city for one week.

READ a daily newspaper from that same city that same week. (Check your public library for copies.)

COMPARE the specific stories covered in each and how those stories are presented.

DISCUSS your observations in class.

To Put It Another Way

CHOOSE a novel that you have been studying in a literature class.

SUMMARIZE the plot and theme of that work, along with the major characters.

PRESENT that summary in a different medium—a poster, a podcast, a video.

DISCUSS with classmates how change of medium does or doesn't affect the message.

Target Audiences

CHOOSE a social-media account you use that displays advertisements. —OR—

VISIT a search engine on your computer or in your account on your family computer.

NOTE the types of advertisements that show up on your page.

ASK friends and relatives to let you see what advertisements show up in their accounts.

DISCUSS in class or at home any differences you note in types of advertisements.

Chapter 16
Creating Internet Literacy
(Inquire pages 257–268)

Teaching Internet literacy skills is often the responsibility of library media specialists; and thus, this chapter will be important to them. However, teachers of content areas will also find a great deal of important information in this chapter, from employing Internet resources in research reports to publishing those reports electronically, from considering the history of Internet technologies to the science of computer networking. The chapter also emphasizes the importance of using Internet resources safely, accurately, and fairly.

Learning Outcomes
- Understand what the Internet is and how it came about.
- Understand Web browsers and their technologies.
- Learn about staying safe online.
- Address effective communication with email, texting, instant messaging, VOIP, and video conferencing.
- Learn about using Internet content effectively and fairly.

Correlations

Common Core State Standards

ELA-Literacy.CCRA.R.1–10	ELA-Literacy.CCRA.L.4–6	Science.Practice.SP2–4
ELA-Literacy.CCRA.W.1–9	Math.Practice.MP2–3	Science.Practice.SP8
ELA-Literacy.CCRA.SL.1–6	Math.Practice.MP5–8	

Partnership for 21st Century Skills

Critical Thinking and Problem Solving
- Reason Effectively and Use Systems Thinking
- Make Judgments and Decisions
- Solve Problems

Communication and Collaboration
- Communicate Clearly

Information Literacy
- Access and Evaluate Information
- Use and Manage Information

Media Literacy
- Analyze Media
- Create Media Products

Information and Communication Technologies Literacy
- Apply Technology Effectively

Life and Career Skills
- Social and Cross-Cultural Skills
- Productivity and Accountability
- Leadership and Responsibility

International Society for Technology in Education

3. Research and Information Fluency
   a. Plan strategies to guide inquiry.
   b. Locate, organize, analyze, evaluate, synthesize, and ethically use information from a variety of sources and media.
   c. Evaluate and select information sources and digital tools based on the appropriateness to specific tasks.

4. Critical Thinking, Problem Solving, and Decision Making
   c. Collect and analyze data to identify solutions and/or make informed decisions.

5. Digital Citizenship
   a. Advocate and practice safe, legal, and responsible use of information and technology.
   b. Exhibit a positive attitude toward using technology that supports collaboration, , and productivity.
   c. Demonstrate responsibility for lifelong learning.
   d. Exhibit leadership for digital citizenship.

6. Technology Operations and Concepts
   a. Understand and use technology systems.
   b. Select and use applications effectively and productively.
   d. Transfer current knowledge to new technologies.

Lesson Plan: Creating Internet Literacy

Day 1

1. Begin a cluster on the blackboard by writing "What is the Internet?" in the middle and circling it.
2. Ask the class to add to the cluster by providing examples of services and technologies related to the Internet.
3. When the clustering session begins to lose steam, ask for a description for each term.
4. Divide students into five groups, pass out the "Extension" activity on the next page of the Teacher's Guide, and allow students time to work on it in class.

Day 2

5. Allow the groups from Day 1 time to practice their presentations.
6. Have them make their presentations, allowing time for questions after each.

Day 3

7. As a class, review "Understanding Web Browsing" on pages 260–261. Refer students to chapter 35 for example projects that employ HTML, CSS, JavaScript, and server-side code.
8. Ask students to volunteer examples of times they have worked with or experienced Web code in the past.
9. Assign pages 262–265 as homework reading.

Day 4

10. Have students write for 10–15 minutes to explain the relative merits of email, text messaging, instant messaging, VOIP, and video chat. What rhetorical situations might call for each?
11. Ask volunteers to share their thoughts. Then consider discussing the "Your Turn" activities on pages 262 and 264 (top). Assign the other activities as appropriate.
12. Open a discussion of Webinars (page 265). Have any students participated in one?
13. If possible, arrange for the class to view a Webinar—whether live or recorded—and discuss the interface. Encourage them to seek out Webinars on topics of their interest.
14. Assign pages 266–267 as homework reading.

Day 5

15. Have students write 5-minute "entry slips" describing what they learned from the assigned reading.
16. Ask them to describe examples of Internet media they may have used in past schoolwork or hobby projects.
17. Discuss the differences among copyright, trademarks, patents, open-source licences, and public domain. Discuss implications for including different types of materials in scholarly work, in business, and in hobby use. Refer students also to the discussion of source abuses on pages 392–395 in chapter 24, "Conducting Advanced Research."

Extension: What Is the Internet?

Name _____   Date _____

Your Turn As a group, follow the "Group Work" directions to prepare definitions for your assigned terms. Then, individually, follow the "Solo Work" directions to ensure you understand all terms.

Group Work

As a group, you will be assigned one of the lettered subject areas below.

1. Read and discuss the explanations on pages 258–259 that relate to your group of topics.

2. Prepare a summary explaining your terms.

3. Choose a spokesperson to make an oral presentation of your terms to the class.

4. Request and answer questions as a group.

Solo Work

With each group presentation…

1. During the presentation, take notes about the terms covered.

2. After the presentation, ask any questions you may have.

3. After class, compare what you learned with the material on pages 258–259.

Group A: Computer Hierarchies
- Mainframes
- Terminals
- Servers
- Clients

Group B: Local Networking
- Modems
- Routers
- LANs, WANs, and WLANs

Group C: Local Connection Types
- Ethernet
- Bluetooth
- Wi-Fi

Group D: Internet Connection Types
- ISPs
- Connections (cable and so on)
- Mobile Telephony
- VOIP Telephony

Group E: Web-Related Terms
- World Wide Web
- The Cloud
- DNS
- Transfer Protocols

Review: Creating Internet Literacy

Name _____ Date _____

Your Turn Answer each of the questions below. Then discuss your answers in class.

1. Define "server" and "client." What are the implications of cloud computing?

   _____

   _____

   _____

2. What is a router in a local network? What types of connectivity might it support?

   _____

   _____

3. How is Bluetooth similar to and different from Wi-Fi? How is mobile telephony different from both?

   _____

   _____

   _____

4. Name at least four possible Internet connection types.

   _____

5. What is the function of HTML? CSS? JavaScript? How does server-side code relate to these?

   _____

   _____

   _____

6. What is the definition of clip art?

   _____

7. How might you incorporate art, photos, and video into your academic work?

   _____

   _____

8. How are copyright, patent, and trademark similar and different?

   _____

   _____

   _____

Science Minilessons: Internet Literacy

Revise a Web Page

CHOOSE a Web site's home page (or other page) that you feel needs revision.

ASK at least three people to interact with the page, individually.

NOTE features they find easy to use and those they find difficult to grasp.

WRITE a summary of those notes.

On paper, **SKETCH** possible changes to the page, to solve any problems.

Extension: **CREATE** an electronic version of the new page for testing.

SUBMIT your work to the site owner as a suggestion, if appropriate.

Design a Fun Video Game that Teaches

BRAINSTORM to decide on a topic or a life skill that you would like to teach.

WRITE a description of how that subject could be shown and practiced on computer.

INCLUDE a list of video games that ideally could be adapted to that purpose.

SHARE your discoveries.

Extension: **CHOOSE** the most appropriate game and use the editing software to make it a teaching tool.

ASK people to test your game.

IMPROVE it as needed.

Experiment with Color

EXPLORE options for including color in HTML and CSS code.

RESEARCH JavaScript functions to change colors dynamically in a Web page.

WRITE a brief report of your findings.

Extension: **CREATE** a Web page that demonstrates different colors and allows the viewer to change them.

SHARE your Web page with classmates.

Compare ISP Features and Prices

RESEARCH home Internet service options in your area.

CREATE a spreadsheet listing connection speed, bandwidth, installation fees, and monthly service costs for each.

INCLUDE any added features in a "Notes" column.

IDENTIFY which plan or plans seem the best choice for your situation.

Build an Internet-Capable Computer

MAKE a list of desired features for a personal computer (processing speed, hard drive size, and so on).

LIST the equipment (tools and components) needed. Remember to include a network card or wireless modem.

SHARE your plan with your classmates.

Extension: **MAKE** a budget and revise your features and equipment to suit.

PURCHASE your equipment.

Carefully **ASSEMBLE** the computer.

TEST it and **INSTALL** an operating system.

Math Minilessons: Internet Literacy

Create an Infographic

INVESTIGATE the variety of infographics available online.

CHOOSE a set of statistics from one of your classes or a recent report you have prepared.

CONSIDER ways that information might best be presented in an infographic.

RESEARCH infographic tools online.

PREPARE your infographic.

PUBLISH it and ask for feedback.

Use Specialized Online Calculators

IDENTIFY a mathematical problem you need to calculate.

SEARCH online for calculators dedicated to that type of problem.

CHOOSE a calculator that seems best for your purposes.

PERFORM the calculation.

REPORT your results and recommendations in class.

Use Web Analytics

On your own blog or Web site, **CHECK** for built-in analytics applications.

ADD one if none exists.

CONDUCT a weekly review of data recorded by the application.

BRAINSTORM changes to improve your site's performance, and apply them.

Extension: **CONTINUE** to review data weekly to identify beneficial changes.

CONTINUE to improve your site.

Explore Math History

CHOOSE a personal hero from the history of math.

SEARCH the Internet for information about that person's life and accomplishments.

CONSIDER how the person's life affected his or her mathematical accomplishments and vice versa.

PREPARE a brief report about the person.

SHARE the report with your classmates.

Explore JavaScript's Math Functions

INVESTIGATE online explanations of JavaScript's Math.random(), Math.round(), and Math.floor() functions.

SAVE the boxed code as an HTML page and open that page in a browser.

GENERATE 50 random numbers with the code and record the results.

CHANGE Math.floor() to Math.round().

Then **GENERATE** and **RECORD** another 50 numbers.

COMPARE the two records and explain any differences you notice.

Extension: **RESEARCH** the use of "forms[0]" and "return false;" and **EXPLAIN** these ideas.

```
<html><head><script type=
"text/javascript">
function randomNumber() {
document.forms[0].elements[0]
.value=Math.floor(Math
.random()*2)+1; }
</script></head>
<body><form><input type=
"text">
<input type="submit" onclick=
"randomNumber(); return false;">
</form></body></html>
```

Social Studies Minilessons: Internet Literacy

Investigate Internet History

INVESTIGATE the history of the Internet.

PREPARE a brief report on what you learn.

EXPLAIN DARPA's role in its origins, the origins of the Web, and the role of Bulletin Board Systems.

SHARE in class what you learn.

Locate Original Documents

CHOOSE a significant person from a period of history you are studying.

IDENTIFY important documents related to that person—writings, birth and marriage certificates, and so on.

LOCATE versions of those documents archived online. (Check LOC.gov, Gutenberg.org, and museum Web sites.)

EXAMINE one of those documents. **SHARE** in class what you have learned.

Extension: **EXAMINE** the other documents.

Use Online Maps

EXPLORE the World Wide Web to locate current maps of a location you are studying.

EXAMINE the maps to see what you can discover.

GIVE a short presentation about what you have learned, projecting electronic copies for your audience or passing out print copies.

REMEMBER to credit the sources for your maps.

Extension: **SEARCH** for archived maps of the same location from earlier times.

COMPARE current and archived versions to identify similarities and differences.

Reveal the Internet's Impact

BRAINSTORM with a partner for ways in which the Internet has made the 21st century different from the 20th.

RESEARCH the topic online to see what you can discover.

CHOOSE the three most significant changes in your opinion.

GIVE a short report in class about the influence of the Internet, focusing on your three choices.

Extension: **INTERVIEW** parents and grandparents for their opinions on the same topic.

Plan a "Flash Event"

RESEARCH the term "social media" and/or "flash event" online. (Also see pages 269–290 and 578–579.)

PRINT out a related news story that you find interesting.

SHARE your story in class.

Extension: **PLAN** a course-related social gathering.

USE social media to arrange who brings what.

ENJOY the gathering.

WRITE an "after action" report explaining what you learned from your research and the experience.

English Minilessons: Internet Literacy

Revise for the Web

CHOOSE a research paper (5 to 10 pages) that you have written for a class.

MAKE a Web site based upon the content of that paper.

BREAK the content into subsections as needed.

CREATE additional headings to improve readability online.

REVISE the text to make shorter sentences and paragraphs.

ADD graphics and multimedia to help convey the message efficiently.

ASK classmates to review the Web site and make comments.

WRITE a journal entry describing what you learned from the process of adapting material to an online medium.

Create an Internet Safety Message

BRAINSTORM a list of hazards involving Internet use.

RANK them from most hazardous to least hazardous.

CHOOSE an item from your list and freewrite about it.

DISCUSS your writing with your classmates.

Extension: **TURN** your freewriting into a short essay (1–2 pages) explaining the dangers and how to avoid them.

Evaluate Ebooks vs. Print

CONSIDER books you have read in traditional print and those you have read in the ebook format.

WRITE a personal commentary comparing the experience of reading books in these two ways.

PUBLISH your commentary online.

Extension: **CONTINUE** to publish commentaries and reviews about the books you read in either format.

Create a Money-Making Blog

CHOOSE a topic of popular culture that you enjoy (i.e. a genre of books, films, or music).

CREATE a blog site devoted to your topic.

CHOOSE a graphic design that suits the topic.

IDENTIFY examples of your topic.

WRITE and **POST** a review of each example.

Extension: **FIND** an online seller that specializes in the topic.

APPLY for an "affiliate" or "associate" account with that seller (with a parent or guardian's permission).

IMPROVE your site regularly by adding linked reviews and by investigating search-engine optimization to guide your efforts.

Chapter 17
Using Social Media

(*Inquire* pages 269–290)

It may be argued that social media is making the various tribes of humankind around the world more aware of one another. These media are certainly making a global conversation more possible than ever before. This chapter prepares students to enter that conversation, both as good listeners and effective communicators.

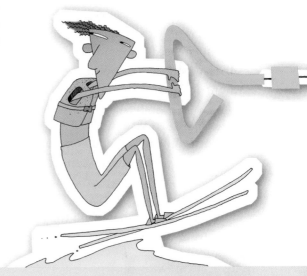

Learning Outcomes

- Understand the purpose of social media.
- Evaluate social-media messages.
- Understand types of social media.
- Create a positive digital footprint.
- Build a personal learning network (PLN).
- Use a PLN to answer project questions.
- Use social media to solve problems.
- Employ social-media etiquette.

Correlations

Common Core State Standards

ELA-Literacy.CCRA.R.1–3	ELA-Literacy.CCRA.SL.4–6	Math.Practice.MP5
ELA-Literacy.CCRA.R.7–9	ELA-Literacy.CCRA.L.3	Science.Practice.SP8
ELA-Literacy.CCRA.W.10	Math.Practice.MP3	

Partnership for 21st Century Skills

Creativity and Innovation
- Work Creatively with Others

Communication and Collaboration
- Communicate Clearly
- Collaborate with Others

Information Literacy
- Use and Manage Information

Media Literacy
- Create Media Products

Information and Communication Technologies Literacy
- Apply Technology Effectively

Life and Career Skills
- Social and Cross-Cultural Skills
- Leadership and Responsibility

International Society for Technology in Education

2. Communication and Collaboration
- Students use digital media and environments to communicate and work collaboratively, including at a distance, to support individual learning and contribute to the learning of others.

3. Research and Information Fluency
- Students apply digital tools to gather, evaluate, and use information.

5. Digital Citizenship
- Students understand human, cultural, and societal issues related to technology and practice legal and ethical behavior.

6. Technology Operations and Concepts
- Students demonstrate a sound understanding of technology concepts, systems, and operations.

Lesson Plan: Using Social Media

Day 1

1. Review the chapter opener on page 269 and lead a class discussion of the bulleted points. Ask students to share their knowledge of social media and to predict the meaning of any unfamiliar ideas in the list.
2. Review page 270 in class and ask students of any other news stories they know in which social media played a part.
3. Review page 271 in class. Explain to students that this page summarizes much of what the chapter will deal with. Ask them to share examples of sharing, learning, interacting, or marketing they have experienced through social media.
4. Have students complete the "Your Turn" on page 270 as an exit-slip exercise.
5. Assign page 272 as homework reading.

Day 2

6. Review the information on page 272. Then present page 273 in class.
7. Divide the class into six small groups. Assign one group to page 274, one to page 275, one to pages 276–277, one to page 278, one to page 279, and one to page 280.
8. Have each group review its assigned section and prepare a 3- to 5-minute summary of that information to share with the rest of the class.
9. Have groups make their presentations.

Day 3

10. Read and discuss page 281 in class.
11. Give students 5 minutes to freewrite about the "Your Turn" on that page.
12. Read and discuss page 282 in class.
13. Lead a class discussion of the "Your Turn" on that page.
14. Assign pages 283–285 as homework reading.

Day 4

15. Discuss the material on pages 283–285.
16. Implement the extension activity on the facing page to allow students to explore PLN possibilities for a research project.
17. If possible, arrange computer time for students to apply the lessons on pages 283–285 to the research project. (See the first activity on page 290 of *Inquire*.)

Day 5

18. Read and discuss pages 286–287 in class.
19. Briefly review pages 288–289 in class.
20. Divide the class into small groups and have them do steps 1–3 of the second activity on page 290 of *Inquire*.
21. Consider allowing future days for the groups to complete their advocacy campaigns (steps 4–8 on page 290 of *Inquire*).

Extension: Using Social Media

Name _____   Date _____

Your Turn Use this sheet to help plan a Personal Learning Network for researching a specific topic.

Our topic: _____

Initial questions to be answered:

1. _____

2. _____

3. _____

4. _____

5. _____

Search Engine Keywords:	Social Media Hash Tags:

Experts and organizations to follow:

Possible social media accounts to begin for this project:

Review: Using Social Media

Name _____   Date _____

Your Turn Answer the following questions.

1. What are the four main purposes of social media?

   _____

   _____

2. Name one way text messaging (instant messaging) is different from writing for school assignments.

   _____

   _____

3. Identify one way a social network can help with your schoolwork.

   _____

   _____

4. What is a hashtag?

   _____

5. What is the word "blog" short for?

   _____

6. Name two ways a group could use a collaborative-documents application such as a wiki or Google Docs for a school project.

   _____

   _____

7. What do the initials PLN stand for?

   _____

   _____

8. List two types of sources you might include in your own PLN.

   _____

   _____

9. List one social-media "Do" and one "Don't" that you would share with a younger student.

   _____

   _____

English Minilessons: Using Social Media

You're the Editor

CHOOSE a topic that is important to you.

SEARCH for microblog messages about it.

SELECT a dozen messages that you believe could be written more effectively.

REVISE and **EDIT** those messages for practice and **KEEP** them in a private file.

USE your experience to carefully craft your own microblog messages in the future.

Build a Brand

IMAGINE that you are the marketing manager for one of your favorite products.

BRAINSTORM ways to promote the brand with social media.

PREPARE a series of social-media messages for that purpose.

PRESENT your plan and messages to a small group of classmates.

ASK them to respond as a focus group.

Virtual Book Club

INVESTIGATE how to start an online book club.

INVITE interested classmates, friends, and relatives to join the club.

ARRANGE a time to chat online, or start a site where comments can be posted.

CHOOSE a book to read and discuss it together.

Math Minilessons: Using Social Media

Top of the Charts

SEND your classmates an email asking them to each identify their favorite band or artist.

MAKE an online survey listing all the bands and artists identified.

ASK your classmates to rank those bands and artists from most liked to least liked.

COMPILE the results into a bar graph.

EXTEND this project by asking classmates to rank songs by the most popular band or artist.

Short and Sweet

GATHER a piece of writing you have done for each of your classes.

CALCULATE in each piece the average number of words contained in 140 characters (including spaces and punctuation).

CHART each class by that average number.

JOURNAL your thoughts about the results.

DISCUSS those results and your thoughts with your classmates.

Math Masters

INVESTIGATE popular mathematicians or scientists who are active on a social-media service.

FOLLOW one of those individuals (with a parent or guardian's permission) and make a record of his or her posts.

RESEARCH an interesting topic mentioned in one or more of those posts.

DESCRIBE your experience to your classmates.

Science Minilessons: Using Social Media

The Shape of an Argument

INVESTIGATE arguments about the effects of the Internet on human cognition.

FIND microblog posts discussing the topic.

CONSIDER longer comments on Web sites and blogs discussing the topic.

DISCUSS the topic in class.

EVALUATE how the experience of discussion in microblogs, on Web pages, and in class are similar and different.

Latest News

CHOOSE a science topic you find interesting.

CREATE a blog, microblog, or other social-media account devoted to that topic.

POST weekly links to the most significant articles or developments in that field.

INCLUDE your own commentary with each post you make.

CRAFT your comments to invite discussion by visitors to your account.

Best Sources

LIST major fields of the sciences.

INVESTIGATE with a small group of classmates the best social media resources for each of those fields of study.

COMPARE your findings with other groups in your class.

Social Studies Minilessons: Using Social Media

News from the Frontier

CHOOSE a famous historical tale of exploration.

IMAGINE the team had cell phones and social media.

PLAN with classmates an online event simulating a report from that team.

CONDUCT your online event.

DISCUSS in class how social media would have changed the mission of exploration.

All About Communicating

CONSIDER the fact that maintaining a marriage requires communication.

ASK people from previous generations in your family or a friend's family about communication in marriage.

TALK with young married people in your community or online about the same topic.

JOURNAL about ways that social media helps or hinders marital communication.

A Question of Timing

CONSIDER a famous revolution in history, prior to the Internet.

JOURNAL about how that revolution might have happened differently if social media were available at the time.

DISCUSS your thoughts with classmates.

Chapter 18
Developing Financial Literacy
(*Inquire* pages 291–314)

There was a time when people could take a job with one company, work there until retirement, and rely upon the company pension plan for their golden years.

Today, careers are more fluid, with people relocating as employers expand, merge, or contract in a global economy. Entrepreneurship and freelancing are at all-time highs. In this new reality, personal financial literacy has become a critical 21st century skill. This chapter will introduce your students to it.

Learning Outcomes
- Develop healthy financial habits.
- Understand earning, saving, and investing.
- Understand purchasing and borrowing.
- Learn about managing money.
- Understand financial terms.

Correlations

Common Core State Standards

ELA-Literacy.CCRA.R.1–6	Math.Practice.MP4–7	Science.Practice.SP4–6
ELA-Literacy.CCRA.L.4–6	Science.Practice.SP2	Science.Practice.SP8
Math.Practice.MP1–2		

Partnership for 21st Century Skills

Critical Thinking and Problem Solving
Reason Effectively and Use Systems Thinking
- Use various types of reasoning
- Analyze how parts of a whole interact with each other to produce overall outcomes in complex systems

Make Judgments and Decisions
- Effectively analyze and evaluate evidence, arguments, claims, and beliefs
- Analyze and evaluate major alternative points of view
- Interpret information and draw conclusions
- Reflect critically on learning experiences and processes

Solve Problems
- Solve different kinds of non-familiar problems
- Identify and ask significant questions that clarify various points of view and lead to better solutions

Communication and Collaboration
Access and Evaluate Information
- Access information efficiently (time) and effectively (sources)
- Evaluate information critically and competently

Use and Manage Information
- Use information accurately and creatively
- Manage the flow of information from a variety of sources
- Apply a fundamental understanding of the ethical/legal issues surrounding the access and use of information

International Society for Technology in Education

Research and Information Fluency
- a. Plan strategies to guide inquiry.
- b. Locate, organize, analyze, evaluate, synthesize, and ethically use information from sources and media.
- c. Evaluate and select information sources and digital tools based on the appropriateness to specific tasks.
- d. Process data and report results.

Critical Thinking, Problem Solving, and Decision Making
- a. Identify and define authentic problems and significant questions for investigation.
- b. Plan and manage activities to develop a solution or complete a project.
- c. Collect and analyze data to identify solutions and/or make informed decisions.
- d. Use multiple processes and diverse perspectives to explore alternative solutions.

Lesson Plan: Developing Financial Literacy

Day 1

1. Have students write freely for 5–10 minutes about their experiences earning money and about plans they have for doing so in the future.
2. Review in class "Developing Healthy Financial Habits" on page 292. Assign the "Your Turn" activity.
3. Discuss page 293 with students. Ask if any students have filled out a W-4 or have received a W-2 or 1099. Assign the "Your Turn" activity.
4. Ask students to predict definitions for employment benefit types (insurance, retirement, day care, profit sharing, paid time off, unpaid leave, housing, meals). Then review "Understanding Benefits" on page 294. Assign the "Your Turn" activity.
5. If time permits, review "Paying Taxes" on page 295.

Day 2

6. Discuss "Saving" on pages 296–297. Assign the two "Your Turn" activities.
7. Discuss student experiences with banking.
8. Review "Purchasing" (pages 298–301) and ask for volunteers to discuss their experiences with the various headings. Have students work on one or more of the "Your Turn" activities.
9. Assign "Borrowing" (pages 302–305) as homework reading. Announce that there will be a quiz after the reading.

Day 3

10. Have students complete the "Borrowing Quiz" on the next page of this book. Review and discuss it. Consider assigning one or more of the "Your Turn" activities on "Borrowing."
11. Review and discuss "Investing" on pages 306–307.
12. Ask students to suggest which instruments (page 307) they might invest in. Encourage them to make the investments they suggest.
13. Consider having student volunteers report near semester's end on the results of their investments.

Day 4

14. Review and discuss "Budgeting" on page 308. Assign the "Your Turn" activity.
15. Review and discuss "Managing Risk" and "Understanding Insurance" (page 309). Assign the "Your Turn" activity.
16. *Special challenge:* As homework, have students investigate the historical origins of insurance.

Day 5

17. Have students write for roughly five minutes about the most surprising detail they discovered from their homework investigation.
18. Briefly discuss those discoveries in class.
19. Review the "Financial Glossary" with students (pages 310–313).
20. Ask each student to share one additional piece of information about any one of the terms.

Extension: "Borrowing" Quiz

Name _____　Date _____

Your Turn Answer the questions below to check your understanding of borrowing.

1. Which of the following is NOT a good tactic for developing credit?
   a. Get a secured loan or a secured credit card.
   b. Apply for an unsecured credit card.
   c. Make payments on time.
   d. Borrow up to 10 percent of your limit, and pay it back each month.
   e. Find a cosigner.
   f. All are valid tactics for developing credit.

2. How is a secured loan different from an unsecured loan?

   _____

   _____

   _____

3. What is the difference between points and fees on a loan?

   _____

   _____

   _____

4. List two ways to avoid credit card pitfalls:

   a. _____

   b. _____

5. List three things that you will be asked on loan applications:

   a. _____

   b. _____

   c. _____

6. What does FICO stand for?
   a. Federal Interest Committee Organization
   b. Fair Isaac Corporation
   c. Fair Interest Community Oversight
   d. None of the above

7. True or False: 700–759 is a "Great" FICO score. T _____　F _____

8. What does FAFSA stand for?
   a. Federal Application For Student Assistance
   b. Fair Aid from Federal Subsidiary Accounts
   c. Free Application for Federal Student Aid
   d. None of the above

Review: Developing Financial Literacy

Name _____ Date _____

Your Turn Respond to the following prompts to check your knowledge of financial literacy.

1. Besides wages, name three other benefits employers may offer to attract employees.

   _____

   _____

   _____

2. Name three taxes that are deducted from your wages.

   _____

   _____

   _____

3. Name one other type of tax.

   _____

4. Explain the difference between banks and credit unions.

   _____

   _____

   _____

5. Name two things included in calculating the Consumer Price Index.

   _____

   _____

6. Explain the difference between layaway and installment purchases.

   _____

   _____

   _____

7. Rank the following in order from low risk and low yield (1) to high risk and high yield (4).

   ____ Certificates of deposit (CDs)   ____ Savings accounts

   ____ Stocks   ____ Bonds

8. Name three types of insurance.

   _____

   _____

Science Minilessons: Developing Financial Literacy

The Sky's the Limit

IMAGINE that you are NASA's director, with a $20 billion budget allowance.

LIST five areas where you would devote those funds.

INVESTIGATE the actual budget for NASA this year.

DISCUSS in class what you have learned from this exercise.

Buy Now!

RESEARCH the psychology of impulse buying.

INVESTIGATE ways supermarkets apply psychology to increase the likelihood of impulse buying by their customers.

CONSIDER the effect of pricing on impulse buying. (E.g., Is a purchase more likely at $3.87, $3.95, $3.99, or $4.00?)

JOURNAL about what you discover.

Cultivating Cash

BRAINSTORM, in a small group, ways that a budget is like and unlike a living organism.

RESEARCH both topics as needed.

WRITE a journal entry summarizing your group discussion and your own thoughts.

SHARE your discoveries with your classmates.

Math Minilessons: Developing Financial Literacy

Cash in on Calculus

INVESTIGATE ways that calculus is used in the world of finance.

CHOOSE a particular application that relates to a chapter you are studying or that is otherwise of interest to you.

JOURNAL about the relationship of "real-world" calculus to what you are studying in class.

DISCUSS in class what you have learned.

Invest in Your Imagination

IMAGINE you have $1,000 to invest.

INVESTIGATE options for investment.

CALCULATE what you would earn on your investment at one year, five years, ten years, and twenty years with each option.

CONSIDER possible detriments to keeping that money invested.

SHARE your investment ideas.

Calculate Profit and Loss

LOCATE online a basic template for a "Profit and Loss Statement."

COMPLETE the form to calculate your personal income, spending, and saving for the current month.

REPEAT the process for an entire semester (or a calendar quarter).

JOURNAL about how the experience has affected your thinking about personal budgeting.

Social Studies Minilessons: Developing Financial Literacy

A Little Credit, Please?

REVIEW *Inquire* pages 303–304 for advice about best uses of credit cards.

INVESTIGATE the origins of credit cards in banking.

DISCUSS in class what role they play that other financial tools do not.

PLAN to use credit cards wisely.

Extension: **TALK** with older relatives about their own experiences with credit cards.

Houses of Cards

READ about the global financial crisis that started in 2006.

CONSIDER the role real-estate investment played in that crisis as well as the effects that the crisis had on personal budgets and long-term savings.

TALK with older relatives about ways the experience has affected their thinking.

JOURNAL your own thoughts about it.

You Can't Take It With You.

INVESTIGATE state and national inheritance laws.

IDENTIFY the benefits and detriments of families passing wealth from one generation to the next.

DISCUSS your thoughts with the rest of the class.

English Minilessons: Developing Financial Literacy

Rags to Riches

CONSIDER a novel in which finances play a central role—for example, *The Count of Monte Cristo, Crime and Punishment, Of Human Bondage,* or *Wuthering Heights.*

CHOOSE a character whose fortunes change dramatically in the novel.

JOURNAL about reasons for those changes.

SUMMARIZE how the difference in fortune affects the character's life.

Extra! Extra!

REVIEW, briefly, the topics covered in the "Developing Financial Literacy" chapter (pages 291–314) of the *Inquire Student Handbook.*

CHOOSE one topic that you learned most about and that you believe everyone should become familiar with.

SUMMARIZE that information for a blog post or in a letter to the editor of a local paper.

The Business of Life

INVESTIGATE the basic elements of a written business plan.

IMAGINE your personal future as a business that needs resources to accomplish its goals and that will pay dividends on investments.

WRITE a business plan outlining your projected future.

DISCUSS your business plan with a trusted adult.

Chapter 19

Succeeding in the Workplace

(*Inquire* pages 315–332)

Just about every day, we read reports about the critical need for an educated, trained workforce. Individuals best suited for jobs now and in the future will be well-versed in the 21st century skills outlined in this resource. They will also have put some thought into a possible career path. In other words, students should keep an eye on the present and the future. This chapter will help students plan for their future with information related to career choices, job searching, interviewing, and much more.

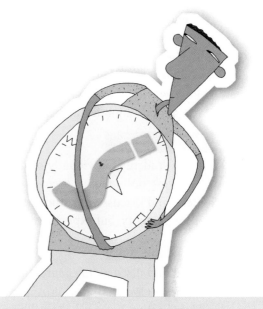

Learning Outcomes
- Plan for possible careers.
- Conduct a job search.
- Prepare for job interviews.
- Understand workplace etiquette.
- Gain entrepreneurial skills.

Correlations

Common Core State Standards

ELA-Literacy.CCRA.R.4–6	Science.Practice.SP1–3	Science.Practice.SP5–8
Math.Practice.MP1–7		

Partnership for 21st Century Skills

Creativity and Innovation
- Work Creatively with Others
- Implement Innovations

Critical Thinking and Problem Solving
- Make Judgments and Decisions
- Solve Problems

Communication and Collaboration
- Communicate Clearly
- Collaborate with Others

Information Literacy
- Use and Manage Information.

Life and Career Skills
- Flexibility and Adaptability
- Initiative and Self-Direction
- Social and Cross-Cultural Skills
- Productivity and Accountability
- Leadership and Responsibility

International Society for Technology in Education

1. **Creativity and Innovation**
   a. Apply existing knowledge to generate new ideas, products, or processes.
   c. Use models and simulations to explore complex systems and issues.
2. **Communication and Collaboration**
   b. Communicate information and ideas effectively to multiple audiences.
   d. Contribute to project teams to produce original works.

3. **Research and Information Fluency**
   b. Locate, organize, analyze, evaluate, synthesize, and ethically use information from sources and media.
4. **Critical Thinking, Problem Solving, and Decision Making**
   a. Identify and define authentic problems for investigation.
   c. Collect and analyze data to identify solutions.
6. **Technology Operations and Concepts**
   a. Understand and use technology systems.
   b. Select and use applications effectively.

Lesson Plan: Succeeding in the Workplace

Day 1

1. State that the 21st century demands skilled entry-level workers. Ask students the following:
   - Why are skilled workers are so important? (Most new jobs are technically oriented, which requires a certain skill level.)
   - What skills should these workers have? (Incoming workers need to be critical thinkers, problem solvers, communicators, and readers. It also helps to have a solid background in science, technology, engineering, and math).

2. Ask for a volunteer to read the chapter introduction on page 315.

3. Review with students the first part of "Connecting with Employers" on page 316 and then have them complete the "Your Turn" activity, listing the 12 abilities and marking their rating next to each ability.

4. Review with students the second part of page 316 and have them complete the "Your Turn" activity, listing the 12 job features and making their rating next to each feature.

Day 2

5. Have students individually read "Career Planning" on page 317 and complete the "Your Turn" by checking online for a career that might interest them.

6. Read and discuss with students "Creating a Plan" on pages 318–319. Have students begin the "Your Turn" activity, but expect them to complete it at a future date.

Day 3

7. Read and discuss "Job Searching" on page 320; then have students complete the "Your Turn" activity.

8. Review "Completing a Job Application" on page 321 with students. They should complete the "Your Turn" activity as needed on their own time.

9. Review "Creating a Résumé" on pages 322–323 with students. If appropriate, have students complete the "Your turn" activity at this time.

10. Review "Acing the Interview" on page 324 with students. Have them complete the two "Your Turn" activities.

11. If time permits, review "Improving Nonverbal Components" on page 325 and assign the "Your Turn" activity. Otherwise, consider it for the next day.

Day 4

12. Read and discuss "Understanding Workplace Etiquette" on page 326; make the first "Your Turn" activity part of the discussion.

13. Read and discuss "Receiving and Giving Instructions" and "Receiving and Giving Criticism" on page 327 and have pairs of students complete the "Your Turn" activities.

14. Review "Innovating on the Job" on page 328 with students and have them complete the "Your Turn" activity.

Day 5

15. Read and discuss "Gaining Entrepreneurial Skills" on page 329 and have students complete the "Your Turn" activity.

16. Review with students "Planning a Product or Service" on page 330 and "Pricing" and "Budgeting" on page 331. If appropriate, have students complete the "Your Turn" activities at this time.

Extension: Succeeding in the Workplace

Name _____   Date _____

Your Turn On pages 317–319, you investigated a career and completed a career plan for it. Extend your career planning by researching a company (corporation, organization, clinic, etc.) that you might want to work for someday. Answer the following questions about this company.

Company Profile

1. What is the name of the company and where is it located?

   _____

   _____

2. Why does this company interest you?

   _____

   _____

3. What product does it make or what service does it provide?

   _____

   _____

4. How many people work there? What would be a profile of a typical employee?

   _____

   _____

5. Who owns the company? How is it organized?

   _____

   _____

6. What would your "dream job" within the company involve?

   _____

   _____

7. What does this company look for in a potential employee?

   _____

   _____

Follow-up: Has investigating this company changed your career plan in any way? If so, how?

Review: Succeeding in the Workplace

Name _____ Date _____

Your Turn Answer each of the following questions.

1. Employers want employees who are flexible. What is meant by workplace flexibility?

   _____

   _____

2. Employees value a strong compensation package. What is meant by compensation in the workplace?

   _____

   _____

3. Which of the following are resources for finding job opportunities?
   - **a.** networking
   - **b.** want ads
   - **c.** online searches
   - **d.** help-wanted signs
   - **e.** all of the above
   - **d.** none of the above

4. What is the difference between chronological and functional résumés?

   _____

   _____

5. The list of nonverbal components of an interview on page 325 begins with promptness. What is meant by promptness, and why is it so important?

   _____

   _____

   _____

6. Workplace etiquette involves respect. Who exactly should an employee respect?

   _____

   _____

7. On page 329, you learned that most businesses try to fill a need that people have. What need does a building contractor fill? How about a beauty salon and spa? A water-treatment facility?

   _____

   _____

   _____

Reflect: How is a career similar to and different from a job? Which one is more important in terms of your long-term goals?

Science Minilessons: Succeeding in the Workplace

Careers in Science and Technology

REVIEW the careers list on page 317 for careers related to science and technology.

IDENTIFY one that especially interests you.

REFER to http://www.bls.gov/k12/azlist.htm to research this career.

Then **PREPARE** a brief career report to share with your classmates. Consider a job description, requirements, opportunities, etc.

Job Searching

STUDY the job-searching resources listed on page 320 and **USE** them to find "career-starter jobs" related to science and technology.

JOT DOWN the information for each job.

Also **DETERMINE** the value that such work experience would offer.

DISCUSS your discoveries with your classmates.

Extension: **MAINTAIN** a list of career-starter jobs in your classroom.

Entrepreneurship

STUDY the pyramid on page 329 that organizes the needs of people.

IDENTIFY existing science- and technology-related businesses that address at least two of these needs.

BRAINSTORM new business ideas (providing a service or making something) in these fields.

SHARE your ideas with your classmates.

Math Minilessons: Succeeding in the Workplace

Careers in Mathematics

REVIEW the careers list on page 317 for careers related to mathematics.

IDENTIFY one that especially interests you, or **SELECT** another one of your own choosing.

REFER to http://www.bls.gov/k12/azlist.htm or a different site to research this career.

Then **PREPARE** a brief career report to share with your classmates. Consider a job description, requirements, opportunities, etc.

Creating a Plan

CREATE a career plan for the career that you identified in the previous minilesson.

REFER to pages 318–319 as a guide (download a template at thoughtfullearning.com/h319.)

FILL IN what you can now from the information that you have already gathered.

CONTINUE working on your plan on your own throughout the school year.

Interviewing

Working with a partner, **CONDUCT** a mock interview for a job that involves mathematics (billing, budgeting, determining quantities, etc.). It could be an actual job from a recent want ad.

DETERMINE who will be the interviewer and the interviewee.

BASE the interview on the questions at the top of page 324.

Afterward, **REVIEW** the interviewee's performance based on the guidelines on page 325.

Then **REVERSE** the roles for a different job.

Social Studies Minilessons: Workplace Success

Careers in Social Studies

REVIEW the careers list on page 317 for careers related to history, government, law, etc.

IDENTIFY one that especially interests you or **SELECT** another one of your own choosing.

REFER to http://www.bls.gov/k12/azlist.htm or a different site to research this career.

Then **PREPARE** a brief career report to share with your classmates. Consider a job description, requirements, opportunities, etc.

Entrepreneurship

IMAGINE your own business that produces a product or service to help people at either the second or third level in Maslow's pyramid. (See page 329.)

IDENTIFY the goals and objectives for such a business. (See page 330.)

Extension: **FILL OUT** a complete planning sheet for your idea. A blank planning sheet is available at thoughtfullearning.com/h330.

Job Searching

STUDY the job-searching resources listed on page 320.

REFER to two or three of them for "career-starter jobs" related to the career you identified in the previous minilesson or to some other aspect of social studies.

JOT DOWN the basic information provided for each job.

Also **DETERMINE** the value that such work experience would offer.

SHARE your discoveries with your classmates for discussion.

Extension: **MAINTAIN** a list of career-starter jobs in your classroom.

English Minilessons: Succeeding in the Workplace

Job Searching

STUDY the job-searching resources on page 320.

REFER to two or three of them for "career-starter jobs" that require strong communications skills.

JOT DOWN information for each job.

DETERMINE the value that such work experience would offer in terms of future careers.

SHARE your discoveries with your classmates.

Extension: **MAINTAIN** a list of career-starter jobs in your classroom.

Creating a Résumé

CREATE a résumé for one of the jobs that you identified in the previous minilesson.

REVIEW pages 322–323 to determine which type of résumé to complete.

DEVELOP as much of the résumé as you can now; **COMPLETE** the rest on your own.

BE SURE your final copy is neat and accurate.

Extension: **CONSIDER** posting your résumé on an online employment Web site.

Interviewing

Working with a partner, **PREPARE** for a job interview using the questions at the top of page 324.

PRACTICE the interview a few times; then **PRESENT** it to a large group for review. (Reviewers should evaluate the interview using page 323 as a guide.)

Part I Answer Key

66

Review: Overview of 21st Century Skills

Name _____ Date _____

Your Turn Answer the questions below.

1. What fact about the brain do you find the most surprising and why?
   Answers will vary.

2. What are some of the essential differences between critical and creative thinking?
   Answers will vary. Sample response: Critical thinking is focused, careful, and intentional thinking. It involves studying a topic closely and narrowly. Creative thinking is expansive thinking. It seeks creative answers to the unknown.

3. Which of the problem-solving steps below require critical thinking (CT), and which require creative thinking (CR)? Label them accordingly.
   - Analyze the problem.   CT
   - Brainstorm solutions.   CR
   - Evaluate solutions.   CT
   - Innovate the solution.   CR
   - Critique the solution.   CT
   - Improve the solution.   CR
   - Implement the solution.   CT

4. Name and define the five parts of a communication situation.
   a. The *sender* is the speaker or writer.
   b. The *message* is the topic and purpose.
   c. The *medium* is the form.
   d. The *receiver* is the listener or reader.
   e. The *context* is the time and place.

5. What is a deductive argument?
   A deductive argument reasons from a general premise to a specific case.

6. To achieve financial literacy, what types of skills do you need? Name two.
   Any of these two: fiscal responsibility; career planning; money management; credit and debt management; risk management; saving and investing

Reflect: What does this Confucius quote mean to you? "Learning without thought is labor lost."
Answers will vary.

74

Review: Critical Thinking

Name _____ Date _____

Your Turn Answer each of the following questions with complete sentences.

1. What does Bloom's Revised Taxonomy show?
   Bloom's Revised Taxonomy shows the progression of thinking skills, from surface thinking (remembering) to deeper levels of thought (creating).

2. How can this taxonomy help you deepen or sharpen your thinking?
   The taxonomy shows the thinking process needed for thinking critical about a subject.

3. How can a pattern help you remember information?
   A pattern helps you fit individual pieces of information into a larger structure and thereby remember the information.

4. What two graphic organizers can help you understand a topic?
   Any two of these; list; time line; similarities/differences chart; Venn diagram; classification chart; cause-effect chart

5. How is a set of instructions like or different from an algorithm?
   Algorithms and instructions both involve a series of steps. An algorithm is a step-by-step problem-solving procedure that skips no steps and makes no assumptions, while instructions often skip steps that would appear obvious to someone who can read the language of instructions.

6. Why is writing a set of instructions a way of applying what you know?
   Instructions involve putting what you remember and understand to use for a specific purpose or output.

7. How can identifying constants and variables help you analyze something?
   Identifying constants and variables forces you to think about the individual parts of something— the parts that remain constant and the parts that may change.

8. Why is a rubric a valuable evaluation tool?
   A rubric helps you judge the value and worth of something by listing desirable traits and using a scale to rate them.

Reflect: Complete your own comparison about critical thinking, using this example as a guide:
Critical thinking is like an onion because it forms in layers, starting with a core of understanding.

82

Review: Creative Thinking

Name _____ Date _____

Your Turn Answer each of the following questions.

1. What is conceptual blending?
   Conceptual blending is a metaphorical thinking strategy that results from a forced connection between two unrelated systems or organization.

2. Write a question that creates an original conceptual blend. Answer it creatively.
   Answers will vary. Sample response: How could a sports team become more like a successful restaurant?

3. What is role-playing?
   Role-playing involves acting out a situation, usually with someone else, to put your knowledge of a topic to work and generate new ideas.

4. Identify three forms of role-playing.
   Any three of these: Game show, debate, interview, party, press conference, scenario

5. What is counterfactual thinking?
   Counterfactual thinking means asking "what if" questions.

6. Write one counterfactual question about a paper clip. Then answer it.
   Answers will vary.

7. What is SCAMPER?
   SCAMPER is a questioning technique for evaluating and improving an idea. The acronym stands for substitute, combine, adapt, magnify, put to other uses, eliminate, and rearrange.

8. Write three questions about a paper clip—one from each of the first three SCAMPER categories.
   Answers will vary.

Reflect: How might thinking creatively about a problem help you to solve it?
Answers will vary.

90

Review: Problem Solving

Name _____ Date _____

Your Turn Answer the following questions.

1. How is creative thinking part of the problem-solving process?
   Creative thinking is needed for imagining solutions, implementing solutions, and improving solutions.

2. Which graphic organizer works well to analyze a problem? Describe it.
   A cause-effect chart is an effective way to analyze a problem. The center of the chart includes the central problem. To its left, it lists the causes of the problem. To the right, it lists potential solutions.

3. What role does a trait evaluation play in the problem-solving process?
   A trait evaluation helps you evaluate, or judge the worth and success, of a solution.

4. Problem solving is actually a version of which other process?
   The inquiry process

5. Scientists follow the scientific method to carry out experiments (and solve problems). Name the steps in this method.
   (1) Identify a question or problem. (2) Create a hypothesis. (3) Identify variables. (4) Identify variables to control. (5) Summarize the experiment.

Reflect: Consider how both critical and creative thinking are a part of the scientific method.
Answers will vary.

98

Review: Communicating

Name _____ Date _____

Your Turn Answer the following questions.

1. Define the following components of a communication situation.
   - Sender: _The sender is the creator of the message._
   - Medium: _The medium is the way the message is expressed._
   - Context: _The context is the place and time of the message._

2. If you are listening at the analytical level, what types of responses might you make? (Name two.)
   Any two of these: You might (1) identify the main point, (2) recognize the support for the main point, or (3) question the purpose of the message.

3. What are the main characteristics of semiformal and formal communication situations?
   - Semiformal: _Characterized by some contractions and personal pronouns and occasional humor_
   - Formal: _Characterized by correct, serious language that uses complete sentences and avoids slang_

4. When speaking in a group, why should you start sentences with "I" instead of "You"?
   Using "I" helps you avoid sounding accusatory and signals that you are speaking for yourself.

5. As a speaker, how can you engage a large audience?
   You can engage a large audience by asking one or more audience members to come up and get involved with a demonstration or an activity.

6. When dealing with stage fright, what does it mean to "get into a wholesome mental space"?
   Get a good night's sleep the day before your presentation. Exercise, shower, eat, and wear comfortable clothing. Then take a deep breath and relax before you begin your presentation.

7. Define *inflection*.
   Inflection is the rise and fall in the pitch of a voice.

Reflect: What two things can you do to improve your listening skills? What two things can you do to improve your speaking skills in a small-group discussion?
   Answers will vary.

106

Review: Collaborating

Name _____ Date _____

Your Turn Answer each of the following questions.

1. Collaboration is a form of which process? Explain.
   Collaboration is a form of problem solving. By collaborating, a whole group takes on the work of finding a solution to an issue or problem.

2. Name three strategies a leader can employ in a group situation.
   a. _Directing_
   b. _Facilitating_
   c. _Collaborating_

3. What are the key parts of a collaboration situation?
   a. _Member (group member)_
   b. _Issue or problem (issue or problem the group is facing)_
   c. _Medium (meeting)_
   d. _Context (time and place)_

4. Which of the following is good advice for resolving a conflict?
   a. Always assume the other person is right.   d. Look for weaknesses and pounce.
   b. Always assume the other person is wrong.   e. Ask the teacher to resolve all conflicts.
   (c.) Allow both sides to calmly explain.   f. Ignore all conflicts and keep smiling.

5. Name two ways to collaborate online.
   a. _Any two of these: (1) use wikis; (2) use blogs; (3) use social media; (4) use chat services; (5) use_
   b. _email; (6) use VOIP services; (7) use forums or message boards_

6. What is netiquette?
   Netiquette refers to behaviors that are considered acceptable and unacceptable online.

Reflect: Why is collaborating such an important skill to master? What information in this chapter will be the most helpful to you?
   Answers will vary.

114

Review: Building Arguments

Name _____ Date _____

Your Turn Answer the following questions.

1. What is the different between a deductive and an inductive argument?
   A deductive argument moves from a general principle to a specific case. An inductive argument moves from a specific case to a general principle.

2. What are three basic elements of an argument, and how would you define each one?
   a. _A premise is a statement taken to be true._
   b. _An inference is a statement derived from previous statements._
   c. _A conclusion is the final inference._

3. What is a mathematical proof?
   A mathematical proof is an argument that starts with givens and asks you to reach a specific conclusion by using logic and mathematical rules.

4. What is the claim in an argument?
   The claim is the main statement made in an argument. It can be a truth claim, a value claim, or a policy claim.

5. What are two types of supporting evidence identified in the chapter?
   a. _Any two of these: facts, statistics, reasons, results, examples,_
   b. _anecdotes, quotations, reflections_

6. What does it mean to answer an objection?
   To answer an objection is to state a position that opposes your claim and then rebut the position, overcome part of it, or concede the objection and move on.

7. What are logical fallacies?
   Logical fallacies distort logic, misuse evidence, or reach false conclusions.

8. What is a *non sequitur*?
   A non sequitur is a statement that does not follow from a previous statement.

Reflect: Why is it important to use logic when developing an argument?   Answers will vary.

122

Review: Succeeding in School and College

Name _____ Date _____

Your Turn Answer the following questions to review your understanding of this chapter.

1. Which of the following is your brain's first job, second job, and third job? (Number them 1, 2, and 3, respectively.)
   Connected __2__   Learning __3__   Alive __1__

2. What are three critical habits for learning (of ten shared in the chapter)? Possible answers:
   1. _sleep,_   2. _eat,_   3. _move,_
   connect, relax, work, wonder, discover, create, or share

3. Finish each of the following sentence starters in your own words:
   Hourly time management means . . . _focusing on the work that you are supposed to be doing, avoiding distractions, and making progress._
   Daily time management means . . . _getting from class to class on time, using your study hall for the most important homework, taking part in extracurricular activities, and meeting a work schedule._
   Weekly time management means . . . _scheduling your activities; planning time for friends, fun, rest; and avoiding overload._

4. In terms of the chapter's advice for completing assignments, what is your greatest strength? Your greatest weakness?
   Answers will vary.

5. List three of the chapter's five techniques for stress management: Possible answers:
   1. _Avoid the problem._   2. _Care for yourself._   3. _Face the problem._
   Get help. Outlast the problem.

6. Does your intended career require any training beyond high school? Explain your educational goals below and how you intend to achieve them.
   Answers will vary.

128

Review: Improving Study Skills

Name _____   Date _____

Your Turn Answer each of the following questions.

1. Why is the two-column format effective for note taking?
   The two-column format allows you to use one column for main points and a second column for asking questions, making comments, and defining vocabulary words.

2. When taking notes, you are instructed to "listen for signal words." What are "signal words"?
   Signal words are words or phrases that signal key concepts that are about to be discussed. Some example signal words include, "Notice how," "Please be aware that," or "There are three kinds of . . ."

3. You are also instructed to "record references." What are "references"?
   References point to additional information on a key idea or concept, such as a page number in a textbook or a useful Web site address.

4. How can writing in a learning log enhance your note taking?
   A learning log can help deepen your understanding of school topics by reflecting on the material and course work you have learned.

5. What is the difference between formative and summative assessment?
   Formative assessments give feedback to the teacher in such forms as journal entries. They are usually ungraded. Summative assessments include tests, quizzes, and exams. They are graded.

6. What tip presented in the "During" section of "Using Test-Taking Skills" seems the most critical to you, and why?
   Answers will vary.

7. Writing prompts usually contain "purpose words." What are "purpose words"?
   Purpose words explain what a responder is supposed to do in her or his response.

8. What is an essential difference between a regular writing assignment and responding to a prompt?
   A regular writing assignment provides more time to use the writing process. A writing prompt requires prompt analysis, gives limited time to respond, and uses a compacted version of the writing process.

Reflect: How would you rate your study habits on a scale of 1 (weak) to 5 (strong), and why?
Answers will vary.

134

Review: Reading to Learn

Name _____   Date _____

Your Turn Answer each of the following questions.

1. How do you analyze the communication situation before you read?
   You can analyze the communication situation of a reading selection by asking questions about its sender (author), message, medium, receiver (audience), and context.

2. What value is there in making predictions about the reading?
   Predictions open your mind to new information. If the reading fulfill your predictions, you can consider why. If the reading does not, you have learned through the contrast.

3. What is the purpose of the SQ3R strategy? What do the letters and number stand for?
   The SQ3R strategy is an active-reading technique that helps you get the most meaning out of what you read. The acronym stands for Survey, Question, Read, Recite, and Review.

4. Will your reading in your science and social studies class be nonfiction or fiction? Why?
   Answers will vary.

5. What are four types of meaning that can be found in a poem? What is "meant" by each one?
   a. Denotative meaning describes what the poem means literally.
   b. Connotative meaning describes the nuances that resonate beyond the poem's literal meaning.
   c. Metaphorical meaning explores the way figures of speech are used in the poem.
   d. Symbolic meaning explores how details represent ideas and things outside of the poem itself.

6. How would you define each of the following terms?
   - Analogy Possible answer: An analogy compares one thing to another thing.
   - Paradox Possible answer: A paradox is a situation that seems contradictory.
   - Genre Possible answer: The genre is the special type of story.
   - Suspense Possible answer: Suspense is the tension of not knowing what's coming next.
   - Alliteration Possible answer: Alliteration is the repetition of sounds at the beginning of words.
   - Free verse Possible answer: Free verse is a style of poem without a specific structure.

Reflect: What type of reading challenges you the most—nonfiction, fiction, or poetry? Explain your choice.
Answers will vary.

140

Review: Building Your Vocabulary

Name _____   Date _____

Your Turn Answer each of the following questions.

1. When keeping a vocabulary notebook, what are three types of information that you could include for each entry? Any three of these:
   a. words,   b. word parts,   c. definitions,
   pronunciations, drawings, examples, synonyms, and sample sentences

2. What does it mean to study a word in context?
   To study a word in context means to look for clues in the text surrounding the word that point to its meaning.

3. Which of the following is not a context clue?
   a. a definition   c. tone   e. antonyms
   b. synonyms   (d.) word length

4. A dictionary provides the etymology of a word. What does the etymology indicate?
   Etymology describes the origins of a word.

5. A dictionary also provides the inflected forms of a word. What are inflected forms?
   Inflected forms are other forms of a word. For example, an inflected form of *child* is *children*.

6. When would you use a thesaurus?
   You might use a thesaurus to find synonyms or antonyms. It is useful for replacing a general word with a more specific synonym.

7. How does a prefix differ from a suffix?
   A prefix modifies before a root word; a suffix modifies after a root word.

8. Refer to the glossary of prefixes, roots, and suffixes to see what you can learn about the following words: Answers will vary.
   - diameter   - ornithology
   - geothermal   - fraction

Reflect: Is there one course in which the vocabulary truly challenges you? If so, why? How might the strategies in this chapter help? Answers will vary.

146

Review: Writing to Learn

Name _____   Date _____

Your Turn Answer each of the following questions.

1. How do writing-to-learn activities help you?
   Writing-to-learn activities help you think more deeply about the subject you are learning.

2. What is meant by these two writing-to-learn activities?
   - Mind mapping is a brainstorming activity in which you make associations or about a word or topic.
   - Nutshelling is writing the main idea of a lesson in a single sentence.

3. Which graphic organizer would you use to consider pros and cons and other two-part structures?
   T-bar

4. Questioning is an important part of the inquiry process. What type of questions require creative responses? And what type require metaphysical (highly abstract) responses?
   Open-ended questions require creative responses; paradoxical questions require metaphysical thinking.

5. In the writing process, how does revising differ from editing? Explain your answer.
   Revising focuses on improving "big-picture" writing traits. Editing focuses on fine-tuning writing for better word choice, smoother sentences, correct copy, and appealing design.

6. What is a thesis? (See "Prewriting.")
   A thesis is a specific thought or feeling about a topic that is explored in a piece of writing.

7. When you revise, what are three "global traits" that you should consider?
   Ideas, organization, and voice.

8. When should you use "amount" versus "number"? (See "Usage Rules" starting on page 192.)
   Use "amount" to refer to things in bulk or mass, "number" for separate things that can be counted.

9. What is a comma splice, and how do you correct one? (See "Sentence Error Rules" on page 196.)
   A comma splice occurs when two separate sentences are combined using only a comma. To correct this error, add a coordinating conjunction after the comma, change the comma to a semicolon, or separate the clauses into two sentences.

10. What is the meaning of the following writing term?
    - Jargon A technical language used by a specific group but not easily understood by outsiders

152

Review: Taking Exit and Entrance Exams

Name _____   Date _____

Your Turn Answer each of the following questions:

1. What does it mean to use "multimodal study forms"?
   Multimodal studying means to use a variety of study techniques, including visual, verbal, and
   written forms, to make new information vivid and memorable.

2. Why is it important to eat breakfast for taking an exam?
   Your brain needs glucose in order to function well. Skipping breakfast limits your ability to think.

3. What is not a basic type of test question?
   a. essay questions   d. short-answer questions
   b. objective questions   e. none of the above
   c. indirect questions

4. In multiple-choice questions, why must you pay careful attention to "negations"?
   Negations can make the question mean the opposite of what you expect.

5. What do the articles "a" and "an" indicate in fill-in-the-blank questions?
   An "a" means that the next word starts with a consonant sound, and an "an" that the next word
   starts with a vowel sound. Both indicate that the word is singular.

6. What is an "inference question"?
   Inference questions ask you to draw conclusions based on evidence.

7. What is a writing prompt?
   A writing prompt is an on-demand writing task that you must analyze and respond to.

8. What is the purpose of the STRAP questions?
   STRAP questions help you closely analyze writing prompts.

9. What should you include in the middle part of a response?
   In the middle part of a response, you should develop your thesis using a variety of supporting
   details in well-formed paragraphs.

Reflect: What part of this chapter will prove especially helpful to you and why? Answers will vary.

158

Review: Developing Visual Literacy

Name _____   Date _____

Your Turn Answer the following questions about the chapter.

1. What is visual literacy?
   Visual literacy is the ability to understand and produce visual images—to interpret images and
   graphic elements and use them to communicate more effectively.

2. How does an individual's "perception cloud" affect his or her ability to interpret an image?
   Individuality, upbringing, and knowledge base filter our perception of visual messages.

3. What is not an element of visual art?
   a. lines   d. space
   b. shapes   e. textures
   c. reflections   f. colors

4. What does it mean for an image to be in balance?
   Balance measures the feeling of evenness of an image. When a visual is balanced, its parts
   complement each other.

5. What is meant by the connotative, or secondary, meaning of a symbol?
   A connotative meaning focuses on personal associations for an image, based on unique experience,
   beliefs, and culture.

6. Which of the following points identify principles of page design?
   a. contrast   d. revising
   b. thoughts   e. pictures
   c. alignment   f. both a and c

7. Which of the graphics presented on pages 228–234 do you find the most interesting, and why?
   Answers will vary.

166

Review: Improving Information and Media Literacy

Name _____   Date _____

Your Turn Answer the following questions to check your information and media literacy.

1. Which of the following are media literacy abilities?
   a. create communication   d. evaluate communication
   b. analyze communication   e. all of the above
   c. access communication   f. none of the above

2. Which of the following is NOT a key concept of media literacy?
   a. Different media use special techniques.   d. Different people interpret media differently.
   b. Many people today can create media.   e. All media sources are equally valid.
   c. Media messages are constructed.   f. Media messages share a point of view.

3. Write a short definition for each of the following:
   Fact: A statement of truth that can be checked for accuracy
   Opinion: A personally held belief
   Claim: A debatable statement that can be supported with evidence and reason

4. Rank the following from fastest delivery to slowest delivery.
   2 TV   4 Book   3 Magazine   1 Blog

5. Rank the following from most reliable to least reliable.
   4 Microblog   2 Newspaper   1 Academic journal   3 Movie

6. Name and explain one way of detecting bias in a message.
   Any of these: (1) The language is extreme; (2) the message appeals to emotion rather than to reason
   and logic; (3) the message simplifies or generalizes information; (4) the message is one-sided.

7. Explain how different people might interpret a message differently.
   People interpret messages differently based on a variety of factors, including age, gender, education
   level, experience, values, beliefs, family, and culture.

8. List one way you could use social media to spread your own message.
   Answers will vary.

172

Review: Creating Internet Literacy

Name _____   Date _____

Your Turn Answer each of the questions below. Then discuss your answers in class.

1. Define "server" and "client." What are the implications of cloud computing?
   A server is a personal computer that functions as a centralized network. Clients are the other
   personal computers or media devices that connect to the server. Cloud computing makes files
   accessible from anywhere with an Internet connection.

2. What is a router in a local network? What types of connectivity might it support?
   A router is a stand-alone device used to network multiple computing devices in one location. It
   might connect to an Ethernet cable or a wireless network.

3. How is Bluetooth similar to and different from Wi-Fi? How is mobile telephony different from both?
   Both Bluetooth and Wi-Fi use wireless modems to send and receive radio waves. Bluetooth
   provides a short-range connection, while Wi-Fi provides a long-range connection. Mobile telephony
   connects to towers wirelessly.

4. Name at least four possible Internet connection types.
   Any four of these: (1) dial-up; (2) DSL; (3) Cable; (4) Satellite; (5) T1

5. What is the function of HTML? CSS? JavaScript? How does server-side code relate to these?
   The function of HTML is to set the content and structure of a Web page. CSS is used for formatting
   and styling Web content. And JavaScript adds interaction to a Web page. Server-side code allows
   you to replicate the formatting of one Web page in a new Web page.

6. What is the definition of clip art?
   Clip art are drawings or graphics that can be cut out and used in other places online.

7. How might you incorporate art, photos, and video into your academic work?
   Answers will vary. Sample answer: To illustrate reports, stories, and other work, or to inspire
   ideas for new projects

8. How are copyright, patent, and trademark similar and different?
   Copyright is legal ownership of a creative work. A patent is a legal right to a unique idea or invention.
   A trademark is a legally recognized symbol, word, or phrase representing a brand, a property, or an
   organization. All of these are intellectual property owned by someone else.

180

Review: Using Social Media

Name _____   Date _____

Your Turn Answer the following questions.

1. What are the four main purposes of social media?
   to share, to learn, to interact, and to market

2. Name one way text messaging (instant messaging) is different from writing for school assignments.
   Answers will vary. Sample answer: Text messaging is more informal than the writing you do in
   school. It is quicker and more conversational.

3. Identify one way a social network can help with your schoolwork.
   Any one of these: Group pages for collaboration; polling and survey services; wall posts and messages
   to communicate with classmates

4. What is a hashtag?
   A hashtag is a keyword with a # in front of it. They help users on Twitter find similar "conversations."

5. What is the word "blog" short for?
   Web log

6. Name two ways a group could use a collaborative-documents application such as a wiki or Google
   Docs for a school project.
   Any two of these: (1) brainstorm ideas; (2) store research; (3) manage a group project; (4) collaborate;
   (5) write collaborative documents; (6) plan and track projects; (7) share writing assignments

7. What do the initials PLN stand for?
   personal learning network

8. List two types of sources you might include in your own PLN.
   Answers will vary.

9. List one social-media "Do" and one "Don't" that you would share with a younger student.
   Answers will vary.

Chapter 18: Developing Financial Literacy   **185**

Extension: "Borrowing" Quiz

Name _____   Date _____

Your Turn Answer the questions below to check your understanding of borrowing.

1. Which of the following is NOT a good tactic for developing credit?
   a. Get a secured loan or a secured credit card.
   b. Apply for an unsecured credit card.
   c. Make payments on time.
   d. Borrow up to 10 percent of your limit, and pay it back each month.
   e. Find a cosigner.
   (f.) All are valid tactics for developing credit.

2. How is a secured loan different from an unsecured loan?
   A secured loan requires collateral, while an unsecured loan does not require collateral but often
   asks for a substantial down payment.

3. What is the difference between points and fees on a loan?
   Points are added to the prime lending rate for borrowers with less than perfect credit ratings, while
   fees are charges for arranging and processing the loan.

4. List two ways to avoid credit card pitfalls: Any two of the following:
   a. (1) Pay off the balance. (2) Avoid making only minimum payments. (3) Pay on time. (4) Don't use
   b. credit card checks. (5) Avoid "reward" purchases. (6) Avoid cards that give perks but charge high fees.

5. List three things that you will be asked on loan applications:
   a. Any three of these: (1) Your name, social security number, marital status, and contact information;
   b. (2) your employment information; (3) a list of your assets; (4) your monthly income and expenses.
   c. _____

6. What does FICO stand for?
   a. Federal Interest Committee Organization
   (b.) Fair Isaac Corporation
   c. Fair Interest Community Oversight
   d. None of the above

7. True or False: 700–759 is a "Great" FICO score. T __X__   F _____

8. What does FAFSA stand for?
   a. Federal Application For Student Assistance
   b. Fair Aid from Federal Subsidiary Accounts
   (c.) Free Application for Federal Student Aid
   d. None of the above

186

Review: Developing Financial Literacy

Name _____   Date _____

Your Turn Respond to the following prompts to check your knowledge of financial literacy.

1. Besides wages, name three other benefits employers may offer to attract employees.

   Any three of these: insurance; retirement; profit sharing; paid time off; unpaid leave; day care;
   housing; meals

2. Name three taxes that are deducted from your wages.

   Any three of these: federal income tax; state income tax; FICA; Medicare; Medicaid;
   unemployment tax

3. Name one other type of tax.

   Any of these: property tax; sales tax; excise tax

4. Explain the difference between banks and credit unions.

   A bank is a for-profit institution open to anyone, while a credit union is a not-for-profit institution
   that functions much like a bank but is open only to certain groups of people.

5. Name two things included in calculating the Consumer Price Index.

   Any two of these: food; merchandise; housing; energy; services

6. Explain the difference between layaway and installment purchases.

   A layaway purchase is when you make a down payment on something, and the seller holds onto
   the item until you can pay the rest of the cost. An installment purchase is when you pay for
   something in portions.

7. Rank the following in order from low risk and low yield (1) to high risk and high yield (4).

   _2_ Certificates of deposit (CDs)   _1_ Savings accounts

   _4_ Stocks   _3_ Bonds

8. Name three types of insurance.

   Any three of these: auto insurance; disability insurance; health insurance; homeowner's insurance;
   liability insurance; life insurance; long-term care insurance; renter's insurance

192

Review: Succeeding in the Workplace

Name _____   Date _____

Your Turn Answer each of the following questions.

1. Employers want employees who are flexible. What is meant by workplace flexibility?

   A flexible employee is able to adapt, prioritize, multitask, learn, and take risks.

2. Employees value a strong compensation package. What is meant by compensation in the workplace?

   Compensation in the workplace involves what you are paid, which benefits you receive, and the
   level to which you are valued in your place of employment.

3. Which of the following are resources for finding job opportunities?
   a. networking   d. help-wanted signs
   b. want ads   (e.) all of the above
   c. online searches   d. none of the above

4. What is the difference between chronological and functional résumés?

   A chronological résumé highlights past work experience in time order. A functional résumé
   highlights skills and qualifications.

5. The list of nonverbal components of an interview on page 325 begins with promptness. What is meant
   by promptness, and why is it so important?

   Promptness means showing up on time for your interview. It is important because it reflects your
   reliability and readiness in the workplace.

6. Workplace etiquette involves respect. Who exactly should an employee respect?

   An employee should respect the organization or company, supervisor, coworkers, customers, job,
   career, and self.

7. On page 329, you learned that most businesses try to fill a need that people have. What need does a
   building contractor fill? How about a beauty salon and spa? A water-treatment facility?

   Answers will vary. Sample answer: A building contractor fills a need for shelter, property, and
   security. A beauty salon and spa fills a need for self-esteem and confidence. A water-treatment
   facility fills a need for water and health.

Reflect: How is a career similar to and different from a job? Which one is more important in terms of your
long-term goals? Answers will vary.

Part II:
Using the Inquiry Process (Lesson Plans)

Learning is hard. It's a journey from ignorance to knowledge, from uncertainty to mastery. The inquiry process guides us on the journey of learning, equipping us with the tools and skills we need to make our way. As students work through the inquiry process, they use all of the 21st century skills they have acquired.

These chapters plot the course, equip students with the resources they need, and send them off to explore the future. Each lesson plan in this section includes the following.

- Learning outcomes and standards correlations
- A daily lesson plan
- An extension activity
- A review that can also serve as a chapter quiz
- Minilessons for math, science, social studies, and English

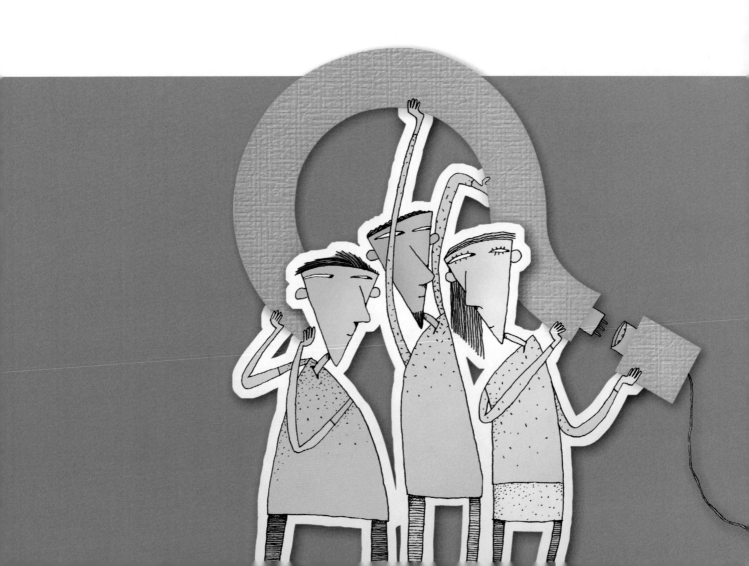

Part II:
Using the Inquiry Process

Chapter 20
Understanding the Inquiry Process

(Inquire pages 335–342)

Students can use the inquiry process across the curriculum to empower their thinking and learning. This chapter gives an overview of the process. As an instructor, you can use this chapter to introduce the process and show how it works. Just as the process empowers student learning, it also empowers the teacher to take a more active role in the classroom by using an inquiry-based approach.

Learning Outcomes

- Understand what the inquiry process is and what steps are involved.
- Follow one student's use of the inquiry process to create a large-scale project.
- Understand how the inquiry process incorporates the 21st century skills.

Correlations

Common Core State Standards

ELA-Literacy.CCRA.W.1–3	Math.Practice.MP8	Science.Practice.SP6
ELA-Literacy.CCRA.SL.1–6	Science.Practice.SP1–3	Science.Practice.SP8
Math.Practice.MP1		

Partnership for 21st Century Skills

Creativity and Innovation
- Think Creatively
- Work Creatively with Others
- Implement Innovations

Critical Thinking and Problem Solving
- Reason Effectively and Use Systems Thinking
- Make Judgments and Decisions
- Solve Problems

Information Literacy
- Access and Evaluate Information
- Use and Manage Information

Media Literacy
- Analyze Media
- Create Media Products

Life and Career Skills
- Flexibility and Adaptability
- Initiative and Self-Direction
- Social and Cross-Cultural Skills
- Productivity and Accountability
- Leadership and Responsibility

International Society for Technology in Education

1. Creativity and Innovation
 (All standards)

3. Research and Information Fluency
 (All standards)

4. Critical Thinking, Problem Solving, and Decision Making
 (All standards)

Lesson Plan: Understanding the Inquiry Process

Day 1

1. Display the definition of the word "inquiry" (a serious and thorough investigation) for students. Ask the class for examples. Note that an inquiry can be done on any topic and that most topics are open to multiple inquiries. Use "blue jeans" as an example. You could investigate how they were first made, the history of different styles, why and when they became popular, etc. Then read the definition on page 335.

2. Lead the class through "Understanding Inquiry" on page 336. Discuss each step as you go. Have students complete the "Your Turn" activity at the bottom of the page.

3. Lead students through "1. Questioning" on page 337. Ask a general question (such as "How could our school improve?") and have students ask specific questions about it. Write down each student's question to show the progression of questioning from general to specific.

Day 2

4. Ask students to write down three goals they have for the semester. Have them choose one to work with.

5. Lead students through "2. Planning" on page 338. Have them complete a planning sheet, asking students to write the goal at the top and establish objectives with the 5W's and H. Then have them list tasks and decide on a schedule. (Go to thoughtfullearning.com/h361 for a copy of the planning sheet.)

6. Discuss the planning sheets students have completed.

Day 3

7. Lead students through "3. Researching" on page 339.

8. Ask for volunteers to explain what tools they use to find new information. Ask what resources they would use if the Internet were not available.

9. Have students turn to "Conducting Basic Research" on pages 363–374 and "Conducting Advanced Research" on pages 375–404. Walk them through the material.

10. Have students complete the extension activity on the next page of the Teacher's Guide.

Day 4

11. Lead students through "4. Creating" on page 340. Let them know that *Inquire* includes many, many projects.

12. Have students flip through Part III of the book (pages 429–606). Ask them to select a project that looks interesting, review it, and share their findings with the class.

Day 5

13. Ask students to pull out their planning sheets from day 2 and review their goals and objectives. Tell them they will use this information to make critical and creative changes.

14. Lead students through "5. Improving" on page 341. Ask students to examine their goal and objectives and the tasks they outlined to achieve their goal. Have them revise their list of tasks by making one critical improvement and one creative improvement.

15. Lead students through "6. Presenting" on page 342. Then have them complete the "Your Turn" activity at the bottom of the page.

Extension: Inquiry Process

Name _____   Date _____

Your Turn Using your library or the Internet, do the following research activity.

Part I

1. What are nanobes? _____

   _____

   Source: _____

2. Where were they discovered? _____

   _____

   Source: _____

3. Who discovered them? _____

   _____

   Source: _____

4. Why are they significant? _____

   _____

   Source: _____

Part II

5. What sports were played in Colonial America? _____

   Source: _____

6. Identify a book that could help you learn more about sports in Colonial America.

   _____

   _____

7. Name the closest library that holds this book. _____

   _____

Follow-up: Name a career that interests you. Identify some ways that this profession involves research. Share your answers with a partner.

Review: Inquiry Process

Name _____   Date _____

Your Turn Complete each item below.

1. Match each step in the inquiry process with its description.

   Questioning

   Planning

   Researching

   Creating

   Improving

   Presenting

   - Using your planning and research to make something new

   - Collecting information and resources for your work

   - Making critical and creative changes to your work

   - Sharing your work with your audience

   - Setting up goals for a project and outlining tasks, time, team, and objectives

   - Exploring possibilities by imagining and brainstorming

2. Think of something you want to do or something you have put off doing for some time. State a goal for this activity.

   _____

   _____

3. Write objectives for your goal, as you would on a planning sheet, by answering the 5 W's and H.

   Who? _____

   What? _____

   Where? _____

   When? _____

   Why? _____

   How? _____

4. Describe the types of research you would need to undertake to achieve your goal.

   _____

   _____

   _____

Science Minilessons: Inquiry Process

Get into the Groove

OBSERVE someone dancing or playing a sport.

QUESTION the physics of movements displayed in the dance or sport.

RESEARCH answers to your question. (See *Inquire* page 339.)

PRESENT your discoveries to your classmates.

Inquire to Discover

BRAINSTORM major scientific discoveries.

CHOOSE one major discovery.

RESEARCH how the discovery was made.

IDENTIFY how each step in the inquiry process was involved in the discovery.

IMAGINE you were a scientist involved in the discovery. **CREATE** an imaginary planning sheet outlining the goal, objectives, tasks, and team involved.

Inquiry into the Scientific Method

LIST the steps of the inquiry process.

LIST the steps of the scientific method.

COMPARE AND CONTRAST the inquiry process with the scientific method. How are they similar? How are they different? How do they both lead to new discoveries?

Math Minilessons: Inquiry Process

What's Then Is Now

RESEARCH the history of the quadratic equation.

WRITE down the equation.

IDENTIFY when, where, and why it was created.

COMPARE how the equation was used then to how it is used today. What was its purpose then? What is its purpose today?

SHARE your findings with a classmate.

Paying at the Pump

OBSERVE the gas prices in your hometown.

RESEARCH gas prices in different regions of the country.

IDENTIFY the factors that determine the price of gasoline. Why is gas cheaper by the gallon in some places in the country compared to others?

CREATE a chart or infographic about national trends in gas prices.

Classroom Architect

CALCULATE the dimensions of your classroom.

IMAGINE the room is empty and you are in charge of redesigning the room.

BRAINSTORM ways to best utilize the space for collaboration and learning.

PLAN AND RESEARCH a new classroom design.

CREATE a detailed blueprint for your new classroom. **PRESENT** it to your class.

Social Studies Minilessons: Inquiry Process

History at Home

READ about the student project to preserve a historic site on *Inquire* pages 338–342.

ASK questions about the history of your hometown.

CHOOSE one question to research.

RESEARCH the question using at least one primary source.

SHARE your findings.

Investigative Reporting

FIND a recent news story.

STUDY the story closely.

WRITE six questions you still have about the story.

CHOOSE one question to investigate further.

RESEARCH your question, gathering and evaluating information.

CREATE a paragraph that asks and answers the question.

Analyzing a Historic Event

SEARCH your textbook for a story about a historic event that interests you.

DOWNLOAD a planning sheet from thoughtfullearning.com/h361.

COMPLETE the planning sheet about the historic event. List the goal, objectives, tasks, and people involved in the historical situation you have chosen.

English Minilessons: Inquiry Process

Literary Brainstorm

CHOOSE a piece of literature you have read or are currently reading.

STUDY the main character's primary traits.

BRAINSTORM ways in which the character develops throughout the piece of writing (changes in motivation, behavior, outlook, personality, and so on).

CREATE a paragraph that summarizes the character's development.

Comparing Processes

EXAMINE the inquiry process (*Inquire* page 336) and the writing process (*Inquire* page 186).

TAKE NOTES, paying close attention to how the two processes are similar and different.

WRITE a reflective paragraph, comparing and contrasting the two processes.

Marking Punctuation Problems

RESEARCH the most common punctuation mistakes, using an Internet search engine.

CHOOSE one problem to investigate further.

CREATE a visual project (poster, video, etc.) that shows the error and explains how to fix it.

MAKE one critical and one creative change to your visual project.

PRESENT it to your class.

Chapter 21
Questioning

(*Inquire* pages 343–354)

Questions drive inquiry, which drives discovery and learning. Students who ask questions take ownership of their learning. They are more engaged in classroom activities and more motivated to delve into difficult concepts. This chapter provides students with many different approaches to questioning. Each strategy used in this chapter is applicable to any class across the curriculum.

Learning Outcomes

Learn about asking . . .

- open, closed, and theoretical questions.
- creative and deep questions.
- journalistic questions.
- sensory and thought questions.
- questions about the world and about the future.
- survey questions.
- SCAMPER questions.
- Socratic questions.

Correlations

Common Core State Standards

ELA-Literacy.CCRA.R.4–9	ELA-Literacy.CCRA.SL.1–6	Math.Practice.MP8
ELA-Literacy.CCRA.W.1–3	ELA-Literacy.CCRA.L.4–6	Science.Practice.SP1–3
ELA-Literacy.CCRA.W.10	Math.Practice.MP1–3	Science.Practice.SP6–8

Partnership for 21st Century Skills

Creativity and Innovation
- Think Creatively
- Work Creatively with Others
- Implement Innovations

Critical Thinking and Problem Solving
- Reason Effectively and Use Systems Thinking
- Make Judgments and Decisions
- Solve Problems

International Society for Technology in Education

1. Creativity and Innovation
- Students demonstrate creative thinking, construct knowledge, and develop innovative products and processes using technology.

4. Critical Thinking, Problem Solving, and Decision Making
- Students use critical thinking skills to plan and conduct research, manage projects, solve problems, and make informed decisions using appropriate digital tools and resources.

Lesson Plan: Questioning

Day 1

1. Ask volunteers to share one question they want answered today. Questions can be about any topic or situation. Do not provide answers, but display the questions.
2. As a class, read the introduction to "Questioning" on page 343. Briefly preview the "Types of Questions" on page 344 and ask students to read the page silently. Categorize the students' earlier questions, pointing out examples of open, closed, and theoretical questions. Assign the "Your Turn" activity.

Day 2

3. Read aloud the top portion of "Asking Creative Questions" on page 345. Next, read the list of questions and ask volunteers to answer them. Then have students complete the "Your Turn" activity.
4. Read aloud the top portion of "Asking Journalistic Questions" on page 346. Discuss with the class how the journalistic questions are different from creative questions. (Answer: Journalistic questions are usually closed ended while creative questions are usually open ended.) Then have students complete the "Your Turn" activity.

Day 3

5. Read aloud "Asking Deep Questions" on page 347. Point out how the questions in the left-hand column of the table move from simple to more complex levels of thinking. If time allows, conduct a class discussion during which you apply those questions to a familiar current event.
6. Review "Asking Sensory Questions" on page 348. Have students complete a sensory chart about the classroom they are in.
7. Review "Asking Thought Questions" on page 349. Have students complete both "Your Turn" activities.

Day 4

8. As a class, review "Asking About Your Future" on page 350. Have students complete the "Your Turn" activity.
9. Ask students to read "Asking About the World" on page 351 silently and then complete the "Your Turn" activity with a partner.
10. Review "Asking Survey Questions" on page 352. As a class, create a survey about a relevant topic in your school. Compose at least one of each type of closed-ended question as outlined on the page.

Day 5

11. Read "Using the SCAMPER Method" on page 353. Give students a topic to work with—a cell phone, a short Web video, a project, or an activity. Then have them answer one of each of the seven types of SCAMPER questions about the topic.
12. As a class, read over "Asking Socratic Questions" on page 354 and have partners complete the "Your Turn" activity at the bottom of the page.
13. Consider assigning the extension activity and the questioning review on the next two pages of the Teacher's Guide.

Extension: Questioning

Name _____   Date _____

Your Turn Choose a topic you are studying in one of your classes and write it below. Then create questions and search for the answers. (If you can't find an answer, ask a different question.)

1. Name of your topic: _____

2. Write one closed-ended and one open-ended question about your topic. (See *Inquire* page 344.)

   Closed-ended question: _____

   Answer: _____

   _____

   Open-ended question: _____

   Answer: _____

   _____

3. Write a creative question about your topic. (See *Inquire* page 345.)

   Creative question: _____

   Answer: _____

   _____

4. Write three deep questions about your topic. Each question should involve a deeper level of thinking than the one before. (See *Inquire* page 347.)

   Deep question 1: _____

   Answer: _____

   _____

   Deep question 2: _____

   Answer: _____

   _____

   Deep question 3: _____

   Answer: _____

   _____

Follow-up: Ask the SCAMPER questions about your topic. (See *Inquire* page 353.)

Review: Questioning

Name _____ Date _____

Your Turn Provide answers for each item below.

1. What is the difference between a closed-ended, an open-ended, and a theoretical question?

   _____

   _____

2. List the journalistic questions. _____

   _____

3. Write a question that would help you evaluate something. _____

   _____

4. List the five sensory questions. _____

   _____

5. Write a creative question about the world. _____

   _____

6. What type of survey question asks participants to rank a list of choices?

   _____

7. Write the word for each letter in this acronym of question types:

   S _____

   C _____

   A _____

   M _____

   P _____

   E _____

   R _____

Reflect: Imagine that you could ask one question about your future that would get a definite and true answer. What question would you ask?

Science Minilessons: Questioning

Experimental Journalist

OBSERVE an experiment you are doing in class.

ASK and **ANSWER** sensory questions about the experiment. (For safety reasons, you may not be able to answer all the questions.)

REFLECT on the experiment and its results.

ASK and **ANSWER** each of the 5 W's and H questions about the experiment. (See *Inquire* page 346.)

Dig into Higgs

READ about the Higgs boson particle.

REVIEW the deep questions that are related to Bloom's thinking scale. (See *Inquire* page 347.)

ASK at least one question about the Higgs boson particle at each level of thinking—remember, understand, apply, analyze, evaluate, and create.

SEARCH for answers to your questions.

RECORD your answers.

SCAMPER in the Lab

LIST all the pieces of lab equipment you have in your science classroom.

CHOOSE one piece that especially interests you.

For each letter of **SCAMPER**, **ASK** and **ANSWER** one question about the item. (See *Inquire* page 353.)

SHARE your ideas for possible improvements or modifications to the equipment with a classmate.

Math Minilessons: Questioning

Applying Deep Questions

IDENTIFY a new idea or concept you are working on in your math class.

REVIEW the deep questions that are related to Bloom's thinking scale. (See *Inquire* page 347.)

ASK at least one question about the idea or concept at each level of thinking.

PRESENT any unanswered questions to your instructor. **SEARCH** for answers.

Thoughtful Solutions

IDENTIFY a specific math idea or concept you find difficult to understand.

REFLECT on the idea, tracing your thoughts about it in a mind map. (See *Inquire* page 349.)

FREEWRITE about the concept.

LIST questions you still have about the concept.

PRESENT the questions to your instructor.

Inquire About Infinity

SEARCH for an answer to this creative question: How big is infinity?

RECORD any answers you find.

WRITE your own creative question about math. (See *Inquire* page 345.)

SEARCH for an answer to your creative math question. If you can't find one, write another creative question to research.

Social Studies Minilessons: Questioning

Ask About Your World

IDENTIFY a conflict that is occurring in a foreign country.

REVIEW the deep questions that are related to Bloom's thinking scale. (See *Inquire* page 347.)

ASK and **ANSWER** at least one question about the conflict at each level of thinking.

REFLECT on the conflict by creating a mind map or freewriting about it.

Question an Event

CHOOSE a current or historical event.

WRITE the journalistic questions about it. (See *Inquire* page 346.)

WRITE a deep question about it. (See *Inquire* page 347.)

WRITE a creative question about it. (See *Inquire* page 345.)

SEARCH for answers to your questions.

Extension: **WRITE** an essay about your findings.

Socratic Conversation

TEAM UP with a partner from your social studies class.

DISCUSS a specific topic or event you are currently studying. **ASK** each other Socratic questions about the topic or event. (See *Inquire* page 354.) One person acts as Socrates, asking questions while the other answers them. Then switch roles.

English Minilessons: Questioning

Revising with SCAMPER

CHOOSE a piece of writing you are drafting for an English course (essay, short story, poem, literary analysis).

ASK and **ANSWER** SCAMPER questions about your first draft. (See *Inquire* page 353.)

REVISE your first draft, using the answers to your SCAMPER questions as a guide.

EDIT your writing and **PRESENT** it to your class.

Setting the Scene

FIND a passage in a piece of literature that uses sensory details.

ANALYZE the description by creating a sensory chart. (See *Inquire* page 348.)

Extension: **ATTEND** an event at your school (game, concert, play, and so on).

ASK yourself what you see, hear, smell, taste, and touch. **RECORD** your observations and write a description of the event.

Reading for Deeper Thinking

STUDY a piece of literature you are reading in an English course.

REVIEW the deep questions that are related to Bloom's thinking scale. (See *Inquire* page 347.)

WRITE at least two questions to help you remember the piece of literature, two to help you understand it, two to help you analyze it, and two more to help you evaluate the piece.

ANSWER your questions and **REFLECT** on what the answers reveal about the reading.

Chapter 22
Planning

(Inquire pages 355–362)

In this chapter, students learn how to plan for success while also allowing for the unexpected "change in plans" along the way. Planning is a key step in the inquiry process—following right on the heels of questioning—and it paves the way for meaningful and successful inquiry-based learning. The proverb "He who fails to plan, plans to fail" rings true when it comes to any type of meaningful work.

Learning Outcomes

- Set goals, objectives, and tasks.
- Schedule time.
- Build a team and gather tools.
- Create a planning sheet.
- Use planning throughout the process.

Correlations

Common Core State Standard

ELA-Literacy.CCRA.W.1–6	ELA-Literacy.CCRA.L.4–6	Science.Practice.SP1–3
ELA-Literacy.CCRA.W.10	Math.Practice.MP1–4	Science.Practice.SP5–8
ELA-Literacy.CCRA.SL.1–6	Math.Practice.MP6–8	

Partnership for 21st Century Skills

Creativity and Innovation
- Think Creatively
- Work Creatively with Others
- Implement Innovations

Critical Thinking and Problem Solving
- Reason Effectively and Use Systems Thinking
- Make Judgments and Decisions
- Solve Problems

Information Literacy
- Access and Evaluate Information
- Use and Manage Information

Media Literacy
- Analyze Media
- Create Media Products

Life and Career Skills
- Flexibility and Adaptability
- Initiative and Self-Direction
- Social and Cross-Cultural Skills
- Productivity and Accountability
- Leadership and Responsibility

International Society for Technology in Education

1. Creativity and Innovation
   (All standards)

3. Research and Information Fluency
   (All standards)

4. Critical Thinking, Problem Solving, and Decision Making
   (All standards)

Lesson Plan: Planning

Day 1

1. Have students spend 5–10 minutes freewriting about the most memorable project they've ever worked on.
2. Ask for volunteers to share their memories.
3. Review the opening page of the chapter (*Inquire* page 355) and engage the class in a discussion about the planning and managing involved in the students' memorable projects.
4. Review "Setting Goals, Objectives, and Tasks" on pages 356–357 as a class.
5. As homework, have students complete items 1 and 2 of the "Extension" activity on the next page of the Teacher's Guide, setting a goal for a project that is related to a topic you are currently studying in class and analyzing that goal according to the SMART guidelines.

Day 2

6. Divide students into small groups to discuss the goals they made for their homework assignment.
7. Have each group choose one of the goals and work together to complete items 3 and 4 of the "Extension" activity, defining their project's objectives and listing the tasks for accomplishing their goal.

Day 3

8. Ask each group to present their plan to the class for discussion.
9. Assign "Scheduling Time," "Building Your Team," and "Gathering Your Tools" (*Inquire* pages 358–366) as homework reading.

Day 4

10. Set a specific due date for the group projects.
11. Allow time in class for groups to create a project schedule, assign team roles, and discuss the tools they will need as directed in the "Your Turn" activities.
12. Near the end of class, review "Creating a Planning Sheet" and "Planning Throughout the Process" with the class as a whole.

Day 5

13. Allow time for groups to fill in a planning sheet (go to thoughtfullearning.com/h361). Sheets must be turned in at the beginning of class on day 1 of the following week.
14. If time remains, allow students to further discuss or begin their project work.

Extension: Planning

Name _____   Date _____

Your Turn Set a goal for a project related to a topic you are currently studying in class. Then analyze the goal, define your objectives, and list your tasks.

1. State your goal: _____

2. Analyze your goal by explaining how the following attributes apply to it.

   Specific: _____

   Meaningful: _____

   Attainable: _____

   Relevant: _____

   Trackable: _____

3. Define your objectives.

Who?	
What?	
Where?	
When?	
Why?	
How?	

4. List your tasks. (Use your own paper if necessary.)

What do we need to do?	What do we need to learn?
1.	
2.	
3.	
4.	
5.	
6.	
7.	
8.	
9.	
10.	

Review: Planning

Name _____   Date _____

Your Turn Answer the following questions to review your understanding of planning.

1. You may use SMART guidelines to set and clarify your goal. What do the letters in SMART stand for?

   S _____   M _____   A _____   R _____   T _____

2. How might you change the following negative situations into positive goals?

   My motorcycle won't run: _____

   _____

   I don't get chemistry: _____

   _____

3. Explain how to schedule a project's tasks in the following situations.

   You have a deadline: _____

   _____

   The project is open-ended: _____

   _____

4. Which two ways of assigning project roles would be poor choices?
   a. Draw roles from a hat.   **c.** Let group members choose.
   b. Have a group leader assign roles.   **d.** Assign roles alphabetically.

5. In your own words, describe the four types of project tools.

   Equipment: _____

   Information: _____

   Materials: _____

   Resources: _____

6. How can a planning sheet help you during each of the following steps in a project?

   Organizing: _____

   Gathering: _____

   Developing: _____

   Evaluating: _____

Science Minilessons: Planning

Stellar Dreams

IMAGINE that your dream is to someday visit the International Space Station.

INVESTIGATE ways that civilians have visited space or will visit it soon.

DEVISE your own plan for achieving your dream.

DISCUSS your plan with a classmate.

Regime Change

INVESTIGATE your family history for any genetic predispositions for conditions such as high blood pressure or diabetes.

RESEARCH preventative measures for those conditions.

PLAN a lifestyle that avoids those conditions or reduces their impact.

FOLLOW your plan to enjoy a healthy life.

The OS with the Most

LIST popular computer operating systems (OS's), from desktop computers to smartphones.

PLAN an approach for predicting their future success based on current user-friendliness, popularity, and market share.

WRITE a blog entry offering your predictions for the future of these computer OS's.

Math Minilessons: Planning

Sport Speak

LIST popular competitive sports in the United States since the nation's birth.

PLAN a way to determine the number of fans for each sport from decade to decade over a 100-year period.

RESEARCH that information.

EXPRESS those numbers as percentages of the nation's overall population on a line graph or bar graph. **DISCUSS** your results.

Color Codes

INVESTIGATE RGB and CMYK color.

LEARN how to apply the mathematical scheme in RBG codes to produce particular colors.

PLAN a Web page to display primary and secondary colors in their natural order on the optical spectrum.

CREATE your Web page.

Extension: **RESEARCH** the CMYK percentages necessary to produce the same colors.

Environmental Equation

LIST fuels used by people to produce heat, light, and power around the world today.

PLAN a research project to determine the amount of usable energy provided, the amount of energy wasted, and the amount of pollution produced with each fuel type.

Extension: **CARRY OUT** the research.

SHARE the results in class.

Social Studies Minilessons: Planning

Social Planning

IMAGINE you will be hosting a weekend meeting of great minds from the past in order to identify major challenges of the present and propose solutions for the future.

PLAN your weekend meeting, considering room and board as well as an agenda to guide discussion.

Extension: **CONSIDER** presenting the meeting with classmates role-playing the historical figures.

A Golden Age

JOURNAL about a period of history you find especially interesting.

DISCUSS in class the significance of arts and crafts as part of a civilization.

PLAN a research project to investigate the design of jewelry (or some other art or craft) made during your chosen period of history and the way it was manufactured.

Extension: **CONDUCT** your research and **SHARE** your work.

Picture This

CONSIDER the topic of photographing and/or videotaping courtroom trials. What personal, public, and professional concerns are involved?

PLAN a class debate about the subject.

Extension: **GATHER** support for your position and hold the debate.

English Minilessons: Planning

Triangulating Titles

LOCATE a short story or novel available in print, as an audio book, and as a film or TV adaptation.

MAKE a schedule to read, listen to, and watch the three versions, leaving time in between the experiences.

FOLLOW your schedule and **JOURNAL** about each version, expressing your reactions.

Unforgettable and Significant

REVIEW a play or another piece of literature that you have read in class.

In a small group, **IDENTIFY** one scene that you find significant, key, integral, etc.

PLAN an enactment of the scene.

Extension: **CARRY OUT** your plan.

Faux Fashion

IMAGINE you are a reporter working for a fashion magazine.

RESEARCH the problem of "fashion piracy."

PLAN an article that includes imaginary interviews with fashion designers and copycat manufacturers. (Or use real interviews, if possible.)

Extension: **WRITE** the article, following your plan.

Chapter 23
Conducting Basic Research

(*Inquire* pages 363–374)

Basic research often begins with asking questions. It continues with finding and organizing information that answers the questions. In this chapter, students will learn how to focus on a topic guided by a central question. They will then learn how to expand upon it with pointed questions, analyze it with journalistic and Socratic questions, and record and organize the answers they find.

Learning Outcomes

- Focus a topic with a guiding question.
- Generate pointed questions to guide research.
- Use questioning to analyze and expand a topic.
- Find answers from various sources.
- Understand how to use keywords.
- Take accurate notes on paper or electronically.
- Organize information.

Correlations

Common Core State Standards

ELA-Literacy.CCRA.R.1–10
ELA-Literacy.CCRA.W.1–10
ELA-Literacy.CCRA.SL.1–6

ELA-Literacy.CCRA.L.3–6
Math.Practice.MP1

Math.Practice.MP3–8
Science.Practice.SP1–8

Partnership for 21st Century Skills

Communication and Collaboration
- Communicate Clearly

Information Literacy
- Access and Evaluate Information

Media Literacy
- Analyze Media

Information and Communication Technologies Literacy
- Apply Technology Effectively

Life and Career Skills
- Productivity and Accountability

International Society for Technology in Education

3. Research and Information Fluency
  a. Plan strategies to guide inquiry.
  b. Locate, organize, analyze, evaluate, synthesize, and ethically use information from a variety of sources.
  c. Evaluate and select information sources and digital tools based on the appropriateness to specific tasks.

4. Critical Thinking, Problem Solving, and Decision Making
  a. Identify and define authentic problems and significant questions for investigation.
  b. Plan and manage activities to develop a solution.
  c. Collect and analyze data to identify solutions.
  d. Use multiple processes and perspectives to explore.

5. Digital Citizenship
  a. Advocate and practice safe, legal, and responsible use of information and technology.
  b. Exhibit a positive attitude toward using technology that supports collaboration, learning, and productivity.

6. Technology Operations and Concepts
  a. Understand and use technology systems.
  b. Select and use applications effectively and productively.
  c. Troubleshoot systems applications.
  d. Transfer current knowledge to new technologies.

Lesson Plan: Conducting Basic Research

Day 1

1. Ask for a volunteer to read aloud the introduction on page 363. Then have students freewrite for 5 minutes to identify topics they are curious about.

2. Ask for volunteers to share their topics, and display them for the class.

3. As a class, review "Identifying Your Guiding Question" on page 364. Have students suggest guiding questions for the topics, and display these as well.

4. Next, review "Generating Pointed Questions" on page 364. Have students choose one guiding question from those on the board and suggest pointed questions to further guide research.

5. Then review "Using Journalistic Questions" and "Employing Socratic Questions" on page 365.

6. Now break the class into groups of 3 to 5 students and ask each group to choose a different topic from the board as a research project.

7. Have the groups identify a guiding question and generate pointed questions to guide their research.

8. Next, to help the groups expand their research even further, direct them to discuss journalistic and Socratic questions about their topics.

9. Assign pages 366–369 as homework reading. Students can complete the "Your Turn" activities individually or in their groups. (The activity on page 369 is optional at this time.)

Day 2

10. Arrange a library tour for the class. (If necessary, provide time for students to complete the "Your Turn" activities from page 366–368.)

Day 3

11. In class, briefly review pages 370–371.

12. Then allow library time for groups to begin researching their topics.

Day 4

13. In class, briefly review pages 372–374.

14. Then allow library time for the groups to finish researching their topics.

Day 5

15. Give each group class time to prepare a presentation about their topic, to be given next week. (Consider combining these presentations with a multimedia project in chapters 32 or 33.)

Extension: Conducting Basic Research

Name _____　　Date _____

Your Turn Consider a topic you have been assigned or one you are personally curious about. Fill out this sheet to plan your research.

1. List a few possible guiding questions about your topic. (See *Inquire* page 364.) Choose one to focus and guide your research.

   _____

   _____

2. Generate several pointed questions to further explore your topic. (See *Inquire* page 364.)

   _____

   _____

   _____

3. Write freely about your topic using the journalistic questions *who? what? when? where? why?* and *how?* to help target your research. (See *Inquire* page 365.)

4. Answer several Socratic questions to expand your thinking about your topic. (See *Inquire* page 365.)

   _____

   _____

   _____

5. List the best sources of information about your topic. (See *Inquire* pages 366–367 and 369.)

   _____

   _____

6. Brainstorm a list of keywords to direct your research. (See *Inquire* page 368.)

   _____

   _____

   _____

7. Take careful notes either on paper or electronically. (See *Inquire* pages 370–371.) Then list below a few good ways to organize your information. (See *Inquire* pages 372–373.)

   _____

   _____

   _____

Review: Conducting Basic Research

Name _____   Date _____

Your Turn Answer the following questions about basic research.

1. What is the purpose of a guiding question?

   _____

   _____

2. What is the purpose of pointed questions?

   _____

   _____

3. What are the six basic journalistic questions?

   _____

   _____

4. What is the value of Socratic questions?

   _____

   _____

   _____

5. Name three types of sources you might use to begin your research.

   _____

   _____

   _____

6. List two Boolean operators and explain how they affect keyword searches.

   _____

   _____

7. Explain the two-column method of taking notes.

   _____

   _____

   _____

Reflect: How are mind maps and corkboard note systems alike and different? What are the strengths and weaknesses of each?

Science Minilessons: Conducting Basic Research

Cradle of Life

READ an article about the Olduvai Gorge.

GENERATE a list of questions you still have about this topic.

LIST keywords for locating answers.

RESEARCH the topic using your own questions.

Extension: **MAKE** a poster, a 3-D model, or an interactive multimedia report to illustrate features of the location.

Near Misses

INVESTIGATE records of comets and asteroids passing near the earth.

GENERATE questions about potential near misses in the future.

RESEARCH your questions.

PRESENT your findings to the class.

Chromatics

GATHER types of food coloring, colored markers, nail polishes, and other coloring agents.

CUT filter paper into strips about 1/2 inch wide and 4 inches long.

MARK each strip with a colored circle 1/2 inch from one end, using different sources of color.

TAPE the opposite end of each strip to the middle of a pencil.

HANG each strip in a container.

POUR water into each container until it touches the end of the strip.

RECORD changes in each colored circle.

REPEAT the experiment with isopropyl alcohol instead of water.

Math Minilessons: Conducting Basic Research

Math History

CHOOSE an important mathematical concept you are studying in class.

GENERATE research questions about the origin, development, or modern applications of the math concept.

RESEARCH to find answers to your questions.

REPORT your findings in class.

Math Scavenger Hunt

READ "Using the Library" on page 369.

LIST places in the library where you might find materials involving math.

VISIT the library and list one math-related example from as many different sections and media as possible.

COMPARE lists of resources with classmates.

Learning to Speak Math

DISCUSS in class how mathematics is like a foreign language . . . and also how it is like a universal language.

IDENTIFY several common uses for math in daily life around the world.

USE Socratic questions to suggest creative ways of applying math to your own life.

FREEWRITE for 5 to 10 minutes about your class discussion.

Social Studies Minilessons: Conducting Basic Research

Where Do Organs Go?

INVESTIGATE briefly online or in the library how organ recipients are chosen.

DRAFT a brief opinion piece about that process.

DISCUSS your opinion and others' opinions in a small group.

USE Socratic questions to consider the topic from different angles.

The First Modern War

CONSIDER what historians mean by calling the U.S. Civil War the world's first "modern war."

MAKE a list of sources that will likely contain information about the idea.

BRAINSTORM keywords that could guide your library or Internet search.

COMPARE your keyword list with a classmate's and **DISCUSS** any differences.

A Personal Retrospective

SELECT a research paper you or someone else wrote on a social studies topic.

CHOOSE either a graphic organizer from this chapter, a mind map, or corkboard software to effectively display some part of the text's main points and details.

CREATE the visual and **PRESENT** it in class.

English Minilessons: Conducting Basic Research

An Attention Catcher

INVESTIGATE historical and modern accounts about the Sargasso Sea.

CONSIDER why people are so fascinated with this region.

WRITE about what you have learned.

DISCUSS your discoveries in class.

A Plague on Your Houses

READ an encyclopedia entry about the Great Plague of London.

CONSIDER where you might look for the best accounts from that period of time.

READ one account, and **SUMMARIZE** what you learned.

Extension: **DISCUSS** in class the possibility of a modern-day plague.

A View from Outside

CHOOSE a novel that you have read for English class or one you are reading on your own.

SUMMARIZE the beliefs of a major character.

CONSIDER how those beliefs match or vary from your own.

USE Socratic questions to find a perspective different from both the character's and your own.

Chapter 24
Conducting Advanced Research

(*Inquire* pages 375–404)

Scholarly research involves a thorough understanding of three basic types of sources: primary, secondary, and tertiary. It also depends upon locating quality sources and accessing information from them accurately and fairly (avoiding plagiarism and other source abuses). And finally, scholarly research requires that the findings follow a particular format and documentation style. This chapter introduces students to these aspects of advanced research.

Learning Outcomes
- Learn about primary, secondary, and tertiary sources.
- Review researching on the Internet.
- Learn about avoiding plagiarism.
- Review journalistic, MLA, APA, and CMS citation styles.
- Learn how to use documentation tools.

Correlations

Common Core State Standards

ELA-Literacy.CCRA.R.1–10	ELA-Literacy.CCRA.L.3–6	Math.Practice.MP3–8
ELA-Literacy.CCRA.W.1–10	Math.Practice.MP1	Science.Practice.SP1–8
ELA-Literacy.CCRA.SL.1–6		

Partnership for 21st Century Skills

Communication and Collaboration
- Communicate Clearly

Information Literacy
- Access and Evaluate Information

Media Literacy
- Analyze Media

Information and Communication Technologies Literacy
- Apply Technology Effectively

Life and Career Skills
- Productivity and Accountability

International Society for Technology in Education

3. Research and Information Fluency
  a. Plan strategies to guide inquiry.
  b. Locate, organize, analyze, evaluate, synthesize, and ethically use information from a variety of sources.
  c. Evaluate and select information sources and digital tools based on the appropriateness to specific tasks.

4. Critical Thinking, Problem Solving, and Decision Making
  a. Identify and define authentic problems and significant questions for investigation.
  b. Plan and manage activities to develop a solution.
  c. Collect and analyze data to identify solutions.

  d. Use multiple processes and perspectives to explore.

5. Digital Citizenship
  a. Advocate and practice safe, legal, and responsible use of information and technology.
  b. Exhibit a positive attitude toward using technology that supports collaboration, learning, and productivity.

6. Technology Operations and Concepts
  a. Understand and use technology systems.
  b. Select and use applications effectively and productively.
  c. Troubleshoot systems applications.
  d. Transfer current knowledge to new technologies.

Lesson Plan: Conducting Advanced Research

1. Ask for a volunteer to read aloud the introduction on page 375. Then have students describe research papers they have written in the past. What challenges and successes did they experience?
2. Then discuss "Understanding Primary, Secondary, and Tertiary Resources" on pages 376–377. Make the "Your Turn" activity on page 376 part of your discussion.
3. Ask students to volunteer examples of the three resource types they have personally used.
4. Discuss ways in which one resource can serve as a primary, a secondary, or a tertiary source, depending upon the research situation.
5. Assign "Using Tertiary Resources" (pages 378–379) as homework reading.

Day 2

6. Have students write entrance slips explaining some of the "do's and don'ts" about search sites.
7. As a class, review "Understanding Nonfiction Books" on pages 380–381. Ask students to explain the value of (or the reason for) each part of a book.
8. Next, review "Understanding Periodicals" on pages 382–383. Ask students to explain the distinctions between newspapers, magazines, and periodicals. Can they think of any real-world examples that blur the boundaries between the three resources? Assign the "Your Turn" activity at this time if it seems appropriate.
9. If possible, allow students library time to research a topic for a paper you will be assigning in the coming weeks, locating helpful nonfiction books and periodicals.

Day 3

10. As a class, review "Using Primary Resources" on pages 384–389.
11. Then have students freewrite for 10 minutes about a memorable event or exhibit they attended, a specific historical item they saw, an interview or survey they conducted, or an experiment they performed.
12. If possible, allow students time in class to share their examples.
13. Assign "Researching on the Internet" (pages 390–391) as homework reading.

Day 4

14. As a class, discuss the homework reading. Then discuss "Avoiding Plagiarism" on pages 392–395.
15. *Extension:* Consider having students research and report on national news accounts of plagiarism.

Day 5

16. As a class, review the four citation styles on pages 396–402 and "Using Documentation Tools" on page 403.
17. Ask students to discuss which citation styles and documentation tools they have had experience with in the past.
18. Allow time for students to discuss which citation styles they prefer and why.

Extension: Conducting Advanced Research

Name _____   Date _____

Your Turn Respond to the following prompts to enhance your understanding of research.

1. Freewrite for 8–10 minutes, exploring your thoughts and feelings about a news topic that concerns you.

2. Discuss your concerns in a small group of classmates. Then note the ways that your classmates agree with and disagree with you.

Agree	Disagree/Question

3. What resources could you use to address your classmates' objections?

    _____

    _____

4. What objections do you think people outside of your group may have to your ideas?

    _____

    _____

    _____

5. What types of sources do you think are most effective for clarifying issues in the face of questions or objections?

    _____

    _____

    _____

Review: Conducting Advanced Research

Name _____ Date _____

Your Turn Answer the questions below about one of your current research projects.

1. What *primary* sources of information would be well suited to this project? How must you prepare to find or use these sources?

   _____

   _____

   _____

2. What *secondary* sources of information does your research project call for? Where can you find them?

   _____

   _____

   _____

3. What *tertiary* sources might be applicable to your project, either for basic information or for a useful overview?

   _____

   _____

   _____

4. What "deep Web" sources might benefit your research?

   _____

   _____

   _____

5. What precautions can you take to avoid source abuses in your research, especially in regard to this particular project?

   _____

   _____

   _____

6. Which of the citation styles discussed in chapter 24 is appropriate for your research project?

   _____

   _____

   _____

Science Minilessons: Conducting Advanced Research

Perchance to Dream

RESEARCH the history of dream theory in psychology.

INVESTIGATE related physiological effects such as rapid eye movement and sleep paralysis.

CHOOSE a main idea/focus to research further.

WRITE a summary of what you have learned about that topic.

A Century from Now

INVESTIGATE recent data from a space probe, satellite, or lander.

CHOOSE one significant discovery from this data.

PROJECT the results of one consequence a hundred years into the future.

WRITE a journal article describing that future.

The Sound of One Hand Clapping

RESEARCH problems that drove the Concorde out of business.

INVESTIGATE research currently underway to solve those problems.

CONSIDER the business reasons behind that research.

DISCUSS what you have learned concerning supersonic commercial flight.

Math Minilessons: Conducting Advanced Research

A Fuel's Journey

INVESTIGATE online the price of gasoline in different regions of the United States, both urban and rural.

MAKE a map that indicates those various prices. Do you see any patterns?

Extension: **RESEARCH** how fuel is transported to each location and where it comes from.

ESTIMATE transport costs for several locales.

DISCUSS implications of your findings.

Exploding TV

RESEARCH changes in television viewing decade by decade since the 1930s.

CHOOSE a focus: numbers of stations, numbers of programs, numbers of viewers, hours watched daily, average viewer age, or some other traceable statistic.

MAKE a line graph showing those changes.

REMEMBER to credit your sources.

DISCUSS your results in class.

Styling Math

INVESTIGATE one or two periodicals that publish articles about mathematics.

CHECK a few of the published essays for content and their submissions guidelines for format and documentation style.

PRESENT your findings in class.

Social Studies Minilessons: Conducting Advanced Research

Animal Testing

FREEWRITE for 5 to 10 minutes, recording your thoughts about animal testing in labs.

INTERVIEW (by email, by phone, or in person) a representative from an animal-rights organization and one from a lab.

PREPARE an in-class presentation treating both sides fairly, and concluding with your opinion.

The County Seat Wars

INVESTIGATE the battles (social, political, legal) that determined a particular county election (your own or any other one).

WRITE a brief report about what you learned.

DISCUSS the effects for citizens of that county.

Extension: **COMPARE** that battle with another one in a different county.

What Might Have Been

CHOOSE a disaster that was caused by human error.

INVESTIGATE that disaster, from its initial cause, through the intervening steps, to the end.

SUGGEST an action that could have prevented the disaster or lessened its effects.

SHARE your findings.

English Minilessons: Conducting Advanced Research

On Location

BRAINSTORM a list of novels that feature a famous setting and **CHOOSE** one novel to read.

FREEWRITE about the setting's importance to the novel.

INVESTIGATE the author's reasons for choosing this setting.

COMPARE the conclusions from your freewriting with the author's stated intent.

Proper Propaganda?

LOOK up the word "propaganda" in a dictionary.

IDENTIFY the main definitions for the word as well as its origins.

RESEARCH examples of propaganda.

SHARE your findings with the class.

How It's Done

CHOOSE a famous author—one you admire or one whose work you dislike.

INVESTIGATE the author's process for writing a book.

CONSIDER how the author's process affects various aspects of his or her work.

WRITE an opinion piece explaining why you believe the process produces work of value or how the process could be changed to avoid creating work of poor quality.

Chapter 25
Creating

(*Inquire* pages 405–414)

After students have completed their planning and research, they are ready to create, putting fingers to the keyboard, eyes and hands to a video camera, paint brushes to canvas. The creating stage in the process can get messy. The key is to encourage students to push forward, to offer assistance as they shape their ideas into something real. This chapter introduces various structures students can use to turn their ideas into effective projects.

Learning Outcomes

- Review the basic three-part structure.
- Understand different informational structures.
- Understand narrative structure.
- Learn about visual structure.
- Learn about producing attention-grabbing projects.
- Learn tips for getting unstuck.

Correlations

Common Core State Standards

ELA-Literacy.CCRA.W.1–6	ELA-Literacy.CCRA.L.3–6	Math.Practice.MP7–8
ELA-Literacy.CCRA.W.10	Math.Practice.MP1–3	Science.Practice.SP1–3
ELA-Literacy.CCRA.SL.4–6	Math.Practice.MP5	Science.Practice.SP6–8

Partnership for 21st Century Skills

Creativity and Innovation
- Think Creatively
- Implement Innovations

Critical Thinking and Problem Solving
(All standards)

Communication and Collaboration
- Communicate Clearly

Media Literacy
- Create Media Products

Life and Career Skills
- Flexibility and Adaptability
- Initiative and Self-Direction

International Society for Technology in Education

1. **Creativity and Innovation**
   (All standards)
2. **Communication and Collaboration**
   (All standards)
3. **Research and Information Fluency**
   (All standards)
4. **Critical Thinking, Problem Solving, and Decision Making**
   (All standards)

Lesson Plan: Creating

Day 1

1. Have students write freely or make a mind map about something they have created, considering the process they used, how the work went, and how they feel about it now. Discuss their responses in class.

2. Read aloud the chapter introduction on page 405. Then have students silently read "A Guide to Creating" on page 406 and reflect on the "Your Turn" activity.

3. Discuss "Creating a Basic Structure" on page 407. Make the "Your Turn" activity part of your discussion. Ask for a volunteer to recall the beginning, middle, and ending of her or his favorite movie, book, or performance. Discuss the purpose of each part and why the three-part structure is effective.

Day 2

4. As a class, carefully read through "Using Informational Structures" on pages 408–410.

5. Brainstorm different projects that could be built with each of the six informational structures mentioned.

6. Have students read "Creating Narrative Structure" (page 411) silently.

7. Assign the "Your Turn" activity at the bottom of the page for homework.

Day 3

8. Read aloud "Creating Visual Structure" on page 412.

9. Show students different pictures or works of art that demonstrate some of the elements discussed on the page.

10. Allow time in the library or computer lab for students to complete the "Your Turn" activity at the end of page 412.

11. Afterward, ask for volunteers to present their discoveries.

Day 4

12. Have students read "Catching Attention" on page 413 silently. Then have them complete the "Your Turn" activity.

13. Review "10 Tips for Getting Unstuck" on page 414 and ask students to complete the "Your Turn" activity in small groups.

14. Assign the extension and review activities on the next two pages as needed.

Extension: Creating

Name _____ Date _____

Your Turn Imagine you must create something with the list of materials below. You can use as many or as few of the items as you wish. Answer the questions below about your creation.

List of Materials

1 flip video camera
3 rolls of duct tape
6 white T-shirts
1 bottle of blue spray paint
1 bottle of pink spray paint
1 toolbox (includes hammer, nails, screws, power drill, tape measure)
1 cordless microphone
1 8 x 12 dry-erase board
1 set of dry-erase markers (red, blue, green, black, purple)
1 volleyball

1. Think about what you could create. Describe it. _____

_____

_____

_____

_____

2. What materials from the list would you use? _____

_____

_____

_____

3. Which informational structure (see *Inquire* pages 408–410) would fit your creation? Explain. _____

_____

_____

4. How could you make your creation more visual? (See *Inquire* page 413.) _____

_____

_____

_____

Special Challenge: If you have access to the materials, build your creation.

Review: Creating

Name _____ Date _____

Your Turn Answer each of the following questions.

1. An essay, a story, or a video should include how many parts? Name them and describe their purpose.

   _____

   _____

   _____

   _____

2. True or false? Comparison-contrast organization is used to shed light on a problem and offer a solution.

   _____

3. What is the purpose of a classification informational structure?

   _____

   _____

4. Which part of the narrative structure offers the most exciting point in a story?
   a. Exposition   **c.** Climax
   b. Rising Action   **d.** Ending

5. What does "value" do for visual structure?

   _____

   _____

6. Describe two ways to attract the attention of the audience with your creation.

   _____

   _____

   _____

7. List two ways to get unstuck during the creative process.

   _____

   _____

   _____

   Reflect: Which strategy or guideline from this chapter do you find most useful, and why?

Science Minilessons: Creating

Unwelcome Visitors

STUDY the causes and effects of an invasive species.

CHOOSE a cause-centered or effect-centered organizational approach to show what you learned. (See *Inquire* page 409.)

Extension: **CREATE** an essay, slide show, or digital story explaining the causes and effects of this particular invasive species.

Flaming Salts

RESEARCH the flame colors of different burning salts.

IMAGINE you are in charge of creating a set for an action movie, and you need to devise a background of blue, red, and green flames.

LIST the materials (salts) you would need to create this effect. Then **CREATE** a sketch or digital representation of the set.

Plant Experimentation

REVIEW the biology of plant life, specifically plant growth.

PLAN an experiment that determines how introducing different variables (color of light, caffeine, soil temperature, etc.) affects plant growth.

Extension: **CONDUCT** the experiment.

PRESENT your findings in a way that catches attention (see page 413).

Math Minilessons: Creating

Recycle Usage

DETERMINE the number of recycling bins at your school.

CALCULATE the amount of recyclable material, by weight, collected each week.

ESTIMATE the amount of recyclable material, by weight, that will be collected throughout the school year.

PRESENT your findings. Include a visual representation of your data.

Beautiful Slopes

DESIGN a picture on graphing paper, using eight lines with positive slope, eight lines with negative slope, four lines with zero slope, and four lines with undefined slope.

RECORD the slope of each line.

Finally, **DETERMINE** an equation for each line using slope-intercept form ($y = mx + b$).

PRESENT your work.

Facility Redesign

DETERMINE the area and perimeter of an athletic facility, performing arts theater, or recreational center at your school.

IMAGINE you are in charge of redesigning this space to improve it.

RESEARCH similar structures and **CHOOSE** an architectural style that interests you.

CREATE a blueprint (*Inquire* page 540) or scale model (*Inquire* page 544) of your new design.

Social Studies Minilessons: Creating

Presenting Propaganda

RESEARCH examples of propaganda posters at the Library of Congress (loc.gov).

CHOOSE one example and **WRITE** an analysis of its visual structure. (See *Inquire* page 412.)

Extension: **CREATE** your own propaganda poster on a topic of your choice, using effective visual elements.

Dear Diary to the Past

RESEARCH an interesting era of world history.

CHOOSE one figure from that era and **RESEARCH** him or her.

CREATE a historical diary entry from that person's perspective.

FOLLOW the narrative structure as you write. (See *Inquire* page 441.)

SHARE your writing with your classmates.

Atlantic to the Pacific

RESEARCH different ways you could classify World War II (by opponents, by battles, by locations). (For more information about classification, see *Inquire* page 410.)

CHOOSE one classification system.

CREATE a line diagram that demonstrates the classification, displaying categories and subgroups.

English Minilessons: Creating

The Personal Essay

PLAN a personal essay about an important event in your life.

USE the narrative structure discussed on *Inquire* page 411 to create your essay.

INCLUDE specific details for each part to create a compelling essay.

IMPROVE the essay by revising and editing.

PRESENT your essay.

Literature Comparison

THINK about two of your favorite authors, literary characters, or pieces of literature.

CHOOSE the pair you know most about.

PLAN a comparison-contrast essay that compares the two, using one of the three comparison-contrast organizational strategies discussed on *Inquire* page 410.

WRITE, revise, edit, and present your essay.

Visual Summary

IDENTIFY a recent book that you enjoyed.

REVIEW its characters and narrative structure.

CREATE an audiovisual or design project summarizing the book. (See *Inquire* pages 507–526 and 527–548.)

IMPROVE the presentation by incorporating visual elements. (See *Inquire* page 412.)

Chapter 26
Improving
(*Inquire* pages 415–422)

Practice makes perfect. But as you know, many students need to understand why that is true, especially when it comes to developing projects. Practice or first attempts allow us to take risks, push ourselves, and do our best thinking. After evaluating our performance, we can improve our initial efforts. In this chapter, students will learn to evaluate and fine-tune their projects by creating and applying rubrics, participating in peer evaluations, identifying critical and creative improvements, and applying the results.

Learning Outcomes

- Learn how to evaluate work.
- Understand how to use a rubric sheet for evaluations.
- Learn how to give and receive peer evaluations.
- Understand making critical and creative improvements.
- Understand how to perfect work according to its application.

Correlations

Common Core State Standards

ELA-Literacy.CCRA.R.4–9	ELA-Literacy.CCRA.SL.1–6	Math.Practice.MP8
ELA-Literacy.CCRA.W.1–6	ELA-Literacy.CCRA.L.1–6	Science.Practice.SP1–8
ELA-Literacy.CCRA.W.10	Math.Practice.MP1–6	

Partnership for 21st Century Skills

Creativity and Innovation
- Think Creatively
- Work Creatively with Others
- Implement Innovations

Critical Thinking and Problem Solving
- Reason Effectively and Use Systems Thinking
- Solve Problems

Information Literacy
- Access and Evaluate Information
- Use and Manage Information

Life and Career Skills
- Flexibility and Adaptability
- Initiative and Self-Direction
- Social and Cross-Cultural Skills
- Productivity and Accountability
- Leadership and Responsibility

International Society for Technology in Education

1. Creativity and Innovation
(All standards)

3. Research and Information Fluency
(All standards)

4. Critical Thinking, Problem Solving, and Decision Making
(All standards)

Lesson Plan: Improving

Day 1

1. Bring to class an early example of something related to your subject area (e.g., a Renaissance map or star chart, the process for adding Roman numerals, an early periodic table of the elements, or a first draft of a famous poem).

2. Lead a class discussion about the example item and its strengths and weaknesses. Then show students a more recent version of the same piece. Ask them what improvements have been made.

3. Also have them consider how future developments might further improve upon the modern version.

4. Read together the chapter opening, on page 415, exploring how making improvements applies to all areas of our lives and how students will soon be applying this important process to their own projects.

5. Have students read "Evaluating" on pages 416–417 and prepare a rubric sheet for a recently completed project. (See the next page in this Teacher's Guide.)

6. Ask them to bring their rubrics to class the next day for discussion. (If students have earlier completed a rubric for the project, have them bring it to class for the next day.)

Day 2

7. Review "Getting a Second Opinion" (pages 418–419) with the class.

8. Consider having two student volunteers model peer reviewing for a project in progress.

9. Then have the rest of the class work in small groups, exchanging projects and evaluating and responding to them.

Day 3

10. Have students read "Making Improvements" (pages 420–421) and fill out an improvement plan sheet or write a journal entry explaining their plans.

11. Ask student volunteers to share their plans for improving their projects.

Day 4

12. Consider giving students class time to make the improvements.

Rubric Sheet

Name _____   Date _____

Project: _____

Goal:	Evaluation:	Rating			Score
		Beat	**Met**	**Didn't**	
		60	40	20	
Objectives:					
1.		**Beat**	**Met**	**Didn't**	
		10	6	2	
2.		**Beat**	**Met**	**Didn't**	
		10	6	2	
3.		**Beat**	**Met**	**Didn't**	
		10	6	2	
4.		**Beat**	**Met**	**Didn't**	
		10	6	2	
5.		**Beat**	**Met**	**Didn't**	
		10	6	2	
6.		**Beat**	**Met**	**Didn't**	
		10	6	2	
				Total:	

Follow-up: What changes will you make to improve your projects?

Review: Improving

Name _____   Date _____

Your Turn Answer the following questions to review what you've learned about improving your work.

1. Explain how a project planning sheet relates to a rubric.

   _____

   _____

   _____

   _____

2. Explain your role as the presenter in a peer-review session.

   _____

   _____

   _____

   _____

3. Explain the responder's role during a peer-review session.

   _____

   _____

   _____

   _____

4. Which two of the following activities are **critical** improvements?
   a. Cutting   **c.** Reworking
   b. Rearranging   **d.** Adding

5. Which two of the following activities are **creative** improvements?
   a. Cutting   **c.** Reworking
   b. Rearranging   **d.** Adding

Reflect: When it comes to making improvements to a work in progress, what do you do best? Which improvement activities do you need to work on?

   _____

   _____

   _____

   _____

Science Minilessons: Improving

Targeting Space

RESEARCH and **DISCUSS** in class the primary goals of space exploration.

CREATE a rubric to measure the attainment of those goals. (See *Inquire* page 417.)

Extension: **INVESTIGATE** the costs and benefits of NASA's program. Also look for benefits not related to the primary goals (e.g., satellite TV).

REPORT your findings.

Species Immigration

LEARN about the intentional introduction of a foreign species into a new environment.

DEFINE the goal of that introduction.

LIST the necessary steps to attain that goal.

CREATE a rubric to evaluate the project.

SUGGEST ways to improve the process in similar undertakings in the future.

CONSIDER how your suggestions may be applied to accidental species introductions.

Protect Your Population

IMAGINE that you and a small group of classmates are on your city's council.

Together, **DRAFT** a plan for protecting citizens from a chemical or biological attack.

INVESTIGATE actual public policies for such an event.

EVALUATE your plan, comparing it with established public policy.

Math Minilessons: Improving

Balancing Act

RESEARCH the target calorie/nutrient intake for your age, height, gender, and activity.

CREATE a rubric to gauge a balanced daily diet.

RECORD everything you eat and drink each day for one week.

EVALUATE your intake, comparing it to your rubric.

IMPROVE your diet as necessary.

Counting Marbles

FILL a glass jar with uniformly sized marbles.

MEASURE the jar and an example marble.

CREATE an equation to predict the number of marbles in the jar.

COUNT the marbles to learn how accurate your prediction is.

IMPROVE your equation based upon what you learn.

Your Turn at Bat

CONSIDER the 2012 baseball batting averages of National League leaders Buster Posey (.336) and Andrew McCutchen (.327).

CALCULATE the minimum number of times at bat each player would need to achieve his average.

INVESTIGATE the actual number of times each player batted in 2012.

EXPLAIN any differences between your calculations and the actual numbers.

Social Studies Minilessons: Improving

Feeding the World

BRAINSTORM a list of possible solutions to the problem of world hunger.

MAKE a rubric for evaluating how well the possible solutions would work.

INVESTIGATE ways in which existing organizations are tackling the problem.

APPLY your rubric to evaluate those organizations' efforts.

SUGGEST ways to improve the existing efforts.

Long Ago and Faraway

CHOOSE a time and place in history that you wish you could visit.

IMAGINE you can travel there in a time machine.

PLAN your trip.

PRESENT your plan to a small group for peer review.

IMPROVE your plan based upon the feedback from your group members.

Trains, Planes, and Automobiles

CONSIDER the importance of transportation for a civilization.

RECORD your thoughts in a journal entry or two.

CRITIQUE in a small group the status of transportation within the United States.

SUGGEST critical and creative changes to public policy to improve U.S. transportation.

English Minilessons: Improving

Pro Peer Review

CREATE a rubric for evaluating the merit of a short story or poem.

CHOOSE a short story or poem that you've read recently.

EVALUATE that short story or poem with your rubric.

ROLE-PLAY a peer review session with another student posing as the author.

SUGGEST ways to improve the work.

"Ad" Things Up

CHOOSE a product that you enjoy.

CREATE a first draft for an advertisement for it (a print ad, TV commercial, or Web video).

PRESENT your ad to classmates and ask them to review it.

IDENTIFY both critical and creative improvements you can make.

Extension: **IMPROVE** your ad and submit it to the manufacturer.

Paper Project

CREATE a rubric for evaluating an essay you have recently finished.

SCORE your essay with that rubric.

ASK a classmate to review your essay and make comments about it.

IDENTIFY critical and creative improvements you could make to the writing.

Extension: **IMPROVE** your essay using the feedback from your rubric evaluation and your peer review.

Chapter 27
Presenting

(*Inquire* pages 423–428)

Twenty-first century technology allows for fast, easy, and affordable presentations to large-scale audiences. This chapter encourages students to learn how to present their school projects on the Web. It also introduces strategies for oral presentations, which are still highly valued in school settings and in the workplace. Use this chapter to build your students' confidence as they present their work online and in person.

Learning Outcomes

- Learn how to review the situation (context) for presenting a project.
- Master presenting in person.
- Learn how to present on the Web.
- Understand how to promote projects.

Correlations

Common Core State Standards

ELA-Literacy.CCRA.W.1–6	ELA-Literacy.CCRA.L.3–6	Math.Practice.MP8
ELA-Literacy.CCRA.W.10	Math.Practice.MP1	Science.Practice.SP1–3
ELA-Literacy.CCRA.SL.1–6	Math.Practice.MP5	Science.Practice.SP6–8

Partnership for 21st Century Skills

Creativity and Innovation
- Think Creatively
- Work Creatively with Others
- Implement Innovations

Critical Thinking and Problem Solving
- Reason Effectively and Use Systems Thinking
- Solve Problems

Communication and Collaboration
- Communicate Clearly

Media Literacy
- Create Media Products

Life and Career Skills
- Initiative and Self-Direction
- Productivity and Accountability

International Society for Technology in Education

1. **Creativity and Innovation**
   - Students demonstrate creative thinking, construct knowledge, and develop innovative products and processes using technology. (a, b, d)

2. **Communication and Collaboration**
   - Students use digital media and environments to communicate and work collaboratively, including at a distance, to support individual learning and contribute to the learning of others. (a, b, d)

3. **Research and Information Fluency**
   - Students apply digital tools to gather, evaluate, and use information. (c, d)

4. **Critical Thinking, Problem Solving, and Decision Making**
   - Students use critical thinking skills to plan and conduct research, manage projects, solve problems, and make informed decisions using appropriate digital tools and resources. (b, d)

5. **Digital Citizenship**
   - Students understand human, cultural, and societal issues related to technology and practice legal and ethical behavior. (a, b, d)

6. **Technology Operations and Concepts**
   - Students demonstrate a sound understanding of technology concepts, systems, and operations. (a, b, c, d)

Lesson Plan: Presenting

Day 1

1. Review the chapter opener on *Inquire* page 423 as a class. Then, using the extension activity on the next page of this guide, engage students in a discussion about their experiences with oral presentations. Also discuss the questions about online presentation.

2. Review "Understanding the Situation" on *Inquire* page 424. Have students fill out a "Situation Analysis" sheet for presenting their latest creation online.

Day 2

3. Read aloud and discuss "Presenting in Person" on *Inquire* page 425.

4. Assign the "Your Turn" activity at the bottom of the page as homework. If the students have not been assigned an oral presentation this year, ask them to prepare one about their family's ancestry. For additional guidelines on oral presentations, see *Inquire* pages 77–79.

Day 3

5. Review "Presenting on the Web" (*Inquire* pages 426–427). Discuss the four factors to consider before posting online—purpose, place, timing, and procedure.

6. Assign the "Your Turn" activity at the bottom of *Inquire* page 427. If students don't have an online project to post, ask them to adapt their oral presentation on family ancestry for the Web.

Day 4

7. Read over "Promoting Your Project" on *Inquire* page 428. Have students discuss how they've promoted themselves or their work in the past.

8. Conduct a brainstorming session to gather new ideas for promoting projects. Consider either or both of the "Your Turn" activities as extended assignments.

Day 5

9. Consider having students continue to work on their oral presentations.

Extension: Presenting

Name _____   Date _____

Your Turn Write about your experiences presenting your work in person and online.

1. How would you describe your experience with giving speeches or oral presentations?

   _____

   _____

   _____

2. Do you feel anxious about talking in front of large groups of people? If so, what strategies have helped to calm your nerves?

   _____

   _____

   _____

3. Have you ever presented school work online? If so, which format did you use (blog, microblog post, online video, etc.)?

   _____

   _____

   _____

4. Has anyone ever commented on your work online? Do you enjoy reading feedback, or would you rather not know how others feel about your work? Explain.

   _____

   _____

   _____

5. Do you prefer presenting work online or in person? Explain your choice.

   _____

   _____

   _____

Review: Presenting

Name _____ Date _____

Your Turn Answer each of the following questions.

1. What questions should you consider before presenting your work?

_____

_____

_____

_____

2. Which do you prefer to use for an oral presentation: note cards, an outline, a slide show, or a manuscript? Explain.

_____

_____

_____

_____

3. Why do you think people post their work online?

_____

_____

_____

_____

4. What are the pros and cons of posting your work on a public online site?

_____

_____

_____

_____

5. How can you use social media to promote your work?

_____

_____

_____

_____

Science Minilessons: Presenting

Changing Climates

RESEARCH the latest information on global climate change.

PLAN a slide show or a video about your findings.

Extension: **CREATE, EVALUATE,** and **IMPROVE** your presentation.

PRACTICE your presentation.

GIVE an oral presentation of your findings.

Then **POST** the presentation online.

Testing Electrolyte Levels in Sports Drinks

GATHER three different sports drinks, copper wire, and a 9-volt battery.

RESEARCH safe ways to create a conductance sensor. **CREATE** your sensor. **CONNECT** one end of the copper wire to the positive terminal of the battery, and, using alligator clips, connect the other end of the wire to your conductance sensor. **DIVIDE** the sports drinks into equal samples, and include an equal sample of distilled water. **PLACE** the conductance sensor into the water, and read and record the current. Do the same for the sports drinks. **RECORD** your results.

PRESENT your findings.

REFLECT on how well the problem-solving method worked for you.

Math Minilessons: Presenting

Soup Volume

MEASURE the diameter and height of an empty soup can to the nearest millimeter.

CALCULATE the total surface area of the can to the nearest 10th of a centimeter squared. Then calculate the volume of the can to the nearest 100th of a centimeter cubed.

PRESENT your findings orally to your class, explaining your order of operations.

Geometrical Marvels

RESEARCH different types of architecture.

CHOOSE a building, space, or structure that you find particularly interesting.

STUDY the structure for geometrical shapes. Then relate the structure to a math concept you are learning in class.

Extension: **CREATE** a slide show including pictures that relate to and explain your findings.

PRESENT the slide show in class or online.

Online Video Presentation

CHOOSE a concept in algebra, geometry, statistics, trigonometry, or calculus to explain.

CREATE a video that explains the concept in an interesting way.

Extension: **POST** the video on different online venues (video-sharing sites, social networks, classroom blogs).

PROMOTE your video using social media.

Social Studies Minilessons: Presenting

I'm a Witness

RESEARCH your county's court schedule.

ATTEND a trial.

TAKE NOTES about the experience.

CREATE an oral presentation about your experience, using note cards, an outline, a slide show, or a manuscript.

PRACTICE your presentation and **PRESENT** it to the class.

A Digital Reconstruction

PLAN a digital story on a topic from America's Reconstruction period.

RESEARCH your topic.

CREATE a storyboard for your digital story.

Extension: **WRITE** your digital story.

POST your story online.

PROMOTE it using social media.

Re-creating a Famous Speech

SEARCH for famous speeches throughout American and world history.

CHOOSE one speech to re-create. Pay close attention to the speaker's emotion and inflection. **PRACTICE** the speech using your preferred preparation tool. (See *Inquire* page 425.)

PRESENT the speech to your class, imitating the original speaker's perspective and feeling.

English Minilessons: Presenting

Measuring Up

READ a book, paying close attention and taking notes about its literary elements (irony, symbolism, foreshadowing, themes, etc.).

CREATE an oral presentation of your literary analysis. The presentation should include visual aids to represent the book's key literary elements.

PRESENT your work in front of the class.

High School Research Conference

CHOOSE a research paper you have written this year, or prepare a new one.

PLAN an oral presentation of your research paper for the students and faculty at your school.

PROMOTE your presentation.

PRESENT your material.

Poetry Slam

CREATE a poem that fits the theme of your school's poetry slam.

PRACTICE reciting the poem.

PROMOTE the poetry slam using local and social-media promotion. (See *Inquire* page 428.)

DELIVER your poem at the poetry slam.

Part II Answer Key

206

Review: Inquiry Process

Name _____ Date _____

Your Turn Complete each item below.

1. Match each step in the inquiry process with its description.

   Questioning — Using your planning and research to make something new

   Planning — Collecting information and resources for your work

   Researching — Making critical and creative changes to your work

   Creating — Sharing your work with your audience

   Improving — Setting up goals for a project and outlining tasks, time, team, and objectives

   Presenting — Exploring possibilities by imagining and brainstorming

2. Think of something you want to do or something you have put off doing for some time. State a goal for this activity.
   Answers will vary.

3. Write objectives for your goal, as you would on a planning sheet, by answering the 5 W's and H.
   Who? Answers will vary.
   What?
   Where?
   When?
   Why?
   How?

4. Describe the types of research you would need to undertake to achieve your goal.
   Answers will vary.

212

Review: Questioning

Name _____ Date _____

Your Turn Provide answers for each item below.

1. What is the difference between a closed-ended, an open-ended, and a theoretical question?
   A closed-ended question seeks a limited response; an open-ended question seeks a longer response; a theoretical question seeks a hypothesis based on broad knowledge.

2. List the journalistic questions. Who? What? Where? When? Why? How?

3. Write a question that would help you evaluate something. Answers will vary.
   Sample response: What is the value of this?

4. List the five sensory questions. What do I see? Hear? Smell? Taste? Touch?

5. Write a creative question about the world. Answers will vary.
   Sample response: Who are the world's power brokers?

6. What type of survey question asks participants to rank a list of choices?
   Ordinal questions

7. Write the word for each letter in this acronym of question types:
   S ubstitute
   C ombine
   A dapt
   M agnify
   P ut to other uses
   E liminate
   R earrange

Reflect: Imagine that you could ask one question about your future that would get a definite and true answer. What question would you ask? Answers will vary.

218

Review: Planning

Name _____ Date _____

Your Turn Answer the following questions to review your understanding of planning.

1. You may use SMART guidelines to set and clarify your goal. What do the letters in SMART stand for?
   S pecific   M eaningful   A ttainable   R elevant   T rackable

2. How might you change the following negative situations into positive goals?
   My motorcycle won't run: Answers will vary. Sample response: How can I fix my motorcycle?

   I don't get chemistry: Answers will vary. Sample response: How can I learn new chemistry concepts?

3. Explain how to schedule a project's tasks in the following situations.
   You have a deadline: Begin with the deadline date and work backward, dividing available time between the various tasks.
   The project is open-ended: List the first task with an estimate of how long it will take, the second with its estimate, and so on.

4. Which two ways of assigning project roles would be poor choices?
   (a.) Draw roles from a hat.   c. Let group members choose.
   b. Have a group leader assign roles.   (d.) Assign roles alphabetically.

5. In your own words, describe the four types of project tools.
   Equipment: Answers will vary.
   Information: Answers will vary.
   Materials: Answers will vary.
   Resources: Answers will vary.

6. How can a planning sheet help you during each of the following steps in a project?
   Organizing: Focuses your thoughts and helps order the tasks needed to finish the project
   Gathering: Guides your resources, team, and tools
   Developing: Reminds you of your project's goals and objectives and keeps you on track
   Evaluating: Provides the goal and objectives that you can use in your evaluation rubric

224

Review: Conducting Basic Research

Name _____ Date _____

Your Turn Answer the following questions about basic research.

1. What is the purpose of a guiding question?
   A guiding question directs the topic and research of an assignment or project.

2. What is the purpose of pointed questions?
   Pointed questions deepen and broaden your research.

3. What are the six basic journalistic questions?
   Who? What? When? Where? Why? How?

4. What is the value of Socratic questions?
   Socratic questions help you think in new ways.

5. Name three types of sources you might use to begin your research.
   Any three of these: direct observations; electronic media, people, print periodicals, reference books, chat applications, email, message boards, search sites, scholarly databases, social media, wikis

6. List two Boolean operators and explain how they affect keyword searches.
   Answers will vary. Sample response: Using and or + results in items that include all keywords in any order or location, while using quotation marks ("") finds the exact phrase within those marks.

7. Explain the two-column method of taking notes.
   The two-column method uses two-thirds of the page for main notes and one-third for headings and documentation.

Reflect: How are mind maps and corkboard note systems alike and different? What are the strengths and weaknesses of each? Answers will vary.

252

230

Review: Conducting Advanced Research

Name _____ Date _____

Your Turn Answer the questions below about one of your current research projects.

1. What *primary* sources of information would be well suited to this project? How must you prepare to find or use these sources?
   Answers will vary.

2. What *secondary* sources of information does your research project call for? Where can you find them?
   Answers will vary.

3. What *tertiary* sources might be applicable to your project, either for basic information or for a useful overview?
   Answers will vary.

4. What "deep Web" sources might benefit your research?
   Answers will vary.

5. What precautions can you take to avoid source abuses in your research, especially in regard to this particular project?
   Answers will vary.

6. Which of the citation styles discussed in chapter 24 is appropriate for your research project?
   Answers will vary.

236

Review: Creating

Name _____ Date _____

Your Turn Answer each of the following questions.

1. An essay, a story, or a video should include how many parts? Name them and describe their purpose.
   They should include three parts: a beginning, a middle, and an ending. The beginning gains the attention of the audience, provides background information, and introduces the main point. The middle provides strong supporting details and develops the storyline. The ending ties everything together.

2. True or false? Comparison-contrast organization is used to shed light on a problem and offer a solution.
   False.

3. What is the purpose of a classification informational structure?
   The purpose of classification is to break a subject into subgroups or categories and then examine the unique properties of each category.

4. Which part of the narrative structure offers the most exciting point in a story?
   a. Exposition   c. Climax
   b. Rising Action   d. Ending

5. What does "value" do for visual structure?
   Value offers the contrast, in terms of lightness and darkness, that creates perspective.

6. Describe two ways to attract the attention of the audience with your creation.
   Make the creation more visual; make it original; make it useful.

7. List two ways to get unstuck during the creative process.
   Any two of these: (1) Step back; (2) review your planning; (3) define the hang-up; (4) list ways around the problem; (5) think upside-down; (6) change your scenery; (7) ask for a second opinion; (8) take small steps; (9) work on a new part; (10) get away.

Reflect: Which strategy or guideline from this chapter do you find most useful, and why?
Answers will vary.

242

Review: Improving

Name _____ Date _____

Your Turn Answer the following questions to review what you've learned about improving your work.

1. Explain how a project planning sheet relates to a rubric.
   Your planning sheet established your goal and objectives. The rubric sheet revisits those goals and objectives, with the purpose of evaluating how well you met them.

2. Explain your role as the presenter in a peer-review session.
   The role of the presenter is to outline the specifics of your project to the responder, and then read and review the responder's feedback, before deciding whether or not to make any changes.

3. Explain the responder's role during a peer-review session.
   The role of the responder is to bring a new perspective the project by giving helpful feedback to the presenter.

4. Which two of the following activities are **critical** improvements?
   a. Cutting   c. Reworking
   b. Rearranging   d. Adding

5. Which two of the following activities are **creative** improvements?
   a. Cutting   c. Reworking
   b. Rearranging   d. Adding

Reflect: When it comes to making improvements to a work in progress, what do you do best? Which improvement activities do you need to work on?
   Answers will vary.

248

Review: Presenting

Name _____ Date _____

Your Turn Answer each of the following questions.

1. What questions should you consider before presenting your work?
   Who will interact with your work? What do you want the audience to get from this experience? Where will you present your work? When will you present your work? Why do you want to present your work? How will your work be presented?

2. Which do you prefer to use for an oral presentation: note cards, an outline, a slide show, or a manuscript? Explain.
   Answers will vary.

3. Why do you think people post their work online?
   Answers will vary. Sample response: A person might present her or his work online to inform, to entertain, to persuade, or to invite discussion.

4. What are the pros and cons of posting your work on a public online site?
   Pros: Broad audience and professional presentation of material
   Cons: Give up some rights, privacy concerns, and spam and advertisements

5. How can you use social media to promote your work?
   Any of these: Share a link to your project on your social network; upload your project to a social network or personal blog; create a group or event on Facebook; send an email or direct message to friends and family; write microblogs containing updates about your project; comment on someone else's blog; post a comment on a message board relate to your project's topic.

Part III:
Developing Projects (Lesson Plans)

The best way to learn critical thinking is to have something to think critically about. The best way to develop inquiry skills is to use them to create something new. Part III of *Inquire* provides guidelines and models for dozens of projects that help students hone these skills while learning about content.

The chapters in this section are not meant to be taught straight through. Instead, you and your students may pick and choose the projects that work best for you. That's why these lessons have a unique set of components.

- Learning outcomes and standards correlations
- Team teaching suggestions
- Project suggestions for science, math, English, and social studies

Part III:
Developing Projects

Chapter 28
Basic Writing Projects

(*Inquire* pages 431–456)

Some people describe writing as a soft skill, but writing is greatly valued in higher education and beyond. The ability to write clearly is an indicator of a strong communicator, a skill coveted by job recruiters. Clear, focused writing isn't easy writing. It is a craft that must be honed through practice and repetition. This chapter introduces the essential writing forms students need to master to succeed as 21st century communicators.

Learning Outcomes

- Question the writing situation.
- Use the inquiry process to complete writing tasks.
- Write for subject areas across the curriculum.
- Produce clear and coherent writing.
- Use paragraphs to build essays.
- Learn the essential forms of business writing.

Correlations

Common Core State Standards		
ELA-Literacy.CCRA.R.1–10	ELA-Literacy.CCRA.L.1–6	Science.Practice.SP1–4
ELA-Literacy.CCRA.W.1–10	Math.Practice.MP3	Science.Practice.SP6–8
ELA-Literacy.CCRA.SL.1–6	Math.Practice.MP5–7	

Partnership for 21st Century Skills	
Creativity and Innovation (All standards)	**Information Literacy; Media Literacy** (All standards)
Critical Thinking and Problem Solving (All standards)	**Information and Communication Technologies Literacy** (All standards)
Communication and Collaboration (All standards)	

International Society for Technology in Education	
1. Creativity and Innovation (All standards)	**4. Critical Thinking, Problem Solving, and Decision Making** (All standards)
2. Communication and Collaboration (All standards)	**5. Digital Citizenship** (All standards)
3. Research and Information Fluency (All standards)	**6. Technology Operations and Concepts** (All standards)

Team-Teaching Suggestions

Writing lends itself to team teaching across the curriculum. You will notice that some of the projects in this chapter deal with highly literary forms (poems and narratives). Both forms can be used outside the English classroom. However, you may wish to team up with a teacher who is more studied in these forms as you move forward with these projects. Below you will find additional team-teaching ideas.

An English or Language Arts Partner

An English or language arts teacher makes an ideal partner for a basic writing project. Collaborating with an English teacher could help answer your questions about grammar and other literary issues. Likewise, you could learn tips for evaluating and grading student writing. Conversely, a partnership could also be valuable for English and language arts teachers, who could seize an opportunity to teach writing outside of a strictly language arts or literary context. This partnership could be beneficial for all parties involved and would work well with all the projects in this chapter, especially **poems**, **essays**, and **narratives**.

A Library or Media Specialist Partner

If your writing project involves library or Internet research, you may consider a partnership with a library or media specialist. This person is an expert on Internet research, including using search engines and navigating academic journals and databases for research subjects. In addition, students would gain a better understanding of the print offerings available at your library. This partnership would likely require class time in the library or at your school's computer lab. Each of the projects in this chapter would benefit from such a partnership, especially for longer forms of writing like **essays** and **narratives**.

A Business or Economics Partner

This chapter deals with three staples of business and professional communication: **email**, **proposals**, and **business letters**. Team teaching with a business or economics teacher would help you provide better context for this type of writing. In addition, this type of partner might be able to demonstrate real-world examples of business writing. Finally, he or she may have tips for using best practices of business and email correspondence.

Social Studies Basic Writing Projects

U.S. History

Summary
Summarize an important speech from American history.

Poem
Write a poem about an important landmark in American history.

Proposal
Write a research project proposal for a topic in U.S. history.

Narrative
Write a historical narrative from the perspective of general, soldier, or volunteer during the Civil War.

Informative Essay
Write an informative essay about an important moment or event in the women's rights movement between 1848 and the present.

World History

Summary
Summarize the key events of the Industrial Revolution.

Poem
Write an ode to a sympathetic figure in world history.

Narrative
Write a fictional narrative about living in Germany during the fall of the Berlin Wall.

Proposal
Write a proposal for a research project involving an important event or period in world history.

Informative Essay
Write an essay about the evolution of allegiances during World War I.

Government and Civics

Summary
Write a summary of a proposed bill in your state's current legislative session.

Professional Email
Write an email message to your local state representative about an accomplishment or particular need at your school.

Business Letter
Write a business letter promoting a cause to a member of your city's city council.

Business Letter
Write a letter applying to volunteer for a political campaign you are interested in.

Informative Essay
Write an informative essay explaining the purpose of the electoral college and why it was formed.

Current Events

Summary
Read and summarize a key news story from the front page of today's newspaper.

Paragraph
Write a paragraph that identifies a current event you want to know more about and explains why.

Email
Write a professional email message to your instructor that includes a link to an interesting story or article on a current event. Explain why your instructor should share the story with your class.

Informative Essay
Write an informative essay that recounts the details of an important current event and predicts how it will end.

Science Basic Writing Projects

Biology/Physical Science

Summary
Summarize the general functions of RNA.

Professional Email
Write a professional email to a local meteorologist asking about the factors influencing the climate in your area.

Paragraph
Write a paragraph that describes what you see as you perform a dissection.

Proposal
Create a proposal for a biology research project or a new biology lab report.

Informative Essay
Research and write an informative essay about an infectious disease.

Narrative
Write a fictional narrative from the perspective of a red blood cell, describing its life as part of the vascular system.

Chemistry

Summary
Summarize the concept of electronegativity.

Paragraph
Write a paragraph on the reactivity of aluminium.

Poem
Write a poem about one of the periodic elements.

Proposal
Write a proposal for a science fair project on a chemistry topic or for a new classroom chemistry experiment.

Informative Essay
Write an informative essay on modern atomic theory, describing the contributions made by scientists in its development.

Physics

Summary
Search for an article in a scientific magazine or journal on a physics topic. Summarize the article.

Paragraph
Write a paragraph explaining the outcome/results of your latest physics experiment.

Proposal
Write a proposal for a new physics lab experiment to be performed in your classroom or on your school's campus.

Poem
Write a poem about Pi to celebrate Pi Day on March 14 (3.14).

Informative Essay
Research and write an informative essay describing a Feynman Diagram.

Math Basic Writing Projects

Algebra/Trigonometry

Summary
Write a paragraph summarizing the concept of absolute value.

Paragraph
Write a paragraph explaining a concept you are learning in your algebra or trigonometry class.

Professional Email
Write a professional email to the admissions department of a college or university you would like to attend, inquiring about the math requirements needed for admittance.

Narrative
Start an algebra diary to log your thoughts, feelings, and questions about the concepts you learn in class. Update it regularly, when ideas are still fresh in your mind.

Informative Essay
Write an informative essay describing how trigonometry concepts such as sine and cosine are used in land surveys.

Geometry

Paragraph
Write a paragraph that explains how to find the angle measurements of a polygon.

Summary
Write a paragraph summarizing the concept of congruent triangles.

Professional Email
Write a professional email to a classmate summarizing a concept in geometry in your own words.

Poem
Write a free-verse poem about a concept you are learning in geometry.

Informative Essay
Write an informative essay on the relationship between geometry and art.

Proposal
Write a project proposal for your geometry class.

Probability and Statistics

Paragraph
Write a paragraph that explains the measures of central tendency.

Summary
Find a current news, business, politics, entertainment, or sports article that involves probability or statistics. Summarize the article and the probability or statistics involved in it.

Informative Essay
Research large data sets at census.gov or fedstats.gov. Compare statistics from your city or state to national averages. Report your findings in an informative essay.

Informative Essay
Research and write an informative essay on the use of probability and statistics in the business of finance and economics.

English Basic Writing Projects

Grammar and Composition

Paragraph

Write a paragraph that explains the proper usage of *its* and *it's*. The paragraphs should include examples that show your knowledge of their proper usage.

Summary

Summarize an article or passage from a book by one of your favorite writers. In your summary, explain the author's writing style and what you enjoy about it.

Business Letter

Write a business letter applying for your dream job. In it, explain your qualifications and why you desire the job.

Poem

Write a poem about something at a grocery store.

Informative Essay

Write an informative essay on what citizenship means in the 21st century.

Narrative

Write a short story.

American/British Literature

Summary

Summarize the key plot points of a piece of American or British literature.

Paragraph

Write a persuasive paragraph in which you take a stance on a character's decision in a piece of literature you are reading for class.

Proposal

Write a project or research proposal for your English or literature course.

Poem

Write a Shakespearean or Petrarchan sonnet.

Informative Essay

Write a critique of a novel or poem you read in your English class.

Narrative

Write a short story from the perspective of a character from one of your favorite novels.

Reading and Literary Analysis

Summary

Write a summary of a piece of writing's narrative structure (see *Inquire* page 411).

Proposal

Write a proposal for a new class reading selection.

Poem

Write a free-verse poem about a reading selection from your class.

Narrative

Write a narrative using the same setting as one from another famous or well-known novel.

Informative Essay

Analyze the theme of a novel or reading selection from your class. Your essay should point to places in the reading selection that demonstrate that particular theme.

Chapter 29
Advanced Writing Projects

(Inquire pages 457–486)

The basic writing projects from the last chapter are the foundation for successful writing. Here, students must deepen their thinking and explore ideas more thoroughly in advanced writing projects. The projects in this chapter challenge students to think more critically, more creatively, and more logically. Two-part essays such as cause-effect are addressed as are literary analysis and research papers.

Learning Outcomes

- Learn to question the writing situation.
- Understand advanced forms of writing.
- Learn to follow the inquiry process to complete advanced-writing tasks.
- Understand critical thinking, creative thinking, and problem solving in writing.
- Learn how to develop ideas thoroughly.

Correlations

Common Core State Standards		
ELA-Literacy.CCRA.R.1–10	ELA-Literacy.CCRA.L.1–6	Science.Practice.SP1–4
ELA-Literacy.CCRA.W.1–10	Math.Practice.MP1	Science.Practice.SP6–8
ELA-Literacy.CCRA.SL.1–6	Math.Practice.MP3–7	

Partnership for 21st Century Skills	
Creativity and Innovation (All standards)	**Information Literacy; Media Literacy** (All standards)
Critical Thinking and Problem Solving (All standards)	**Life and Career Skills** (All standards)
Communication and Collaboration (All standards)	

International Society for Technology in Education	
1. **Creativity and Innovation** (All standards)	3. **Research and Information Fluency** (All standards)
2. **Communication and Collaboration** (All standards)	4. **Critical Thinking, Problem Solving, and Decision Making** (All standards)

Team-Teaching Suggestions

The advanced writing projects in this chapter are large-scale projects that offer many opportunities for collaboration. The projects require students to explore complex ideas; use a variety of research methods; and write clearly, correctly, and persuasively. Below are suggestions for using teacher partnerships to administer the projects in this chapter.

A Library or Media Specialist

If you, as an instructor, are not well versed in advanced research techniques, you may find a partnership with a library or media specialist helpful. All of the projects in this chapter require students to use a variety of print and Web resources to explore topics more fully. A media specialist can impart her or his expertise on advanced research techniques for your students, including tips for exploring content-rich Web resources. In addition, a library specialist can aid students in their search for print resources available in your school's library.

An English or Language Arts Partner

If your advanced writing project involves a writing form that you are not familiar with, you may find it helpful to collaborate with an English or language arts specialist. Since most of the projects in this chapter deal with research, an English partner could aid you in teaching students how to integrate sources within their writing and how to avoid plagiarism. In addition, this person would be helpful for questions about guiding and evaluating writing. This partnership would work best with **cause-effect essays, comparison-contrast essays, argument essays, problem-solution essays, literary analysis**, and **research papers**.

A Science/Math Partner

When a project topic is related to a specific content area, especially one in science or math, an appropriate content-area teacher should be involved. This teacher can offer advice about understanding the topic, conducting research, assisting in experiments, and so on. She or he can also check the validity and accuracy of the findings in the finished product.

English Advanced Writing Projects

Composition

Comparison-Contrast Essay
Create an essay that compares and contrasts two different neighborhoods in your hometown.

Argument Essay
Argue for or against the use of drones by the U.S. Department of Defense in other parts of the world.

Problem-Solution Essay
Write an essay about a problem facing today's high school students. End the essay by offering a reasonable solution.

Research Paper
Write a research paper on a significant person or an event that happened on your birthday.

American Literature

Cause-Effect Essay
Analyze the causes and effects of the naturalism movement in American literature.

Comparison-Contrast Essay
Write an essay comparing and contrasting American novels or authors.

Literary Analysis
Analyze Mark Twain's depiction of Jim in *Huck Finn.*

Research Paper
Write a research paper about a famous American author. The paper should consider how real events from the author's life influenced her or his writing.

British/World Literature

Cause-Effect Essay
Explore one part of a cause-effect theme in Homer's the *Iliad* or *Odyssey.*

Comparison-Contrast Essay
Compare and contrast Petrarchan sonnets to Shakespearean sonnets.

Comparison-Contrast Essay
Choose two pieces of British literature. Compare and contrast how the two pieces portray men and women.

Literary Analysis
Analyze "gender" and "chivalry" in *Le Morte d' Arthur* by Sir Thomas Malory.

Argument Essay
Construct an essay that sympathizes with an anti-hero or villain from a piece of British or world literature.

English I and II

Cause-Effect Essay
Write about the causes and effects of an event that changed your perspective on life.

Comparison-Contrast Essay
Write a comparison-contrast essay comparing heroines from two different novels.

Problem-Solution Essay
Write a problem-solution essay that describes a problem in your community and offers a solution.

Literary Analysis
Write a literary analysis of a theme from Shakespeare's *Romeo and Juliet.*

Science Advanced Writing Projects

Physical Science

Cause-Effect Essay
Write about the causes and effects of a natural disaster.

Comparison-Contrast Essay
Compare and contrast the merits of biodiesel, oil, and natural gas.

Lab Report
Write a lab report in which you test the density of liquids.

Comparison-Contrast Essay
Write an essay comparing and contrasting transverse and longitudinal waves.

Argumentative Essay
Write an argument essay that supports or opposes the practice of fracking as a means of obtaining natural gas.

Lab Report
Write a lab report on using matchstick rockets to observe Newton's laws of motion.

Biology

Comparison-Contrast Essay
Write an essay comparing and contrasting white blood cells to red blood cells.

Lab Report
Write a lab report based on the dissection of a sea cucumber. Include a diagram of its parts in your report.

Problem-Solution Essay
Write an essay in which you examine the loss of biodiversity in a specific ecosystem and offer a solution for preventing future losses.

Cause-Effect Essay
Write an essay describing the causes and effects of natural selection.

Comparison-Contrast Essay
Write an essay comparing and contrasting diffusion and osmosis.

Research Paper/Report
Write a research paper on the human genome project.

Chemistry / Physics

Comparison-Contrast Essay
Write an essay that compares and contrasts metals, non-metals, and metalloid elements.

Cause-Effect Essay
Explore the cause-effect relationship between the molality of solute in a solution and the solution's freezing point or boiling point elevation.

Lab Report
Create an effective lab report for an experiment in your chemistry or physics class.

Research Paper / Report
Explore a recent development in quantum physics. Research as much as you can about it and report your findings in a research paper.

Math Advanced Writing Projects

Algebra / Trigonometry

Comparison-Contrast Essay

Write an essay comparing and contrasting the graphing of a linear inequality versus graphing a linear equation. Show examples.

Cause-Effect Essay

Use algebra to explore the causal relationship between outside temperature, inside temperature, and electricity bills. Report your findings in a cause-effect essay.

Argumentative Essay

Argue for or against the truthfulness of the following statement: "Algebra matters in the real world."

Compare-Contrast Essay

Write an essay comparing and contrasting the different methods for calculating irrational decimal place values of the constant Pi.

Research Report

Write a research report on the background and history of the Pythagorean Theorem.

Probability and Statistics

Cause-Effect Essay

Examine the causes and effects of omitted-variable bias in relation to economics.

Argument Essay

Choose your favorite sport. Write an argument essay that uses statistics to make a case for one athlete being the greatest of all time in that sport (i.e.: *The greatest football player of all time is…*).

Comparison-Contrast Essay

Research and study the use of probability and statistics in two different careers. Report on your findings in a comparison-contrast essay.

Problem-Solution Essay

Write an essay in which you describe a difficult probability or statistics question and explain the steps for solving it.

Geometry

Comparison-Contrast Essay

Write an essay comparing and contrasting different types of quadrilaterals.

Lab Report

Create an experiment that explores projectile motion with unit vectors. Write a lab report to publish your findings.

Argument Essay

Some schools require students to take math courses in this order: Algebra I, Geometry, and Algebra II. Other schools prefer this order: Algebra I, Algebra II, and Geometry. Write an essay that explains why one sequence is preferable to the other.

Research Paper / Report

Explore the concept of Euclidean geometry. Learn about its history and report your findings in a research paper or report.

Social Studies Advanced Writing Projects

U.S. History

Problem-Solution Essay

Study health problems experienced by soldiers during the American Revolution. What solutions were attempted to remedy the problems? How effective were the solutions? What solution worked best? Report your findings in a problem-solution essay.

Cause-Effect Essay

Write an essay exploring the causes and effects of the United States' involvement in the Korean War.

Literary Analysis

Write a literary analysis exploring *education, knowledge, ignorance,* or *empathy* in *Narrative of the Life of Fredrick Douglass, an American Slave.*

Research Paper

Use a variety of primary and secondary resources to write a research paper on the birth of America as a world empire.

U.S. Government / Civics

Argumentative Essay

Imagine you could steal attributes (leadership style, policies, character traits, etc.) from any U.S. president and combine them to mold the ideal president. Write an argumentative essay in which you describe which attributes you would steal from which president(s) and why.

Cause-Effect Essay

Research significant Supreme Court cases from the 1960s. Choose one case and write an essay about its causes and effects.

Comparison-Contrast Essay

Research and write an essay in which you compare and contrast the concept of democracy in two different countries.

Problem-Solution Essay

Brainstorm problems with the current political environment in the United States. Use historical evidence and visionary thinking to come up with a solution. Write a problem-solution essay based on your findings.

World History

Cause-Effect Essay

Write a cause-effect essay exploring the causes and lasting impacts of the Glorious Revolution in the British Isles.

Compare-Contrast Essay

Write an essay comparing British or French colonialism to the current role of the United States in foreign affairs. How is it the same? How is it different?

Literary Analysis

Read one of the Four Books and Five Classics used in Confucianism studies. Write a literary analysis in which you explore the influence of the teachings on Chinese culture.

Research Paper

Write a research paper about a significant revolution or demonstration and its impact on world history.

Chapter 30
Data and Graphing Projects

(*Inquire* pages 487–506)

In an age of information overload, graphic analysis and presentation are increasingly important. This chapter provides students an overview of the graphic tools available for their use to present information graphically. They will learn how to create graphs, tables, diagrams, time lines, and more.

Learning Outcomes
- Create pie, line, and bar graphs.
- Create tables.
- Create diagrams, time lines, and flowcharts.
- Create infographics.
- Perform data mining.

Correlations

Common Core State Standards

ELA-Literacy.CCRA.R.1–3	ELA-Literacy.CCRA.SL.1–6	Math.Practice.MP1–7
ELA-Literacy.CCRA.R.7–10	ELA-Literacy.CCRA.L.1–6	Science.Practice.SP1–8
ELA-Literacy.CCRA.W.1–10		

Partnership for 21st Century Skills Common Core State Standards

Creativity and Innovation (All standards)	**Information Literacy** (All standards)
Critical Thinking and Problem Solving (All standards)	**Media Literacy** (All standards)
Communication and Collaboration (All standards)	**Life and Career Skills** (All standards)

International Society for Technology in Education

1. **Creativity and Innovation** (All standards)	3. **Research and Information Fluency** (All standards)
2. **Communication and Collaboration** (All standards)	4. **Critical Thinking, Problem Solving, and Decision Making** (All standards)

Team-Teaching Suggestions

The expression "can't see the forest for the trees" has been around for a long time. Nevertheless, it is especially apt today. The sheer mass of information available means students can get lost in details and miss the grander scope of things. Data and graphing projects help students sort out all the details and present them in effective ways. Team teaching can help students make the best use of data in graphic formats.

A Math Partner

Math teachers are well practiced in presenting information graphically. Tools commonly associated with math include **pie charts**, **line graphs**, **bar graphs**, and **tables**. They are also well prepared to help students with the logic of **flowcharts**. In addition, a math partner can be of great aid as students perform **data-mining** projects.

A Social Studies Partner

A social studies teacher can help to put knowledge within a historical or cultural context using **time lines**, **line graphs**, **pie graphs**, and **line graphs.** They are all common tools for presenting historical information. Social studies teachers can also be of aid in developing more modern infographics that capture and present a grand picture.

A Media Specialist or Computer Science Partner

Many computer tools now exist for analyzing and presenting data. Even word-processing programs now integrate with spreadsheet programs and with basic drawing software, making integration of text and graphics easier than ever before. What's more, the rise of cloud computing makes ever more data readily available to students.

A media specialist or computer science teacher can train students to put these tools to best use creating **pie charts**, **line graphs**, **bar graphs**, **tables**, **diagrams**, **time lines**, **flowcharts**, and **infographics**, and performing **data mining**. Meanwhile, the teaching partner can focus on the larger picture—the gathering and analysis of data.

Math Data and Graphing Projects

Geometry

Infographic

Research the five regular solids, discovering where they came from and finding real-world examples of each. Create an infographic describing these five solids.

Bar Graph

Do a geometry scavenger hunt in your classroom or school, looking for plane and solid geometric forms: circles and spheres, squares and cubes, rhombuses and diamonds, and so on. Create a bar graph comparing the frequency of occurrence for each form. What patterns do you notice?

Algebra

Line Graph

Calculate answers to a series of quadratic equations. Map each result on a line graph. Note which variables and constants affect which dimensions of the resulting parabolas.

Infographic

Create an infographic, using what you discovered in the project above. The infographic should teach others about quadratic equations and parabolas. Use words, graphics, and numerical values to clearly communicate the concepts.

Mathematics

Line Graph

Investigate the sales history of Lays brand potato chips since the 1980s. Create a line graph mapping sales. Create a similar line graph for competitors to Lays.

Pie Graph

Research the federal budget for the current year, listing the main areas of expense. Create a pie graph showing the proportion of the budget used by each budget item.

Bar Graph

Roll two six-sided dice 100 times, recording each result. Plot the results on a bar graph, comparing the number of times that each numerical value from 2 to 12 resulted. Report on any patterns you see and the reason for them.

Statistics

Table

Create a table that lists the age and height of a sampling of students from your school. Try to get height measurements from multiple grades so that you have a range of ages.

Scatter Diagram

Create two scatter diagrams to plot the information you found in your table above. Use one diagram to plot the ages and heights of male students and the other to plot the ages and heights of female students. Run age across the X axis and height up the Y axis, and then plot points. What trend do you see in the points? Are age and height positively correlated? What differences are there between the two diagrams?

Science Data and Graphing Projects

Space Science

Pie Graph

Investigate the geological ages of the moon. Make a pie graph demonstrating those lunar changes.

Investigate the geological ages of the earth. Make another pie graph demonstrating those terrain changes.

Size the pie charts proportionately and superimpose the moon chart over the earth chart.

Discuss differences and similarities in the development of the moon and earth.

Stacked Bar Graph

Research the elemental composition of our solar system's eight planets. Create a stacked bar graph comparing the composition of those planets side-by-side, as percentages of each planet.

Make a second stacked bar graph that compares the composition of the four inner planets in terms of total volume.

Do the same for the four outer planets.

Biology

Time Line

Research a significant breakthrough, discovery, or change related to biological science. Learn as much as you can about the chronology of your topic. You will want to discover what happened and when. Then compile a time line that shows the critical actions or events related to your topic.

Pie Graph

Research the biomass of the earth—the total weight of living things on the planet. Discover how much of the biomass is attributable to microorganisms, how much to plants, and how much to animals. Create a pie graph to show the result of your research.

Discover how much of the animal biomass is attributable to insects, fish, birds, amphibians, reptiles, mammals, and "other." Create a pie graph to show the result of your research.

Infographic

Build an infographic about biomass, incorporating the two pie graphs you created above as well as other graphics, images, words, and statistics.

Science

Infographic

In a small group, brainstorm a list of sciences. Be as thorough as possible.

Using a cluster or outline, organize those sciences by their relationships to one another.

Research the origins of each field of science.

Create an infographic that shows how our current fields of scientific inquiry descended from earlier fields of scientific study.

Include major historical milestones from other disciplines, such as the arts, in the margins of your infographic.

Social Studies Data and Graphing Projects

World History

Table

Choose two major cities from a historical period you are studying. (They could be ancient cities such as Babylon and Troy, or modern ones like London and Paris.)

Create a table comparing features of the cities, such as their origins, their longevity, their populations, their major trades, and so on.

Infographic

Use the two tables that you created above to develop an infographic comparing the two cities. Draw data from the tables to generate other graphics such as pie graphs, bar graphs, and time lines to make the comparisons visual and vivid.

Stacked Bar Graph

Investigate the origins of the domestication of cattle. Create a stacked bar graph that shows the expansion of cattle raising, continent by continent, from prehistory to today.

Pie Graph

Investigate the major oil producers on the globe, noting the number of barrels produced per year. Make a pie graph showing total oil production and the proportion produced by the top five producers (and "others").

U.S. History

Flowchart

Review the "EMR Flowchart" on page 499. Research the possible paths a bill must take in your state government to become law. Create a flowchart illustrating that process. Have another student check your flowchart for possible errors or unclear steps. Publish your flowchart online, in a blog, or elsewhere.

Line Graph

Study immigration records in your community, county, and/or state as far back as you can go. Look specifically for immigration trends for different ethnic groups. Create a line graph tracking the number of immigrants from different groups arriving each year/decade over a period of time.

Pie Graph

Study income figures for the United States, seeking the number of households at different levels of income:

- $0 to $49,999
- $50,000 to $99,999
- $100,000 to $149,999
- $150,000 to $199,999,
- $200,000 to $249,999

Create a pie graph to show your results.

Ancient History

Time Line

Investigate the major periods in human history, from the Neolithic Age to present time. Create a time line that shows the progression.

Line Graph

Research the growth of human populations over the course of history, from the Neolithic Age to the present. Create a line graph showing the fluctuations of human populations over that time period.

Infographic

Use the time line and line graph you developed above to create an infographic that tracks the periods and populations in human history.

English Data and Graphing Projects

World Literature

Infographic

Choose a novel with a plot that covers at least a few years of events. *Angle of Repose* and *The Count of Monte Cristo* are two possible examples. Read the novel.

Create a poster-style infographic that uses a time line on the left, major events from the novel in the middle, and historical notes or other notes of interest along the right.

Display your poster in class or publish an electronic copy online.

Word Cloud

Choose a piece of literature that is available in the public domain, such as material from Shakespeare, Ovid, the Bible, Milton, Melville, Poe, or other famous sources. Read the selection and write a journal entry on your thoughts about the passage.

Block copy and paste the material into a word-cloud program. Consider the word cloud in light of your journal entry.

Write a new journal entry indicating whether the word cloud supports your previous impressions or presents new ideas and thoughts to you.

Reading

Line Graph

Investigate the history of reading over the past 1,000 years: What percentage of the population has been literate century by century? Create a line graph showing those percentages.

Bar Graph

Research the current literacy rates in English speaking nations: the U.S., Canada, the U.K., Ireland, Australia, and New Zealand. Create a bar graph showing the current literacy rates of these nations. Reflect on reasons for any differences you see.

Stacked Bar Graph

Investigate what people are reading (fiction and nonfiction) in English speaking nations: the U.S., Canada, the U.K., Ireland, Australia, and New Zealand. Create a stacked bar graph that shows the types of reading by nation.

Infographic

Combine the three graphs above into a poster-style infographic, reporting on the history of reading, current literacy across the English speaking world, and current reading patterns. Add other graphics, words, and figures to draw conclusions.

Writing

Spreadsheet

In each class throughout your day, record the amount of time you spend writing. Compile the figures into a spreadsheet or table of data.

Bar Graph

Using the data from your spreadsheet or table above, create a bar graph that indicates the amount of time spent writing in each class.

Chapter 31
Audio-Visual Projects

(Inquire pages 507–526)

With today's explosion of affordable audio and video recorders, powerful editing software, and portable computers, students can easily record, produce, and publish their own multimedia works. Instead of being just consumers of media, they become producers. This chapter provides many example projects and instructions to help them do just that.

Learning Outcomes
- Create slide shows.
- Create a Pecha Kucha presentation.
- Create "how-to" videos.
- Create public service announcement videos.
- Create documentaries.

Correlations

Common Core State Standards

ELA-Literacy.CCRA.R.4–10	ELA-Literacy.CCRA.SL.1–6	Math.Practice.MP1–8
ELA-Literacy.CCRA.W.1–10	ELA-Literacy.CCRA.L.3–6	Science.Practice.SP1–8

Partnership for 21st Century Skills

Creativity and Innovation
- Think Creatively
- Work Creatively with Others
- Implement Innovations

Critical Thinking and Problem Solving
- Reason Effectively and Use Systems Thinking
- Solve Problems

Communication and Collaboration
- Communicate Clearly
- Collaborate with Others

Information and Media Literacy
- Use and Manage Information

Media Literacy
- Analyze Media
- Create Media Products

Information and Communication Technologies Literacy
- Apply Technology Effectively

Life and Career Skills
- Flexibility and Adaptability
- Initiative and Self-Direction
- Productivity and Accountability
- Leadership and Responsibility

International Society for Technology in Education

1. **Creativity and Innovation**
   (All standards)
2. **Communication and Collaboration**
   (All standards)
3. **Research and Information Fluency**
   (All standards)
4. **Critical Thinking, Problem Solving, and Decision Making**
   (All standards)
5. **Digital Citizenship**
   (All standards)
6. **Technology Operations and Concepts**
   (All standards)

Team-Teaching Suggestions

Audio-visual projects allow students to marry their knowledge of a subject with their 21st century media-making skills. When posted online, such projects help students to view themselves as part of the knowledge-making community and as lifelong learners. Students also begin to see the practical value of what they are learning. All of this makes an audio-visual project a great tool for studying core subjects and for team teaching.

A Science Partner

A science partner might help students prepare a **video podcast** to demonstrate a scientific principle in action. **Slide shows** are also effective tools for presenting research results, while a **Pecha Kucha presentation** might be used for a public demonstration of a scientific concept.

Students can also be encouraged to indulge their scientific curiosity by preparing a **documentary** about ongoing research at a university or a corporate laboratory. (This can also make them better aware of career opportunities in science.)

Finally, students might make a **how-to video** about an experimental process or give lab-safety instruction in a **public-service announcement**.

A Social Studies Partner

A social studies partner can help students to prepare a **podcast** reporting on an important current event or a historical figure. (Many example podcasts can be found online for inspiration.) This teacher might also arrange an evening of **slide shows** or **Pecha Kucha presentations** for public edification and to let parents know what their students are studying.

More ambitious projects might include video **documentaries** about historical topics, **public-service announcements** about current events, or **how-to videos** presenting solutions to current social problems.

An Arts Partner

Whatever your subject matter, an arts partner can help students with production values of an audio-visual project. A music teacher can make students aware of the importance and effects of background music or other sound in an **audio podcast**. Visual arts teachers can help students to design slides for a **slide show** or a **Pecha Kucha presentation**, making sure visuals aid in communication rather than detract from it. A drama instructor or photographer can provide guidance for producing video projects such as **documentaries**, **public-service announcements**, and **how-to videos**.

Social Studies Audio-Visual Projects

World History

Podcast
Create a podcast that tells the story of an important historical figure, introducing the person to an unfamiliar audience.

Pecha Kucha Presentation
Create a Pecha Kucha presentation explaining the history of an empire.

Documentary
Make a documentary about an invention that has affected the entire world.

Public-Service Announcement
Develop a message to prepare time travelers for visiting a historical event of your choice.

How-To Video
Make a video showing how citizens can set up a new representative democracy.

World Geography

Slide Show
Use public domain photos (wikimedia.org or flicker.com/creativecommons) to create a slide show about a major geographical feature you would like to visit.

Documentary
Make a documentary about a geographical feature close to your own home.

Public-Service Announcement
Make a public-service announcement about the hazards of earthquakes, volcanos, or other geographical dangers specific to a particular locale.

How-To Video
Create a video showing how to prepare for travel to a geographical feature that is not easily accessible.

American History

Podcast
Make a podcast explaining a significant event from American history to people from foreign lands.

Slide Show or Documentary
Prepare a slide show or a documentary about Civil War reenactors. Include details of how they became involved in the hobby, how they prepare their equipment, and what battles they portray. If possible, compare reenactors near you to those in a different region.

How-To Video
Choose a period from American history and make a video showing how to accomplish a common task from that time (such as plowing a field by horse or building a log cabin).

American Government

Podcast
Create a podcast in which two or more people debate an issue currently being considered by local or national government. Include a moderator to keep the discussion moving smoothly.

Pecha Kucha Presentation
Make a Pecha Kucha presentation explaining how decisions are made and implemented by your county board. Be sure to request permission of the board to take pictures during the proceedings.

Public-Service Announcement
Create a public-service announcement encouraging people to vote. Address any reasons they might have for not voting.

Science Audio-Visual Projects

Earth Science

Slide Show

Create a slide show revealing how natural fires play a role in the health of some forests.

Pecha Kucha Presentation

Make a Pecha Kucha presentation about geothermal energy produced in Iceland or elsewhere on the globe.

Documentary

Make a documentary about a waterway of your choice, explaining the role it plays for the region.

Public-Service Announcement

Create a public-service announcement about the role an endangered species plays in the overall biosphere.

How-To Video

Make a how-to video explaining safety procedures to use during an extreme weather event or another sort of natural disaster.

Biology

Podcast

Make a podcast explaining why it is important for people to understand the basics of cellular function or some other aspect of biological science taught in high school.

Documentary

Create a documentary debating the use of laboratory animals in scientific research. Be sure to fairly portray all sides of the issue. If possible, include interviews of experts on the subject.

Public-Service Announcement

Make a public-service announcement that educates people about the importance of using prescription medicines correctly. (Possible topics might include creation of "super-bug" microorganisms when antibiotics are used incorrectly and tainting of public water supplies when medications are disposed of improperly.)

Space Science

Podcast

Create a podcast about the latest developments in space exploration. If possible, make this an ongoing project rather than a single episode.

Pecha Kucha Presentation

Make a Pecha Kucha presentation about a past or future space mission, explaining how it was conceived and carried out.

Public-Service Announcement

Explain the benefits of space science to other fields of study and to our society in general.

How-To Video

Create a video explaining how to build and operate a model rocket or other space-related project.

Math Audio-Visual Projects

Algebra

Podcast

Make a podcast exploring the idea of discussing algebra with a creature from an alien civilization. Would all civilizations develop algebra in a similar way? Would all separate algebra, trigonometry, and geometry as we do, or would they divide them differently?

Slide Show

Create a slide show that demonstrates how to factor binomial equations.

Documentary

Make a documentary that explores the origins of algebra in history. Explain elements that drove its development. Also include examples of how algebra plays a role in daily life.

How-To Video

Develop a series of how-to videos that demonstrate the workings of algebraic equations you have learned.

Trigonometry

Podcast

Make a podcast discussing common uses of trigonometry in our society.

Slide Show

Make a slide show comparing historical methods for quickly referencing sine, cosine, and tangent. Include tables, slide rules, and modern calculators, as well as equations for calculating these values exactly.

Pecha Kucha Presentation

Create a Pecha Kucha presentation that explains the origins and current applications of trigonometry. Present it to your family and friends. Hold a question and answer session afterward.

Public-Service Announcement

Make a public-service announcement advocating effective ways to further interest female students in mathematics. Feature in your PSA applications of trigonometry.

Calculus

Podcast

Interview someone who works in banking, insurance, or some other financial field, asking them to describe the role of calculus in their work.

Slide Show

Create a slide show for beginning calculus students, showing them the sorts of things they will learn in their study.

Pecha Kucha Presentation

Make a Pecha Kucha presentation revealing how some particularly interesting feature of calculus was developed.

How-To Video

Prepare a how-to video that demonstrates how to calculate and graph a function of your choice.

English Audio-Visual Projects

Writing Process

Podcast
Create an ongoing podcast that explores the many uses of writing in careers today. Be sure to cover the ways in which teams of people—writers, editors, and proofreaders, among others—work together to take a piece from initial concept to polished publication.

Slide Show
Create a slide show that teaches the steps in the writing process. Include advice for best practices at each stage.

Documentary
Make a series of documentaries about famous fiction and nonfiction writers, revealing what they have to say about their own writing process.

Public-Service Announcement
Create a public-service announcement about the importance of the writing process. Include apt quotations from famous figures. (Such quotations can easily be found online.)

American Literature

Podcast
Create a podcast series in which you read or perform favorite works of American literature in the public domain. This can be a great project for a team of people. Each podcast can be one short story, one chapter from a book, a scene from a play, or one or more poems. (Visit Librivox.org for examples of such literature read by volunteers.)

Pecha Kucha Presentation
Make a Pecha Kucha presentation that encapsulates a novel or a play. Use public-domain images from wikimedia.org or flickr.com/creativecommons to illustrate your presentation, or take photographs of your own.

Public-Service Announcement
Choose a literary work that warns against some sort of private or public behavior. Make a public-service announcement based on that piece of literature.

World Literature

Slide Show
Write a review of a famous piece of world literature. (Don't be shy about revealing a difference of opinion with other reviewers, as long as you support your own with evidence.) Make a slide show summarizing your review. If possible, post your slide show online for others to view.

Documentary
Produce a documentary about a figure you admire from world literature. You might choose a particular author or an individual character from a work. Explain the importance of this figure to world culture.

How-To Video
Make a video explaining how to succeed as an author, based on a historical example. Include problems the author faced and solutions to those problems.

Chapter 32
Design Projects
(Inquire pages 527–548)

Designs don't come to existence in a vacuum. Every design fills some need that gives it shape. This reciprocity makes design projects effective in engaging students with content. Students can see real applications for what they are learning and how that learning in turn shapes their futures. This chapter introduces students to a wide range of design projects they may put to use.

Learning Outcomes
- Create print designs.
- Create fashion designs.
- Design games.
- Create blueprints and prototypes.
- Design tools and machines.

Correlations

Common Core State Standards		
ELA-Literacy.CCRA.R.4–10	ELA-Literacy.CCRA.SL.1–6	Math.Practice.MP1–8
ELA-Literacy.CCRA.W.1–10	ELA-Literacy.CCRA.L.3–6	Science.Practice.SP1–8

Partnership for 21st Century Skills	
Creativity and Innovation (All standards)	**Information and Media Literacy** (All standards)
Critical Thinking and Problem Solving (All standards)	**Life and Career Skills** (All standards)
Communication and Collaboration (All standards)	

International Society for Technology in Education	
Creativity and Innovation (All standards)	**Research and Information Fluency** (All standards)
Communication and Collaboration (All standards)	**Critical Thinking, Problem Solving, and Decision Making** (All standards)

Team-Teaching Suggestions

Design projects often involve drawing, drafting, measuring, using proportions, rapid prototyping, building, bench testing, and similar experimental activities. These projects may also require unfamiliar tools and materials, as well as special work and storage space. As a result, some design projects are best done in collaboration with teaching partners. Here are some suggestions.

An Art Partner

An art instructor can be invaluable for projects that involve lots of graphic design, especially when it comes to theater costumes and sets. Graphic design also plays a major role in print layout, from the artwork of a book cover to the font choice of the text inside. Game designs also require a strong graphic sense to help create a pleasurable experience. Even blueprints, models, tools, and machines benefit from an artist's vision.

A Theater Partner

Many of the design projects described in this chapter find perfect application in a theater setting. For any play, actors must be costumed with clothes and jewelry. Printed posters, flyers, and programs (perhaps even T-shirts for advertising) must be developed. Stage sets must be drawn and constructed. A play can even provide a reason for a more formal blueprint or diorama. Theater instructors are used to managing these various elements that go into making a production.

An Industrial Arts or an Engineering Partner

For the "heavier" projects in this chapter—especially tool and machine designs—an industrial arts instructor or an engineering specialist can be of great assistance. Such a partner is best prepared to instruct students in safety procedures and in proper uses of tools and equipment. The instructor or specialist can also best explain the creation and use of blueprints and prototypes.

Social Studies Design Projects

European History

Poster

During much of medieval history, kings and queens ruled Europe, and the British royal family still enjoys much popularity.

Decide whether you support monarchy or oppose it. Create a poster to express your views.

T-Shirt

The Industrial Revolution transformed the Western World, creating both wealth and misery. If you lived in an agricultural community that was industrializing, would you support the change oppose it?

Design a T-shirt expressing your position for or against the Industrial Revolution.

U.S. History

Game

The Jamestown Colony and the Plymouth Settlement were established and developed in very different ways.

Choose one of the colonies and create a board game or card game to simulate the establishment of that settlement.

Blueprint or Scale Model

From grade school on, most students know of Christopher Columbus' *Niña, Pinta,* and *Santa Maria.* These ships were actually quite small and open to the elements.

Research the design of one of these ships and create a blueprint or scale model to show how it was built. Present your design to the class.

World History

Poster

Create a brochure that captures the essence of a ruler's reign.

Costume

Hold a costume party that portrays a historical period. Discuss the relation of fashion to the character of the time period.

Game

Design a game that communicates important facts about your favorite civilization.

Scale Model

Study the sketches of Leonardo Da Vinci's inventions, from flying machines to tanks to giant crossbows. Create a blueprint or prototype of one of his inventions.

Science Design Projects

Anthropology

Tool

Research techniques for creating stone tools during the Neolithic Period.

Using similar materials and techniques, create a replica stone tool.

Game

Create a game that simulates the way to grow and sustain an agriculture-based society. Make sure to allow for factors such as drought, fire, disease, invasion, and social unrest.

Chemistry

Model

Investigate complex molecules. Choose one and build a model showing the elements involved, their positions, and their bonds. Present your model to classmates.

Game

Make a memory game of flash cards about the periodic table of the elements. On one side, include the name of the element. On the other side, include the element's symbol and any other details you want to memorize.

Biology

Poster

Make a poster demonstrating the expression of a passive gene (such as red/green color blindness) across at least three generations.

Game

Create a game that pits a healthy cell (player 1) against a viral assault (player 2). Depict actual cell defenses against viruses.

Scale Model

Build a scale model of the skeletal structure of an animal's limb. Make sure that the joints in the scale model work they way they do in the actual animal—ball and socket, hinge, pivot, sliding, condyloid.

Environmental Science

Brochure

Investigate the history and the scientific explanation of acid rain.

Choose a specific geographic locale that it continues to affect.

Locate photographs of the area before it was damaged by acid rain, at the worst of that damage, and in its present condition.

Make a brochure illustrating those changes and educating the reader about the causes of acid rain and possible solutions to it.

Math Design Projects

Mathematics

Book Cover
Create a cover for an imaginary book about a famous mathematician. Include back copy that makes people want to read more about that person.

T-Shirt
Design a T-shirt that celebrates the importance of the number 0.

Tool
Research different abacuses from history. Build one and demonstrate how to use it.

Algebra

Brochure
Choose an algebra concept or formula you recently learned. Design a brochure that explains and demonstrates that concept or formula to someone learning it for the first time.

T-Shirt
Choose a graph function that you find attractive. Make a T-shirt that pictures that graph. Include the function equation below the graph.

Trigonometry

Game
Create a concentration game by writing trigonometry terms (*sine, cosine, tangent,* etc.) on some cards and definitions of the terms on other cards. Lay all cards facedown on a table and challenge a classmate to a game of concentration. Each player lifts a card and tries to match it to the right definition or word. A match allows the player to continue; otherwise play goes to the other person.

Prototype
Create a car chassis that uses only triangular forms. Use a computer-aided design program to do your work, or build the chassis out of cardboard and tape.

Tool
Design a tool that is not a compass and that allows you to draw a triangle of any shape and any size from 1 centimeter per side to 20 centimeters per side.

Geometry

Scale Model
Use triangles, squares, pentagons, hexagons, and octagons to design a geodesic dome. (Search online for examples.)

Calculus

Scale Model
Research calculus equations for determining the trajectory of a stone hurled from a trebuchet (a medieval throwing device). Research trebuchets and build a scale model. Safely fire the trebuchet repeatedly and measure the trajectory of each flight. Compare actual flights to figures from trajectory calculus.

English Design Projects

American Literature

Poster

Research a genre of American literature: western, science fiction, fantasy, horror, mystery, and so on.

Create a poster that promotes the genre, using an engaging image and powerful text.

Diorama

Build a diorama of a significant location in a piece of literature, for example, the drawing room in "The Telltale Heart" or the hideaway in *The Diary of Anne Frank*.

Book Cover

Create a new book cover (front and back) for a novel you have read. Make sure the back cover copy describes the story and makes readers eager to read.

Language Arts

Game

Create a game show that presents contestants with grammatical terms and asks them to provide definitions, or presents them with sentences and asks them to identify the parts of speech of each word.

Tool

Create a balance scale for weighing the quality of a piece of writing. Create a weight for each of the following: ideas, organization, voice, words, sentences, correctness, and design. As you analyze a piece of writing, place each weight either in the "pro" or the "con" balance. When you are done assessing, decide what changes can shift the balance, moving traits out of "con" and into "pro."

World Literature

Brochure

Create a brochure that promotes a certain period in literature or the body of literature from a particular nation.

Jewelry

Make a beaded necklace or bracelet that represents the characters and plot of a favorite book.

Game

Host a role-playing game that casts players in the roles of characters from a story they have not read. Afterward, hold a discussion about the actions they took compared to the actions of the characters in the actual story.

Poster

Research great speeches from history. Choose one that interests you and create a poster that promotes the speech. Give viewers a reason to want to attend the speech.

Costume

Create a costume to deliver the great speech you chose above. Memorize the speech and deliver it.

Chapter 33
Performing Projects

(*Inquire* pages 549–568)

Public speaking has been important from Pericles to the present. Our new interconnectedness makes this skill vital not just for speaking to groups in a room but also for speaking to groups in online environments. As a result, instructors need to provide students with a wide variety of speaking opportunities such as the ones presented in this chapter. These performance skills enhance student confidence and influence.

Learning Outcomes

- Prepare for different types of speeches.
- Participate in interviews.
- Prepare regular and character debates.
- Hold simulations.
- Stage plays.

Correlations

Common Core State Standards

ELA-Literacy.CCRA.R.1–10	ELA-Literacy.CCRA.L.3–6	Science.Practice.SP1–4
ELA-Literacy.CCRA.W.1–10	Math.Practice.MP3	Science.Practice.SP6–8
ELA-Literacy.CCRA.SL.1	Math.Practice.MP5–7	

Partnership for 21st Century Skills

Creativity and Innovation (All standards)	**Media Literacy** (All standards)
Critical Thinking and Problem Solving (All standards)	**Life and Career Skills** (All standards)
Communication and Collaboration (All standards)	

International Society for Technology in Education

1. **Creativity and Innovation** (All standards)	3. **Research and Information Fluency** (All standards)
2. **Communication and Collaboration** (All standards)	4. **Critical Thinking, Problem Solving, and Decision Making** (All standards)

Team-Teaching Suggestions

Performing projects often involve researching, writing, speaking, producing, and designing, which means they cross specific content boundaries. For example, presenting content-driven speeches could evolve into a cross-curricular project. Here's how a team of teachers could provide assistance to students preparing demonstration speeches, such as the one presented on pages 556–557.

A Math Partner

If the speech demonstrates a particular mathematical process or formula, then a math instructor should assist in the initial research and development. The instructor can ensure that the student has a clear step-by-step understanding of the process so that he or she can carry out an effective demonstration. The instructor can also check the student's math that will be displayed at each step in the demonstration. In short, the math instructor's contributions should focus on the details related to the subject matter.

An English Partner

While preparing a demonstration speech, students should either develop a word-for-word manuscript or prepare an outline to guide them. An English instructor can assist them in shaping their speeches, no matter what format they choose to use. Students will also need guidance in terms of pace, voice quality, posture, eye contact, and so on. The instructor can provide this guidance as well as observe and assess practice runs. In short, the English instructor's contributions should focus on the craft of speech making.

A Computer or Technology Partner

Visuals and/or props are key elements in a demonstration speech. When demonstrating a math process, students may want to show the steps in a PowerPoint presentation. A computer or technology specialist should be on hand to offer assistance as needed. A specialist can also make sure that the necessary equipment is available (computer, projector, screen) for the speech, plus provide any other equipment that might be necessary. In short, the specialist's contributions should focus on the technical support.

Social Studies Performing Projects

U.S. History

Persuasive Speech
Argue for or against the importance of a particular historical event that wasn't covered in great detail in your class.

Demonstration Speech
Develop a demonstration speech that shows how a particular task (preserving food, providing refrigeration, attending school) was carried out during an earlier time in our history.

Live Interview
Interview a local historian about a particular topic related to the history of your community or region.

Debate/Round Table
Research a controversial issue in our history, and debate or discuss the issue as if you lived during that time period.

Play
Stage a play that addresses a time, place, or event in our history.

World History

Persuasive Speech
Convince your audience of the significance of an ancient culture. Focus on a culture that may be somewhat new to them.

Demonstration Speech
Demonstrate how an earlier political system (such as the feudal system) worked.

Character Debate
Develop a debate between an important world figure you have learned about in World History and someone equally important alive today.

Simulation
Re-enact an important scene in history such as the signing of the Magna Carta.

Play
Stage a play that addresses a time, place, or event in a period of world history that intrigues you.

Sociology/Psychology

Persuasive Speech
Defend a position on a timely social issue such as yearlong schooling, gun control, or health care.

Interview
Interview a sociologist or psychologist about an important aspect of his or her profession.

Simulation
Simulate a peer-pressure scenario such as a bullying confrontation, or a team conflict.

Play
Stage a play that explores a modern social problem such as racial marginalizing or the rights of children.

Government

Persuasive Speech
Argue for or against a citizen's participatory responsibilities in our political/governmental system.

Demonstration Speech
Show the steps involved in a behind-the-scenes governmental/political process such as the voting process.

Live Interview
Interview a local politician about the key points in his or her legislative agenda.

Simulation
Simulate the trial of a political figure such as President Nixon during the Watergate investigation.

Science Performing Projects

Biology

Demonstration Speech

Discuss and show an important cycle in human life (birth, brain development, infection, digestion, aging, etc.).

Live Interview

Interview a physician about the key aspects and goals of preventative medicine, holistic medicine, and so on.

Debate/Round Table

Debate or discuss a timely biological issue such as the loss of genetic diversity of wild crop strains; the loss and degradation of grasslands, forests, and wetlands; or harmful residues in drinking water.

Simulations

Create a simulation in which the participants interact in a particular biotic community.

Physics

Persuasive Speech

Argue for or against the Common Core State Standards for physics.

Demonstration Speech

Prepare a demonstration related to a topic such as thermodynamics, electricity and magnetism, or oscillations and waves.

Interview

Interview a scientist or engineer about a cutting-edge topic such as lithium-ion technology that could help produce inexpensive batteries for electric cars.

Round Table

Form a group of classmates to research a topic of interest such as the connection between black holes and existence. Then discuss the topic in front of a live audience.

Chemistry

Persuasive Speech

Argue for the importance of green chemistry in today's world, perhaps as it pertains to the petroleum and energy industries.

Demonstration Speech

Prepare a demonstration of a topic of interest such as the foaming capacity of soaps, the contents of a soft drink, or water purification.

Interview

Interview a chemist in a local business about his or her background, job description, challenges, and so on.

Character Interview

Research a famous chemist such as Marie Curie or George Washington Carver. Then script an interview with this person. Perform the interview with a classmate.

Round Table

Form a group of classmates to research a topic of interest and importance such as the detection of insecticides and pesticides in the produce that we eat. Then discuss the topic in front of a live audience.

Math Performing Projects

Algebra

Persuasive Speech

Argue for or against the Common Core State Standards for mathematics, especially as they pertain to algebra.

Demonstration Speech

Demonstrate how to complete an algebraic function such as working with linear equations or dividing and factoring polynomials.

Interview

Interview a math instructor or professor about the origins of algebra and what impact its discovery has had in the field of mathematics.

Debate/ Round Table

Debate or discuss the following topic.

Resolved: Algebra is an essential component in the high school math curriculum.

Simulation

Simulate a review session for a critical algebra exam. Roles should include a tutor, students of varying abilities, and perhaps an instructor who makes a brief appearance or two.

Geometry

Persuasive Speech

In a persuasive speech, argue for a project-based approach to geometry rather than one driven by textbooks and tests.

Demonstration Speech

Demonstrate how to complete a geometric function such as solving proportions or working with ratios or proofs.

Interview

Interview a math instructor or professor about the origins of geometry and what impact its discovery had in the field of mathematics.

Roundtable

Invite local contractors, builders, engineers, landscapers, and so on to join in a roundtable discussion of the application of geometry in the workplace.

Simulation

Simulate a real-life situation in which geometry is used to solve a problem, answer a question, or carry out a job.

Calculus

Demonstration Speech

Demonstrate how to work with decimal expansion, differential equations, applications of the derivative, or some other calculus formula.

Character Debate

Research the Leibniz-Newton calculus controversy. Then create a debate between the two individuals based on this controversy.

Roundtable

Invite math educators to join you and your classmates in a discussion of the expectations for calculus students, as well as math students in general, in other countries.

Simulation

Simulate a situation in which a group of retirees want to be re-introduced to a basic study of calculus.

Play

Stage a historical play (serious or satiric) based on your research on the origins of calculus.

English Performing Projects

American Literature

Persuasive Speech

In a persuasive speech, argue for your choice of the "Great American Novel."

Demonstration Speech

Demonstrate an effective process for analyzing a poem by Emily Dickinson, Robert Frost, Carl Sandburg, or other great American poet.

Interview

Interview a literature instructor, local author, or bookstore owner about his or her favorite piece of American literature.

Character Debate

Create a character debate involving a past American author (Mark Twain, Stephen Crane, etc.) and a modern one (Tom Wolfe, Toni Morrison, etc.) in which they discuss writing style and technique.

Simulation

Simulate a trial in which a literary character (Hester Prynne, Huck Finn, Holden Caulfield) is being judged for his or her actions.

British/World Literature

Demonstration Speech

Demonstrate an effective process for analyzing a poem by one of the Romantic poets (Blake, Byron, Keats, Wordsworth, etc.).

Interview

Interview an English instructor or professor about the history and origins of the novel as an important genre.

Debate

Debate the following issue.

Resolved: Shakespeare is the authentic author of the plays and poetry attributed to him.

Simulation

Re-enact a critical scene in an important piece of literature such as *A Tale of Two Cities, A Doll House, Madame Bovary, Don Quixote, Heart of Darkness,* and so on.

Play

Research an important European, African, or Asian author. Then stage a play that captures a significant time in this person's life.

Language/Composition

Persuasive Speech

Argue for or against a particular language-related issue such as the value of having one standard dialect (Standard American English).

Demonstration Speech

Demonstrate an effective process for editing and proofreading a composition.

Interview

Interview a local author about his or her personal process of writing. Or interview the person about one particular part of the process, perhaps revising.

Character Debate

Create a debate between two individuals from different eras who may have differing attitudes about language and writing, such as Virginia Woolf and Stephen King.

Simulation

Create an editing session between a present-day English teacher and someone with a unique set of the language skills, such as Huckleberry Finn.

Chapter 34

Community Projects

(*Inquire* pages 569–588)

Community projects help students develop collaboration skills, demonstrate leadership, practice teamwork, and accomplish goals that individuals can't achieve alone. These projects also connect students to the world outside the classroom. The greatest achievements of human civilization—from building pyramids to building the World Wide Web—result from collaborative effort. Community projects equip students to succeed in any century, but especially our own.

Learning Outcomes

- Organize fund-raisers and service projects.
- Arrange flash events.
- Run contests and campaigns.
- Create clubs.

Correlations

Common Core State Standards		
ELA-Literacy.CCRA.R.7–10	ELA-Literacy.CCRA.SL.1–6	Math.Practice.MP1–8
ELA-Literacy.CCRA.W.1–10	ELA-Literacy.CCRA.L.3–6	Science.Practice.SP1–8

Partnership for 21st Century Skills	
Creativity and Innovation (All standards)	**Information and Media Literacy** (All standards)
Communication and Collaboration (All standards)	**Critical Thinking and Problem Solving** (All standards)

International Society for Technology in Education	
1. Creativity and Innovation (All standards)	**3. Research and Information Fluency** (All standards)
2. Communication and Collaboration (All standards)	**4. Critical Thinking, Problem Solving, and Decision Making** (All standards)

Team-Teaching Suggestions

Community projects require long-term and large-scale thinking to be successful, so students will need all the help they can get. Therefore, teachers should work together as advisors and managers so that the students' efforts develop into meaningful and productive experiences for everyone. Some community projects may involve technology and design components that lend themselves to team teaching. Here's how teachers might collaborate:

A Social Studies Partner

When it comes to understanding the feasibility of community project ideas, students will benefit from the advice and guidance of a social studies instructor or a community outreach person. What students might initially think is a good idea may turn out to be impractical or redundant after consulting with an advisor.

An Art Partner

Most promotional material for community projects will involve art, especially posters, fliers, T-shirts, bumper stickers, and Web sites. An art instructor can offer design advice, help students procure the necessary materials, and guide students in the actual art work. Effective visuals are important because they draw attention and create a positive buzz.

An English Partner

Community projects almost always involve some type of printed material—fliers, announcements, speech manuscripts, and so on. An English instructor can advise and assist in the develop of these texts. Advice would be especially helpful when dealing with persuasive texts. An English instructor can also coach students as they prepare to deliver speeches or make announcements.

A Computer or Technology Partner

To promote most community projects, students will need a Web site, a PowerPoint presentation, and a social media marketing plan. A computer or technology specialist can work with students in these areas. In addition, a specialist will be helpful during the setup of equipment at an event or presentation.

English Community Projects

Literature

Fund-Raisers

Stage and sell tickets to dramatic readings from literature, the proceeds going toward the purchase of electronic readers for the school.

Service Projects

Establish a service in which interested literature students read to young students and help them with their reading skills.

Flash Events

Create a flash event in which participants enact an important scene from a famous novel.

Contests

Create a game show in which contestants must answer questions based on literature. Award book prizes to winners.

Clubs

Start a book club that focuses on particular genre: mystery, fantasy, biography, and so on.

Language/Composition

Service Projects

Create a writing lab in which composition students can tutor others in their writing.

Flash Events

Create a flash poetry slam. The slam could be part of a poetry-awareness celebration.

Contests

Plan a short story contest based on a particular theme, genre, or style of writing. Promote the contest in school and online.

Campaigns

Assign student writers to assist candidates in crafting speeches and campaign literature.

Clubs

Establish a writing club in which students and instructors gather to share their writing in progress and to discuss new techniques, writing challenges, and so on.

Journalism

Fund-Raisers

Plan a school-wide paper drive, selling the paper to a local recycling company. Use the proceeds to start an account for purchasing tablet or notebook computers or other paperless technology.

Service Projects

Establish a volunteer service in which student journalists help community groups and organizations create newsletters and promotional literature.

Flash Events

Create a flash event in which the participants in some way celebrate newspapers and/or the important role that journalists play in an open society. This event could be part of a campaign promoting the Fourth Estate.

Contests

Plan a news writing contest, perhaps with participants crafting creative headlines for a series of stories or writing leads for stories.

Campaigns

Put together a team of student journalists offering public-relations advice and promotional literature for school campaigns.

Math Community Projects

Algebra

Service Projects

Establish a volunteer service in which algebra students serve as tutors at various community centers.

Flash Events

Plan a flash event in which students celebrate/honor/promote some aspect of algebra.

Contests

Carry out an algebra contest, perhaps modeled after the Final Four, in which participants are placed in a bracket. As the contest progresses from week to week, the initial 64 contestants would be reduced to 32, then 16 and so on. The final four could draw significant interest.

Clubs

Establish an algebra club in which interested students enrich their math experiences.

Geometry

Fund-Raisers

Plan a fund-raiser in which the proceeds go toward new math equipment, such as new calculators or new math apps.

Service Projects

Establish a service in which interested geometry students offer their math expertise free of charge in the community.

Contests

Run a contest in which participants find the area and perimeter of various structures in the community.

Clubs

Establish a geometry club in which interested students enrich their math experiences.

Statistics/Probabilities

Service Projects

Establish a service in which interested students use statistical analysis to measure anything from traffic flow at intersections to purchasing patterns at local businesses.

Flash Events

Plan a flash event using probability and statistics to determine when the highest number of spectators will be present to view the experience.

Contests

At the beginning of the week, offer a statistics puzzler for students to solve. Draw a winner at the end of the week.

Campaigns

Create a team of math students who monitor surveys and polls during a school, local, state, or federal campaign and use statistics to predict outcomes.

Clubs

Establish a statistics/probability club in which students enrich their understanding in this field of mathematics.

Social Studies Community Projects

History

Fund-Raisers
Organize a fund-raiser, with the proceeds for establishing or repairing a historical marker or monument.

Service Projects
Form a group of interested students to research the history of the community and write feature stories for the local newspaper.

Flash Events
Plan a flash event in which students reenact an important event in history. The event could coincide with a national holiday.

Contests
Create a history game show. Provide appropriate "historical" prizes to award to winners.

Clubs
Establish a history club in which interested students enrich their understanding of local, state, national, or world history.

Sociology/Psychology

Fund-Raisers
Organize a fund-raiser with the proceeds going to a community group or organization in need of funds.

Service Projects
Form a group of interested students to volunteer at service organizations in the community—youth groups, senior centers, rehab centers, and so on.

Flash Events
Plan a flash event in which the performance heightens public awareness of an important social issue.

Contests
Organize a writing or visual contest in which participants express their thoughts and feelings about some aspect of social media.

Campaigns
Run a campaign that addresses a social/psychological problem—bullying, alienation, depression, and so on.

Government

Flash Events
Plan a flash event in which the performance addresses an important issue in a current political campaign.

Contests
Organize a Trivial Pursuit contest in which participants answers questions about the different branches of government, famous as well as infamous elected officials, and so on.

Clubs
Create clubs affiliated with the different political parties. Members can investigate and discuss pressing political issues, invite party members to meetings, and offer their services during local elections.

Economics

Fund-Raisers
Plan a fund-raiser, with the proceeds going to community and church groups that provide assistance to the unemployed.

Campaigns
Run a campaign that focuses on responsible money management (planning, budgeting, saving, etc.) for high school students.

Clubs
Create an investment club with members studying the market and making investments, whether in reality or in simulation.

Science Community Projects

Biology

Fund-Raisers

Plan a fund-raiser in which the proceeds go toward a worthy cause such as a local wildlife refuge or an urban-garden project.

Service Projects

Form a group of interested students to offer their services to environmental clean-up efforts, animal shelters, and so on.

Flash Events

Plan a flash event in which the performance heightens public awareness of an important issue such as animal rights, biodiversity, or preventative medicine.

Contests

Run a "green thumb" contest where student participants enter their homegrown veggies or flowers for judging. Award ribbons as prizes.

Clubs

Create a garden club in which club members learn about and practice different gardening and growing techniques.

Chemistry

Fund-Raisers

Form a group of students to create and sell eco-friendly household cleansers. Use the funds to buy new chemistry equipment.

Flash Events

Plan a flash event in which the performance illustrates an important concept related to chemistry, such as models of the structure of atoms or a process such as oxidation.

Contests

Organize a contest in which participants answer chemistry-related brainteasers. Award prizes to weekly winners.

Campaigns

Run a campaign focusing on the awareness of harmful chemicals in the environment, in foods, and so on.

Clubs

Establish a chemistry club in which interested students enrich their understanding in this area of science.

Physics

Service Projects

Form a group of students who create instructional videos for middle schoolers, teaching about energy, mechanics, and so on.

Flash Events

Plan a flash event in which the performance demonstrates a basic concept such as the generation of electricity.

Contests

Organize a contest in which teams of physics students compete before a live audience.

Campaigns

Run an awareness campaign on an appropriate topic, perhaps the current state of battery- and hydrogen-powered transportation.

Clubs

Establish a physics club in which students enrich their understanding in this field of science.

Chapter 35
Web Projects

(*Inquire* pages 589–606)

The information age is fully upon us, and its backbone is the Internet. Even scholarly writing is now published online, where results of new research can be quickly disseminated and easily discussed.

Consequently, not only will students often find themselves drawing upon online sources in their research, they will also need to understand how to interact with that information and even publish their own work. This chapter familiarizes students with common technologies for publishing online.

Learning Outcomes

- Use HTML to build a Web page.
- Plan a multipage Web site.
- Use Wiki and Blog software to build a Web site.
- Use CSS to style a Web page.
- Use JavaScript and PHP to make a Web page interactive.

Correlations

Common Core State Standards

ELA-Literacy.CCRA.R.1–10	ELA-Literacy.CCRA.SL.1–6	Math.Practice.MP1–8
ELA-Literacy.CCRA.W.1–10	ELA-Literacy.CCRA.L.3–6	Science.Practice.SP1

Partnership for 21st Century Skills

Communication and Collaboration
- Communicate Clearly
- Collaborate with Others

Media Literacy
- Create Media Products

Information and Communication Technologies Literacy
- Apply Technology Effectively

International Society for Technology in Education

1. Creativity and Innovation
- Students demonstrate creative thinking, construct knowledge, and develop innovative products and processes using technology. (a–d)

2. Communication and Collaboration
- Students use digital media and environments to communicate and work collaboratively, including at a distance, to support individual learning and contribute to the learning of others. (a–d)

3. Research and Information Fluency
- Students apply digital tools to gather, evaluate, and use information. (b–d)

4. Critical Thinking, Problem Solving, and Decision Making
- Students use critical thinking skills to plan and conduct research, manage projects, solve problems, and make informed decisions using appropriate digital tools and resources. (b, d)

5. Digital Citizenship
- Students understand human, cultural, and societal issues related to technology and practice legal and ethical behavior. (a, b, d)

6. Technology Operations and Concepts
- Students demonstrate a sound understanding of technology concepts, systems, and operations. (a–d)

Team-Teaching Suggestions

Web projects are often exciting for students because this sort of publishing presents student work outside the classroom. It also provides an opportunity to learn how text, graphic design, and computer skills work together to communicate a message effectively.

These projects afford great opportunities for team teaching, allowing each teacher to focus on one aspect of the overall project.

A Language Arts Partner

Text online usually requires a different approach than text in print. Online, reader attention span is shorter, eyes scan pages for main ideas, and deeper information is assumed to be available behind hypertext links or searchable by key words.

The rapid nature of online publishing can make attention to accurate spelling, punctuation, grammar, and word use difficult. At the same time, the potential widespread viewership makes these mechanics crucial. Poorly crafted language can lead readers to dismiss an otherwise valuable message.

For these reasons, a language arts teacher can be a great partner for guiding students during a Web project in any content area.

An Arts Partner

Like the cover of a magazine or brochure, the home page of a Web site, blog, or wiki has to quickly attract attention and direct readers to points of interest. Interior pages must continue to hold readers' attention and lead them to a conclusion or a call to action.

To maximize visual impact, consider partnering with an arts instructor. He or she can teach visual design and guide GUI (graphical user interface) development. An arts instructor with experience in Web languages such as HTML for structure and CSS for style can be especially helpful. (See *Inquire* pages 594–595 and 602–603 for more about HTML and CSS.)

A Mathematics or Computer Science Partner

Computers are amazing calculating machines, capable of prodigious mathematical feats in science, finance, architecture, social engineering, and more. Virtually every field of endeavor uses computers in some way. At heart, computers run on math. Math dictates the binary nature of chips, the functions of computer languages, and the hexadecimal code controlling the colors displayed on monitors.

So whatever your content area, a math or computer science partner can help deepen your students' understanding of and appreciation for a Web project's application to their futures.

Social Studies Web Projects

U.S. History

Web Page

Create a Web page that features the current U.S. Cabinet members, with a short description of duties for each, followed by one paragraph of biography.

Web Site or Wiki

Expand the Web page above to a full site, featuring one cabinet position per page, with a history of its establishment and members who have filled the post.

Blog or Message Board

Make a series of blog or message board posts, featuring one or more U.S. Cabinet positions, and arguing for or against their existence.

Sociology/Psychology

Web Page

Investigate the history of studies considering a link between genetics and crime.

Write a position essay about what you have learned.

Post it as a Web page, with links to your sources.

Web Site, Wiki, or Blog

Gather your Web page (above) with other students' pages to create an online journal discussing the topic.

Construct your journal as a Web site, a wiki, or a blog.

Current Events

Web Site or Wiki

As a class, investigate the evolution of modern media from traditional forms.

Brainstorm a list of specific topics.

Assign each topic to a small group of students for further research.

In each small group, prepare a Web or wiki page about the assigned topic.

Arrange those pages into a class report about modern media, and release it to the public.

Blog or Message Board

Maintain a class blog or message board where teacher and students alike can post links to news items about developments in news media.

Use the comments feature of that space to discuss those items.

20th Century History

Web Page

Design a two-column Web page with side-by-side, 3- to 5-paragraph biographies of President John F. Kennedy and Premier Nikita Khrushchev.

Introduce the page with a brief summary of these two leaders' interaction.

Web Site or Wiki

Build a class Web site, wiki, blog, or message board that discusses modern repercussions of the 20th century Cold War.

Include discussion of how the personalities of President John F. Kennedy and Premier Nikita Khrushchev influenced that competition.

Science Web Projects

Physics/Technology

Web Page

Which invention came first, the wheel or fire? Document your answer in a short paper about the significance of each invention for humankind.

Web Site or Wiki

As a class, brainstorm a list of the 50 most important inventions in human history.

Assign one invention to each student for a one-page research paper. (Use journalistic documentation style; see *Inquire* page 397.)

Assemble your class papers into a Web site or wiki.

After reading all entries, vote in class to rank the inventions in order of importance.

Then vote to determine the top 10 write-ups by your classmates.

Discuss how the quality of write-ups did or did not influence the vote for most important inventions.

Chemistry

Web Site or Wiki

As a class, create a Web site or wiki featuring an online, interactive periodic table of the elements.

Use the site's home page to display the overall table.

Reserve an individual page for each element, linked to that element's position on the home page.

Assign 2–3 elements per student, or work on more in small groups.

Write a brief overview of each element, defining its properties, discussing its scientific history, and explaining its uses to humankind.

Finish the Web site or wiki with a separate page discussing the history of the periodic table of elements itself.

Blog or Message Board

As a class, create a blog or message board where students can post news stories about chemistry and discuss its effects.

Space Science/Astronomy

Web Page

Create a series of images showing the relative position of the planets, month by month, over the course of one Earth year.

Create a Web page that uses JavaScript to determine the current month and display the appropriate image.

Add more images for months in future years and adjust your JavaScript code to suit.

Consider expanding your page to include planetary positions from both the past and the future, and to allow your visitor to input a month and year to view.

For an added challenge, include code to output clickable areas for each planet, using either image map markup or CSS-positioned layers.

Math Web Projects

Algebra

Web Page

Investigate the claim that without specific number words, the human brain cannot recognize groups larger than three. Write your conclusions as a Web page, with illustrations included.

Web Site or Wiki

Investigate number systems and vocabulary in other cultures—modern and ancient. Choose one example and research ways that it shaped, empowered, or constrained the use of mathematics. Write a Web page about what you learned, and add it to a Web site or wiki with other student's examples.

Blog or Message Board

Find examples of math blogs or message boards available online. Choose a topic you find interesting and get involved in the discussion. Tell your classmates about the experience.

Calculus

Web Site or Wiki

As a class, brainstorm a list of real-world uses for calculators.

Search for examples of free calculators online.

Create a Web Site or Wiki cataloging what you find and offering advice and commentary about each resource.

Web Page

Build a Web page using JavaScript allowing the visitor to add two numbers and generate a total. (Hint: You will need a form with three text boxes and a submit button.)

Expand your code to a four-function calculator with Add, Subtract, Multiply, and Divide buttons.

Add other functions as you can to make this a full-featured scientific calculator.

Vocational Math

Blog

Use an online job board to make a list of math-related careers.

Choose one that appeals to you.

Write a blog entry describing the career.

Also explain what you must accomplish to achieve that career.

Include a time line to guide and track your progress toward that career.

Web Site or Wiki

Polish your blog entry (above) to serve as a page on a class Web site or in a class wiki.

Discuss in class any careers that may be missing from the site or wiki.

In small groups, create descriptions for those careers as well.

English Web Projects

American Literature

Web Page

Make a Web page comparing an American novel you recently read and enjoyed to a movie based upon it.

Web Site or Wiki

In a small group, brainstorm a list of recent novels you have read. Have each student select a favorite novel and generate catalog copy and a sample cover for it. Then design a proposed Web site to advertise those books. Discuss your finished proposal in class with other groups.

Blog Reviews

Write a series of blog posts, comparing books you have read to films based upon them. Consider allowing visitors to comment upon your posts. (Comments help to generate traffic.) If possible and with a parent's permission, create an associate's account with an online store, and link your posts to the products you review.

World Literature

Web Page

Search online to find famous dystopian novels in world literature.

Include a brief (1–3 sentences) description of each title.

Choose one novel, read it, and write a review about it. In your review, express your opinion about the role of dystopian stories in world literature. Post your review online as a Web page.

Web Site or Wiki

With classmates or friends, join the Web page above with others to create a Web site or wiki that focuses on dystopian world literature.

Add an introductory page to the site or wiki.

Include a message board or comments feature and encourage discussion of dystopian themes.

South American Literature

Web Site or Wiki

As a class, brainstorm a list of South American novelists, poets, and essayists whose work has been influential in the U.S.

Arrange small groups for further study.

In small groups, investigate your assigned author's life and work.

Have each group member write a short critical review of one publication by the author.

As a group, prepare a short biography (one printed page) of your author, including a summary of your critical reviews.

Assemble the entire class's work into a Web site or wiki devoted to South American writers.

Planning Sheet

Name _____   Date _____

Project _____

Your Turn Complete this sheet in order to plan a project. (See *Inquire* page 350 for an example.)

Goal: _____

Objectives: Who? _____

_____

What? _____

_____

Where? _____

When? _____

Why? _____

_____

How? _____

_____

Tasks: **Time:**

1. _____   _____

2. _____   _____

3. _____   _____

4. _____   _____

5. _____   _____

6. _____   _____

7. _____   _____

8. _____   _____

Team: _____

_____

Tools:

Equipment: _____

Materials: _____

Information: _____

Resources: _____

Rubric Sheet

Name _____ Date _____

Project _____

Your Turn Write your goal and objectives in the first column. Then evaluate the goal and each objective, rate them, and total your score. (See *Inquire* page 417 for an example.)

Goal:	Evaluation:	Rating			Score
		Beat 60	**Met** 40	**Didn't** 20	
Objectives:					
1.		**Beat** 10	**Met** 6	**Didn't** 2	
2.		**Beat** 10	**Met** 6	**Didn't** 2	
3.		**Beat** 10	**Met** 6	**Didn't** 2	
4.		**Beat** 10	**Met** 6	**Didn't** 2	
5.		**Beat** 10	**Met** 6	**Didn't** 2	
6.		**Beat** 10	**Met** 6	**Didn't** 2	
				Total:	

Trait-Evaluation Sheet

Name _____ Date _____

Your Turn Write down what you will be evaluating. In the first column, list the traits. In the second column, evaluate each trait. In the third column, list suggestions for improvement. (See *Inquire* page 66 for an example.)

Evaluation for: _____

Traits	Evaluation	Improvements

Categories Chart

Name _____   Date _____

Your Turn Write the 5 W's and H, the five senses, or other categories about your topic in the left column. In the right column, provide details about your topic. (See *Inquire* pages 17 and 348 for examples.)

Topic: _____

T-Chart

Name _____   Date _____

Your Turn Label the following T-chart to make a problem/solution, pro/con, or before/after chart. Then fill it in. (See examples on *Inquire* pages 17 and 183.)

Topic: _____

Cause-Effect Chart

Name _____ Date _____

Your Turn Write the event in the center circle. Then list causes on the lines to the left and effects on the lines to the right. (See *Inquire* page 17 for an example.)

Causes: **Effects:**

Event

Venn Diagram

Name _____ Date _____

Your Turn List the two topics you are comparing. Write what is unique to each topic in its own space. Write what is common to both topics in the shared space. (See *Inquire* page 17 for an example.)

Topic 1: _____   **Topic 2:** _____

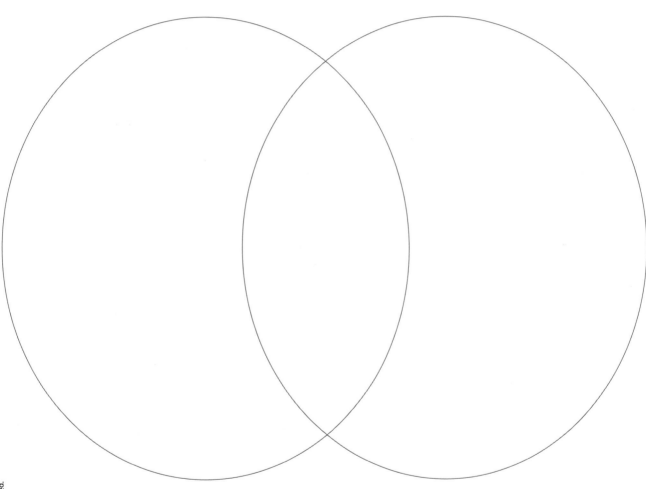

Time Line

Name _____ Date _____

Your Turn Identify the overall topic. Then note increments of time on the left of the time line and write events on the right. (See *Inquire* pages 16, 183, and 372 for examples.)

Topic: _____

Cycle Diagram

Name _____   Date _____

Your Turn Identify the overall process. Then write steps in the process in their appropriate positions around the circle. (See *Inquire* pages 182 and 372 for examples.)

Topic: _____

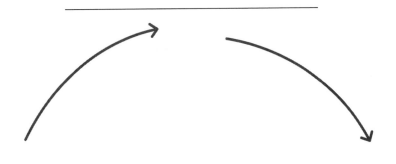

Budget Sheet

Name _____ Date _____

Your Turn In the first cell below, fill in the purpose of the budget. In the first rows, record types of income, the budgeted amount, and the actual amount. In the later rows, record types of expenses, the budgeted amount, and the actual amount. Calculate the difference and totals. (See *Inquire* pages 331 and 574 for examples.)

Budget for _____	Budget Amount	Actual Amount	Difference
Income			
Expenses			

Revising Checklist

Name _____   Date _____

Your Turn Use the following checklist to revise your writing. When a line is true, check it off. Continue revising until all lines are true. (See *Inquire* page 189 for more information.)

Ideas

- [ ] **1.** The writing focuses on one part of an interesting topic.
- [ ] **2.** The thesis is clear, concise, and compelling.
- [ ] **3.** A variety of details develops the thesis.
- [ ] **4.** Each paragraph focuses on a main point.
- [ ] **5.** The writing achieves its purpose (inform, persuade, entertain).

Organization

- [ ] **6.** The beginning captures the reader's attention and provides the thesis.
- [ ] **7.** The middle develops the thesis.
- [ ] **8.** Details are arranged effectively (time, location, importance), and paragraphs appear in the best order.
- [ ] **9.** The ending sums up the thesis and provides a final thought.

Voice

- [ ] **10.** The voice is appropriate to the topic and purpose of the writing.
- [ ] **11.** The voice connects with the reader.
- [ ] **12.** The level of language is appropriate to the writing form.

Editing Checklist

Name _____ Date _____

Your Turn Use the following checklist to edit your writing. When a line is true, check it off. Continue revising until all lines are true. (See *Inquire* page 190 for more information.)

Words

- [ ] **1.** Nouns are specific and verbs are active.
- [ ] **2.** Modifiers are used sparingly and only to improve clarity.
- [ ] **3.** Words show respect for gender, ethnicity, age, and ability.

Sentences

- [ ] **4.** Sentences vary in length and begin in different ways.
- [ ] **5.** Sentences flow smoothly.
- [ ] **6.** Most sentences use active voice.
- [ ] **7.** All sentences include a subject and a predicate and express a complete thought. (See pages 195–196.)

Correctness

- [ ] **8.** All sentences end with correct punctuation.
- [ ] **9.** Commas are used correctly. (See page 191.)
- [ ] **10.** Subjects and verbs agree. (See page 194.)
- [ ] **11.** Pronouns and antecedents agree. (See page 194.)
- [ ] **12.** Spelling and capitalization are correct.

Design

- [ ] **13.** The document follows the requirements of the assignment or form.
- [ ] **14.** The typeface is easy to read.
- [ ] **15.** White space (margins, blank lines) creates accessible blocks of text.
- [ ] **16.** The overall design enhances the clarity of the piece.